THE END OF ICELAND'S INNOCENCE

THE END OF ICELAND'S INNOCENCE

The Image of Iceland in the Foreign Media during the Financial Crisis

Daniel CHARTIER

University of Ottawa Press
Presses de l'Université du Québec

Library and Archives Canada Cataloguing in Publication

Chartier, Daniel, 1968-

The end of Iceland's innocence : the image of Iceland in the foreign media during the financial crisis / Daniel Chartier.

Translation of: La spectaculaire déroute de l'Islande.

Co-published by: Presses de l'Université du Québec.

Includes bibliographical references.

ISBN 978-0-7766-0760-3

1. Financial crises--Iceland. 2. Global Financial Crisis, 2008-2009--In mass media. 3. Iceland--In mass media. 4. Iceland--Foreign public opinion. 5. Iceland--Economic conditions--21st century. 6. Bank failures--Iceland--History--21st century. 7. Iceland--Economic policy. I. Title.

HB3722.C4213 2011   330.94912'090511   C2010-907366-5

THE END OF ICELAND'S INNOCENCE

The Image of Iceland in the Foreign Media during the Financial Crisis

Original title: *La spectaculaire déroute de l'Islande.*
L'image de l'Islande à l'étranger durant la crise économique de 2008
(Québec, Presses de l'Université du Québec, 2010, ISBN 978-2-7605-2539-9).

DISTRIBUTION

Canada, United States, Australia and New Zealand: University of Ottawa Press

Other countries: Citizen Press (Reykjavík and London, U.K.)

Design: Grafisk hönnun / Helgi Hilmarsson

All rights reserved. No reproduction, translation, or adaptation without authorization
© Presses de l'Université du Québec
© Daniel Chartier – First English version

ISBN 978-0-7766-0760-3

To my Icelandic friends

TABLE OF CONTENTS

INTRODUCTION: A MEDIA CRISIS 9
Excessiveness 11
The Research 15
The Role of the Media—Dramatisation of the Crisis 25

PART ONE: ASSETS IN JEOPARDY 37
An Egalitarian, Progressive and Peaceful Country—An Independent Utopia 39
The Impact of the Crisis Abroad—A General Dislike of Iceland 47
A Casualty of the Global Crisis—The First Domino to Fall 55
Communication Problems—An Atmosphere of Mistrust 60
Ethics—In Great Disarray 66
Free-Thinking Artists—Björk and Olafur Eliasson 73
Humour—'Ctrl-Alt-Del. Welcome to Iceland 2.0' 78

PART TWO: BANKRUPTCY 85
Numerous Warnings—A Foreseeable Collapse 87
Bankruptcy—*Iceland* Became Synonymous with *Crisis* 92
Social and Economic Incest—A Closely-Knit Economy 99
Davið Oddsson and the Central Bank of Iceland—Political Intervention in Economics 104
Arrogance—Excessive Confidence 109
Iceland's Very Loyal Friend—Richard Portes 113
The New Vikings—Yesterday's Heroes, Today's Villains 118
Gender Issues—Women: The Antidote to the Crisis 129

PART THREE: THE REST OF THE WORLD 135
Scandinavia—Our Nordic Friends 137
Russia—Our New Friend 143
The Conflict with the United Kingdom—One of Us, Not One of Them 152
Europe—Seeking Protective Shelter 161
A Very Small Country—Big Is Not Always Beautiful 170

CONCLUSION: THE HUMILIATED COUNTRY 183
Violence—Icelanders' Anger 185
Returning to Traditions—Fishing, Morality and Anti-Consumerism 191
Irresponsibility—Who Should Pay the Price? 198
Humiliation—The Wounded Tiger 207

CHRONOLOGY 218

BIBLIOGRAPHY 227

INTRODUCTION

A MEDIA CRISIS

EXCESS

'The country's international reputation is ruined.'
Financial Times, October 19, 2008[1]

Until very recently, Iceland was known for its extraordinary landscapes—made up of volcanoes, geysers, glaciers, lava fields and deep fjords—and the rich cultural heritage left by descendants of the Vikings through the sagas. At the turn of the 21st century, this small country of 330,000 inhabitants surprised the West with its unprecedented economic growth, propelling it to the ranks of the richest nations on the planet. The short period of prosperity that ensued, during which the sky was the limit, constitutes Iceland's 'New Viking' period, a time referred to as such because the dozen businessmen behind the growth have been likened to the Vikings given their appetite for conquest.

Then, in late September 2008, the world witnessed the swift and spectacular fall of the empire built by these men, and the collapse of Iceland, which sank into a crisis that was first financial, then economic, moral and ethical in nature. And last but not least, Iceland is faced with an identity crisis. Within a few days, thousands of articles appeared in the foreign media, describing Iceland as bankrupt, the first casualty of a growing worldwide crisis, a country humiliated and ruined. The surprise was so great that the media could only wonder how a Western country could be hit by a crisis of that scope, as the following article appearing in *Le Monde* indicates:

---

[1] Sarah O'Connor, 'Glitnir chief rolls up her sleeves for mammoth task', *Financial Times*, October 19, 2008.

Yes, how did it come to this? Iceland is not an emerging country; it's a very modern society of 330,000 inhabitants, the richest Nordic nation after Norway, ranking high in all the international indices. It is a constitutional state whose institutions are similar to those of the Scandinavian countries. And yet, it did come to this.[2]

A number of assumptions were put forward in an attempt to explain the collapse of Iceland's economy—inordinate borrowing by companies, banks and individuals; foreign conspiracy; collusion between political and economic powers—but one factor in particular was singled out: excess. Excessive confidence, excessive lack of restraint, excessive finance in light of the real economy. The economists observing the country—which could be described as a laboratory for neo liberalism—were able to foresee what would happen in a situation where value mechanisms, such as new rules for the production of wealth, were pushed to the limit. Before the collapse, borrowing opportunities seemed endless, and the profits were thought to be inevitable. All of Iceland´s natural resources were suddenly in the role of collateral and to be exploited at once. As an adviser with the country's Chamber of Commerce said, 'Iceland has valuable resources in abundance, ranging from fish to clean energy and, as such, they can be leveraged for the good of the nation'.[3] After the collapse, columnist A.A. Gill summarized the situation tongue in cheek, saying 'there is something invigorating about Iceland at this moment—like being with people waking from a dream. It's exciting and instructive.'[4]

---

2 Gérard Lemarquis, 'L'Islande au bord du gouffre', *Le Monde*, October 9, 2008, p. 3. The original quote read: 'Oui, comment en est-on arrivé là? L'Islande n'est pas un pays en voie de développement, c'est une société très moderne de 330 000 habitants, la plus riche des nations nordiques après la Norvège, qui caracole en tête de tous les palmarès internationaux. C'est un État de droit dont les institutions sont analogues à celles des pays scandinaves. Et pourtant, on en est arrivé là.'
3 Finnur Oddsson, quoted by David Ibison, 'Iceland wealth fund is proposed', *Financial Times*, April 25, 2008, p. 2.
4 A.A. Gill, 'Iceland: frozen assets', *Sunday Times*, December 14, 2008.

With hindsight and historical perspective, there were signs warning of what was to come—signs that people seemed either unable or unwilling to heed in the frenzy of the economic boom. In 2006, Jeremy Batstone published an article in *Money Week* cautioning about the very situation Icelanders found themselves in a few months later:

> Given the relatively small size of the country's economy, a sharp fall in GDP would feed its way quickly into the public finances. The budget surplus would be expected to turn swiftly into a deficit (as is the way with emerging economies). If the crisis widened to engulf the banking sector (although regional banks are vehemently denying any risk at present) the government would almost certainly end up having to shoulder a good part of the bank's increased debt burden.[5]

In March 2008, David Ibison issued a warning in the *Financial Times*, stating that 'the country's banking assets have grown at a speed rarely seen in the modern world. ... By 2006 they had risen to eight times GDP and the ratio is now thought to be near 10 times'.[6]

What was foreseen actually occurred in autumn 2008: the entire New Viking empire collapsed in a few hours like a flimsy house of cards. Foreign journalists struggled to describe the scope of the crisis. Gérard Lemarquis, for example, summarized the situation as follows, even before the crisis had reached a peak:

> A potentially bankrupt country with its hand out to other countries for short-term financing, two of the three main banks urgently nationalised, 15% inflation, and a currency, the Icelandic krona, which has lost

---

[5] Jeremy Batstone, 'Is Iceland facing a meltdown?' *Money Week*, May 18, 2006.
[6] David Ibison and Gillian Tett, 'Indignant Iceland faces a problem of perception', *Financial Times*, March 27, 2008, p. 13.

60% of its value in one year: that is Iceland's present situation.[7]

Then, an abundance of increasingly disastrous statistics began appearing in the foreign media: the Reykjavík exchange had lost 94% of its value;[8] as many as 20,000 Icelanders may have declared bankruptcy.[9] In the end, the social and financial toll was completely mindboggling. Norwegian-French judge, Eva Joly, wrote in August 2009 that Iceland was 'shouldering a $100 billion debt that the vast majority of the population had in no way incurred and had no way of paying down'.[10] One hundred billion dollars of debt for 330,000 inhabitants, i.e., more than $300,000 for every man, woman and child in the country. As A.A. Gill wrote, that was a rude awakening for a country that a few months earlier was one of the richest nations in the world.

Today, beyond the statistics, the people of Iceland are angry and worried. The country, which had taken tremendous pride in its success, looked on powerlessly as its international image underwent a spectacular reversal. As Sarah O'Connor wrote in October 2008, 'the country's international reputation is ruined'.[11] The story of this collapse, both fascinating and unsettling, is found in the narrative woven by the thousands of articles that appeared about Iceland in the foreign press during the crisis of 2008.

---

7 Gérard Lemarquis, 'L'Islande au bord du gouffre', *Le Monde*, October 9, 2008, p. 3. The original quote read: 'Un pays en faillite potentielle mendiant à l'étranger un financement à court terme, deux des trois grandes banques nationalisées en catastrophe, une inflation à 15% et une monnaie, la couronne islandaise, qui, en un an, a perdu 60% de sa valeur : telle est la situation actuelle de l'Islande.'
8 Vincent Brousseau-Pouliot, 'Les gagnants et perdants d'une année folle', *La Presse* (Montréal), December 24, 2008.
9 *IcelandReview.com*, 'Default claims in Iceland pile up', January 13, 2009.
10 Eva Joly, 'L'Islande ou les faux semblants de la régulation de l'après-crise', *Le Monde*, August 1, 2009. The original quote read: 'voit peser aujourd'hui sur ses épaules 100 milliards de dollars de dettes, avec lesquelles l'immense majorité de sa population n'a strictement rien à voir et dont elle n'a pas les moyens de s'acquitter'.
11 Sarah O'Connor, 'Glitnir chief rolls up her sleeves for mammoth task', *Financial Times*, October 19, 2008.

THE RESEARCH

> We figured the driver taking us to a New York airport didn't know much about our destination when we said we were going to Iceland and he asked us to spell it.
>
> 'Oh', he said. 'The bankrupt country.'
>
> Yes, the bankrupt country. Not the volcanic island south of the Arctic Circle with the near-lunar terrain that astronauts once practiced on. Not the home of a swinging Reykjavik nightlife, and other-worldly native musicians like Bjork and Sigur Ros. Not the land with spectacular scenery and bubbling geothermal pools.
>
> The bankrupt country.
> *Daily Times*, January 6, 2009[1]

This book is intended to provide an analysis of the changes in Iceland's image, through the thousands of articles appearing in the international media in 2008. It does not take a specific position on the crisis that rocked the country—a crisis that was financial and economic, but also moral, ethical and an identity crisis all in one—or delve into Iceland's internal political issues. Rather, it takes an analytical look, as objectively as possible, at the media coverage of the highly complex events that took place in Iceland.

It does not judge the veracity of what was said in the foreign press about Iceland (even if in some case, the facts and the points of view

---

[1] David Bauder, 'Dollar goes a long way on winter trip to Iceland', *Daily Times* (Delaware), January 6, 2009.

might be questionable). Rather, it organizes, comments and relays the key themes in what has been said abroad about Iceland. This foreign discourse might seem, for an Icelander, very far from his own perception of reality or even sometimes in contradiction with facts, but nevertheless, it has constructed for millions of people abroad the only image of Iceland they will ever get.

Why was so much said about such a small country in 2008? Iceland is viewed as a model, laboratory, counterexample or warning, depending on the perspective. For the British, French, Quebecers, Americans, Danish, Canadians and Germans, what happened in Iceland can indicate the worst of what could happen within their own borders. Who doesn't like Iceland? Before the crisis: almost no one except a few environmentalists condemning the fact that such a rich country could practise whaling. After the crisis? So many people that it's impossible to name them all: British, Belgian and Dutch depositors; employees of companies acquired by Icelandic conglomerates; the country's economic partners; Scottish nationalists who lost a model; social democrats around the world who considered Iceland's wealth as evidence of the superiority of its economic system; right-wing economists who thought the system reflected the success of neo liberalism. And, of course, Icelanders themselves, humiliated and ruined by the illusions brandished by a few of their countrymen, viewed as the modern reincarnation of the Viking. And yet, just months before, this country, liked by all, was at the top of happiness, wealth and equality indices. The media reported and exaggerated the facts, relayed rumours and accounts of the crisis, and disseminated a flood of true and false information, swamping Iceland and helping overturn the image of a country often idealised abroad. Ultimately, what happened in Iceland is a fascinating case of a country that fall was not only abrupt but of epic proportions. In that respect, the crisis there concerns us all.

* * *

Based on the imageology work of the 'Iceland and Images of the North' (INOR) research project and a pluridisciplinary approach to the sources and functions of national images, this study is intended to provide a detached, discursive analysis of the evolution of Iceland's image in the foreign media in 2008, a year in which the country experienced an unprecedented economic crisis in a particularly turbulent global context. It is not concerned with reviewing the facts of the crisis or explaining them, but rather with determining, through a dialectic approach, the main themes and topics of the articles written about Iceland during this period. It looks at these themes and topics from the perspective of image making—through the process of accumulation and concurrence—in order to measure the impact of what was said on Iceland's image abroad. In addition to imageology, this study relies on the hermeneutics of reception (Hans Robert Jauss[2] and Wolfgang Iser,[3] in particular), an ideological and sociological analysis of discourse (Marc Angenot[4] and Pierre Bourdieu[5]), and applications of such an analysis in a 'national' context (Micheline Cambron,[6] Dominique Perron[7] and Régine Robin[8]).

The 'material' for this study was selected from the thousands of articles published on Iceland in foreign newspapers. Most of the articles were culled through a systematic scan of nine major English- and French-language dailies—the *New York Times*, *Le Devoir*, the *International Herald Tribune*, the *Financial Times*, the Glasgow *Herald*, the *Globe and Mail*, the *Australian*, *Le Monde* and the *Guardian*—which are briefly described below. Other articles were collected on

---

2 Hans Robert Jauss, *Pour une herméneutique littéraire* (Paris: Gallimard, 1988); *Pour une esthétique de la réception* (Paris: Gallimard, 1990).
3 Wolfgang Iser, *The act of reading* (London: Routledge and Kegan Paul, 1978).
4 Marc Angenot, *1889 : un état du discours social* (Longueuil: Le Préambule, 1989); *La propagande socialiste : six essais d'analyse du discours* (Montréal: Éditions Balzac, 1997).
5 Pierre Bourdieu, *Les règles de l'art* (Paris: Seuil, 1992).
6 Micheline Cambron, *Une société, un récit* (Montréal: L'Hexagone, 1989).
7 Dominique Perron, *Le nouveau roman de l'énergie nationale* (Calgary: University of Calgary Press, 2006).
8 Régine Robin, *Berlin chantiers* (Paris: Stock, 2001); *La mémoire saturée* (Paris: Stock, 2003).

an ad hoc basis from some 30 other media sources, in order to round out the information and viewpoint. While it would have been impossible to include every article appearing in every daily newspaper worldwide—some of which may have had a bearing on the making of Iceland's image—the corpus compiled for this study nonetheless contains some 3,000 articles from different cultural, political and national contexts.

The crisis that shook Iceland in the fall of 2008 was, without a doubt, a media event. During the months preceding the crisis, the above-mentioned nine newspapers together published an average of 50 articles a month on Iceland; at the peak of the crisis in October and November 2008, they produced more than 900 articles. For a country like Iceland, whose role is said to be 'negligible' from a global standpoint, such numbers represent an excessive amount of discourse that battered the country's image, which had been patiently polished over the years.

* * *

One of the difficulties inherent in research of this nature is that new modes of circulation ultimately blur the line between editorial, news item, column and letter. The web sites of newspapers often mix the print version of articles with electronic texts, which may be written by the editorial team (e.g., journalists' blogs), readers or other sources. As a result, the newspaper's point of view gets lost in the shuffle, rather than being presented on the editorial page as it was in traditional, 20th century newspapers. *Le Monde*, for example, moved the blogs of its journalists and readers to the front page—in the space of one edition—to show that such 'new voices ... now seem to be fundamental forums for information and democratic debate'.[9]

---

9   Boris Razon, 'La journée des blogueurs', *Le Monde*, November 27, 2009. The original quote read: 'voix nouvelles ... paraissent aujourd'hui des lieux fondamentaux de l'information et du débat démocratique'.

This approach certainly provides for a better flow of information and more interactivity, but it also creates confusion about sources, opinions and viewpoints. The weight of media rumour increases, along with repeated expressions and republished news items—whether verified or not—all of which affect our understanding of a person, place or thing. The image of countries—people and situations—can thus be eroded by the flow of information and the ambiguity of sources; at the same time, it can be more easily altered. The circulation of articles (from large agencies like Associated Press, Agence France-Presse, etc., and media networks) also obscures editorial content: for example, it becomes very difficult to pinpoint the source of an article published by *Le Devoir*, obtained from *Le Monde* which, itself, is supplied by various print and television news agencies. For the purpose of this analysis, a text appearing in a newspaper (whether written by that paper's editorial team or not) was considered part of that newspaper's discursive corpus, as it was deemed to be a statement about which an editorial choice was made: the decision to publish an article, letter or excerpt of a blog remains the intellectual responsibility of the newspaper in question. The abundance of sources of media discourse is a modern-day phenomenon; these sources should be considered in an inclusive manner, and not be sorted according to principles established for times gone by.

In analysing the articles selected from the foreign media, a number of topics came to light. These topics—which form the subject matter of the chapters of this book—were then studied from a dialectic standpoint that was both synchronic (status of the topic in 2008) and diachronic (evolution of the topic from before, during and after the crisis). They concern the reactions reported from Iceland (violence, irresponsibility, humiliation), the function of discourse circulation (warning, arrogance, communication problems, humour), Iceland's relations with other countries (Scandinavia, Europe, Russia and the United Kingdom), and components of Iceland's image (equality, gender issues, traditions), as well as elements of the economic crisis, often shaded with moral and ethical concerns (the new Vikings, bankruptcy, social and economic incest and the impact of the crisis abroad). The goal here is to provide food for thought about the role of the media in the creation of crisis discourse by focusing on a fascinating case: that of the complete and sudden reversal of the image of a 'small' country, formerly admired by all. Of course, for Iceland, it is also a matter of grasping the effect of the deluge of foreign discourse that has defined it, the sum of which represents a burden that it can no longer ignore today.

* * *

Here is a brief description of the nine newspapers on which this study is based and their coverage of Iceland in 2008:

The *NEW YORK TIMES* (New York, United States) published about 75 articles on Iceland in 2008, i.e., feature analyses and short news items on the financial crisis in Europe, which also discussed Iceland. Founded in 1851, this daily is known for its editorial excellence (its journalists have won the Pulitzer Prize more than a hundred times) and has become a journalistic benchmark worldwide. It sells on average a million copies a run, and its articles are often published by other newspapers. Showing little interest in Iceland's problems, its journalists attempted to place the country's crisis in the broader context of Europe and the world to gain an understanding of the issues. They also endeavoured to determine the impact on Iceland's image abroad.

LE DEVOIR (Montréal, Québec, Canada) published some 40 articles on Iceland in 2008. Founded in 1910, this newspaper is one of the few independent dailies in Canada. Its importance in Québec lies more in its intellectual credibility than in its circulation (about 40,000 copies). Politically left, it advocates the role of the State, the right to political autonomy, and protection of the environment. Most of the articles appearing in this newspaper were favourable toward Iceland, perceived as a small sovereign country, a model of the struggle against social exclusion. The crisis was understood through the moral and ethical questions it raised for both Iceland and the rest of the world.

The *INTERNATIONAL HERALD TRIBUNE* (Paris, France, and New York, United States) published some 30 articles on Iceland in 2008. Founded in Paris in 1887 and originally intended for American expatriates, it became an international newspaper in the late 20th century. Supplied by its own correspondents and those of the *New York Times*, it is published in 35 different locations, circulated in 180 countries, and has a print run of about 250,000 copies. This newspaper favours analyses over editorial positions; however, its journalists took a cold, dark look at Iceland. Described as an isolated island, a small state of fragile sovereignty, Iceland was compared to other countries in crisis (the Ukraine, Argentina, Pakistan and Hungary). This newspaper was concerned about Iceland's approaching Russia and its conflict with the United Kingdom; it felt that Iceland's leaders should take responsibility for their actions.

The *FINANCIAL TIMES* (London, United Kingdom) published more than 400 articles concerning Iceland in 2008, close to 250 of which focused exclusively on the country. Founded in 1888, published in London and having a worldwide circulation of more than 400,000, it is one of the most highly respected financial newspapers in the world. Its exhaustive coverage of Iceland included an overview of the situation, an account of its daily evolution, and analyses by its expert journalists, David Ibison, Tom Braithwaite and Sarah O'Connor. Moderate in stance, this newspaper was interested in particular in the relations between Iceland and the United Kingdom, as well as in the connection between the events in Iceland and the global economic crisis.

The *HERALD* (Glasgow, United Kingdom) published some 30 articles on Iceland in 2008, for the most part positive and favourable toward the country. Founded in 1763, this newspaper is one of the world's oldest English-language dailies still in operation. It has a circulation of 60,000, is centre-left in orientation, and constitutes a forum for ideas. Its coverage of the crisis closely followed changes in Iceland's role, as a model or counter model, for Scottish independence.

The *GLOBE AND MAIL* (Toronto, Canada) published about 170 articles about Iceland in 2008, including 40 feature articles. Founded in 1844, this daily has a circulation of 350,000, is distributed nationally, and is the largest-circulation national newspaper in English Canada. Its journalists wrote articles that were rigorous, direct and bore fine distinctions, but were sometimes tinged with sarcasm. In them, Iceland was described as a desperate, arrogant country, ridiculed by the economic world and responsible for its own fate. The articles mentioned the effects of the crisis on Canada and its impact on Iceland's identity. Little mention was made of the conflict with the United Kingdom.

The *AUSTRALIAN* (Sydney, Australia) published about 70 articles on Iceland in 2008, the majority of which were very critical of the country's economic model and the conduct of its elite. Founded in 1964, this daily is centre-right, considers itself a national newspaper, and sells 200,000 copies on average. Located far from Europe and the Americas, its journalists view Europe and social democracy with scepticism. They focused on the moral aspect of the crisis in Iceland, the irresponsibility of the country's leaders, and the climate of political and economic collusion. For this newspaper, Iceland is an example of financial failure.

LE MONDE (Paris, France) published more than 110 articles on Iceland in 2008. Founded in 1944, this daily is known for its editorial quality and independence. With a circulation of 350,000, it is the

French-language daily that is best known internationally. Its journalists were interested in Iceland's models of social equality and wealth distribution, which they considered exemplary. They were concerned, however, about the financial difficulties that rocked the island and the collusion between authorities. *Le Monde* is pro-European Union and often referred to the advantages of the euro for countries like Iceland.

The *GUARDIAN* (London, United Kingdom) published close to 500 articles dealing with Iceland in 2008, over 130 of which were devoted exclusively to the country. Its journalists, David Teather among them, were interested in all aspects of Iceland (culture, society, international relations) and not only the economic issues. Traditionally labour-oriented and published by a foundation, the *Guardian* is one of the few independent dailies in the United Kingdom. It has a circulation of about 350,000. Reflecting Britain's concerns about Iceland, it was careful to avoid sensationalism and took a critical look at Iceland's situation.

In addition to the coverage of Iceland provided by these nine newspapers, ad hoc research was conducted in the following newspapers, periodicals and web sites: Agence France-Presse (AFP) (France), Associated Press (AP) (United States), *Aftenposten* (Norway), *BBC News* (United Kingdom), *Bloomberg* (United States), *BusinessWeek* (United States), *Channel 4 News* (United Kingdom), the *Chicago Tribune* (United States), *CNN Money.com* (United States), *Cyberpresse* (Québec), the *Daily Telegraph* (United Kingdom), the *Daily Times* (United States), *Dagsavisen* (Norway), the *Dallas Morning News* (United States), the *Detroit News* (United States), *Earthtimes*, the *Economist* (United Kingdom), the *Financial Mail* (South Africa), *Forbes* (United States), *Gawker*, *Groundreport*, the *Huffington Post* (United States), *Iceland.org* (Iceland), *IcelandReview.com* (Iceland), *Icenews* (Iceland), *L'Express* (France), the *Independent* (United Kingdom), *La Presse* (Québec), *Money Week* (United Kingdom), *Moscow News* (Russia), the *New Yorker* (United States), *NRC Handelsblad* (Netherlands), *Politiken* (Denmark), Canadian Press (CP) (Canada), Reuters (United Kingdom), RIA Novosti (Russia), *Sedlabanki.is* (Iceland), the *Sunday Times* (United Kingdom), the *Telegraph* (United Kingdom), *Télérama* (France), the *Times* (United Kingdom), *Time* (United States), *Vanity Fair* (United States), the *Wall Street Journal* (United States), the *Washington Post* (United States), *Wikileaks* and *Yahoo News*.

THE ROLE OF THE MEDIA
DRAMATISATION OF THE CRISIS

'A crisis? That's the media's fault!'
Le Devoir, January 8, 2009[1]

In the spring of 2008, foreign journalists reported a possible conspiracy against Iceland, led by media. This idea, which later disappeared, provided food for thought about the role of the media, its power and its ability to stir people up or calm them down in times of crisis. During the events of 2008, politicians and bankers worldwide accused the media of not properly gauging its impact and of sensationalising events, in some cases to the point of creating crises then reporting on them. This idea could well apply not only to Iceland's situation, but to any crisis, as Mark Fenton-O'Creevy, a professor at Open University, suggests: 'media stories on the current turmoil are not just reflecting events, they are also creating them'.[2] Yet, journalism is essential: it provides information, issues warnings, produces analyses and offers an outside point of view on events; it also provides a daily chronicle of events which is revealed from one article and media to another and constitutes a sort of day-to-day record of contemporary times: 'journalism, so the adage goes, is the first draft of history'.[3]

During the crisis in Iceland, the banks, governments and financiers were very aware of the importance of communications and used

---

[1] Canadian Press, 'La crise? C'est la faute aux médias!', *Le Devoir*, January 8, 2009.
[2] Mark Fenton-O'Creevy, quoted by Tim Harford, 'Shock news? The media didn't get us into this mess', *Financial Times*, December 13, 2008, p. 12.
[3] Lionel Barber, 'How gamblers broke the banks', *Financial Times*, December 15, 2008.

them extensively in an attempt to influence perceptions. For example, while signs of the crisis were growing, Baugur Group simply claimed the contrary in a news release: 'Baugur has maintained that it is not affected by the economic turmoil in Iceland.'[4] As if *saying* so were enough to *create the fact* or reality. Similarly, when Moody's rating agency downgraded its rating of the Icelandic State and banks in March 2008, the government responded with a communication strategy rather than an economic one: according to an article in *Le Monde*, 'The Prime Minister, Geir Haarde, and the Icelandic banks waged a communication battle against what they called irrational mistrust.'[5] Using battle language, the Chairman of the Board of House of Fraser, a company affiliated with Baugur Group, declared at the peak of the crisis in October that 'like in the war—"dangerous talk costs lives".'[6] Poland's Deputy Finance Minister also believed that the media's coverage of the reaction of financial markets was 'an "infection" ... based more on psychology than on economic fundamentals.'[7] The chief economist of the Conference Board of Canada also alluded to the 'psychology of recession', stating that 'if [the media] continues to say that the sky is going to fall, people think that the sky is going to fall.'[8]

No one doubted that the economic crisis rocking Iceland in the fall of 2008 was real—certainly not Icelanders, for whom exaggerated media discourse in no way helped ease their worries about the very practical problems facing their country—or that it could have serious repercussions abroad. However, the way in which it was reported

---

4 Lucy Killgren, 'Moss Bros says Baugur talks continue', *Financial Times*, April 3, 2008.
5 George Hay, 'Le sang se glace dans les veines de l'Islande', Économie, *Le Monde*, October 7, 2008, p. 17. The original quote read: 'Le premier ministre, Geir Haarde, et [l]es établissements bancaires [islandais] ont engagé une bataille de communication contre ce qu'ils qualifient de défiance irrationnelle'.
6 Don McCarthy, quoted by Tom Braithwaite, 'Baugur evades Icelandic chill', *Financial Times*, October 4, 2008, p. 19.
7 Katarzyna Zajdel-Kurowska, quoted by Jan Cienski and Thomas Escritt, 'New EU members spared worst of crisis', *Financial Times*, October 11, 2008, p. 13.
8 Glen Hodgson, quoted by Canadian Press, 'La crise? C'est la faute aux médias!', *Le Devoir*, January 8, 2009. The original quote read: 'Si [les médias] continuent à dire que le ciel nous tombe sur la tête, les gens pensent que le ciel leur tombe sur la tête'.

by the foreign media—in terms of implosion, chaos and collapse—worsened the situation and made Iceland a pathetic example of the financial failure the world was experiencing.

The power of the media is considerable. Sometimes there is a significant difference between the words reported and the reality of a situation. Sometimes events are considered, first and foremost, *media* events—produced, communicated and used strictly by the media. The tone and style adopted by newspapers can magnify the facts, giving them a dramatic or tragic aspect, creating an *ethos* to make the news more appealing to readers.

The crisis in Iceland was the subject of a media storm, a blitz of articles, rumours, explanations, reports, biases, etc. that dramatised the situation by using disaster scenarios in particular. These scenarios ultimately forged the 'Icelandic crisis' like an ethos, shaping a narrative supplied by daily news from all over the world into a vast and powerful discursive network. In all the hubbub, the small voice of Iceland—that of the government, businesses and people—seemed to serve only the purpose of providing an air of tragedy to the story. Portrayed through oversized lens, the country stood by, powerless, as its image underwent a complete and sudden reversal.

Such dramatisation was based, in some cases, on personal accounts, which made events seem more plausible. The *Globe and Mail*, for example, used an interview with a modest sheep farmer, Bragi Vagnsson, to indicate that the crisis was forcing Icelanders to abandon sometimes ancestral traditions, in this case an occupation practised for 500 years. The example raised concern about the loss of Iceland's identity and values, threatened by the country's financial turmoil, referred to as 'Iceland's meltdown'.[9] The comments of politicians also dramatised the situation, making it seem critical; Reykjavík city councillor Oddný Sturludóttir was quoted as saying that 'the tension

---

9 Robert Jackson and Brian Milner, 'Iceland's meltdown', *Globe and Mail*, June 3, 2008, p. B-1.

is incredible. ... I am really afraid of what is going to happen'.[10] Since politicians are sensitive to what the media says, the way in which the media reports the facts can influence the words and deeds of leaders. Thus, when the British government invoked anti-terrorism legislation to freeze Icelanders' assets, foreign journalists interpreted the move as confirmation of the disaster scenarios which they, themselves, had contributed to spreading. In addition to grappling with an internal economic crisis, Iceland found itself at the centre of a situation that threatened to extend far beyond its borders.

At certain times, foreign readers may have wondered whether what they were reading was really about Iceland or about an unprecedented global economic crisis *based on the case of Iceland*, which had become an icon of the worse-case scenario, a warning of a cataclysm that threatened the world. Foreign journalists were certainly not shy about using strong images to describe Iceland as a country in the grips of its financiers. Nor were they reluctant to use disaster vocabulary—such as *abyss, implosion, paralysis, catastrophe, sinking, crash, chaos, lost values, lost generation, risk of depopulation, depression, uprising* and even *civil war*—to qualify the difficulties experienced by Iceland. It is not surprising that foreign readers ultimately perceived Iceland as the most extreme case, which reassured them about what was going on in their own country. Here are a few examples of the images and scenarios reported:

> *On the brink of the abyss,* Iceland *is making a tremendous effort on all fronts,* from Moscow to the International Monetary Fund (IMF), to find the liquidities it desperately needs to *escape bankruptcy.*[11]

---

10 Oddný Sturludóttir, quoted by Matthew Hart, 'Iceland's next saga: The wounded tiger's tale', *Globe and Mail*, November 15, 2008, p. F-4.
11 Agence France-Presse, '*Au bord du gouffre,* l'Islande *se démène sous tous les fronts*, de Moscou au Fonds monétaire international (FMI), pour trouver les liquidités qui lui font cruellement défaut et *échapper à la faillite*', *Le Devoir*, October 16, 2008 (italics added).

The *entire* banking system of Iceland had *imploded*.[12]

All imports have been blocked. Short of currencies, the Central Bank is refusing outflows of kronur. *There is a shortage of many products in stores.* Only the food and pharmaceutical sectors have been spared. Without money, *Iceland is paralysed.*[13]

Blood is freezing in Iceland's *veins.* ... Iceland is about to sink.[14]

Look at Iceland: ... a housing market *in crisis, distressed* banks and a market *crash*.[15]

It was the day Iceland *came crashing down to earth*. A team of British treasury experts flew into Reykjavik, *like emergency doctors at a car crash*.[16]

Iceland's *descent into financial chaos* accelerated last night as the Government took over a third bank.[17]

---

12 Terry McCrann, 'Treasury is no longer a bastion of reason', *Australian*, November 1, 2008 (italics added).
13 Élise Vincent, '*Toutes les importations sont bloquées.* À court de devises, la Banque centrale refuse les sorties de couronnes. *Beaucoup de produits manquent dans les boutiques.* Seuls les secteurs alimentaire et pharmaceutique sont épargnés. Privée d'argent, *l'Islande est un pays paralysé*.' *Le Monde*, October 24, 2008, p. 21 (italics added).
14 George Hay, '*Le sang se glace dans les veines* de l'Islande, [...] L'Islande est au bord du *naufrage*.' Économie, *Le Monde*, October 7, 2008, p. 17, http://www.breakingviews.com/ (italics added).
15 Derek DeCloet, 'Credit crisis. Smells like Norway in 1990', *Globe and Mail*, July 17, 2008, p. B-2 (italics added).
16 Roger Boyes, 'Iceland braces for Brits wanting their money back', *Australian*, October 13, 2008 (italics added).
17 Correspondents in London and Reykjavik, 'Another Iceland bank for rescue by Government', *Australian*, October 10, 2008 (italics added).

> The small insular state *collapsed* as soon as foreign investors deemed that the Icelandic government was incapable of *rescuing* its *crushed* banks. ... The country's currency *sank like a lead ingot*.[18]

The following description, appearing in a *Globe and Mail* article, provides an apocalyptic picture of the situation:

> *In real terms*, the gross domestic product *has crashed* by 65 per cent. The island faces *a sudden spasm of depopulation* as *Icelanders prepare to flee* in search of work. *Anger, shame and dread* have spread like *pathogens*. They *depress the mood* of this northern capital as much as the *empty construction sites* and the gallows of idle cranes.[19]

The rumours and exaggerations that were circulated may have actually caused panic, as Tom Braithwaite suggested: 'Iceland's capital was enduring a psychological battle as talk of food and oil shortages was being dismissed as irresponsible by government ministers, anxious to damp the threat of panic.'[20] *Psychological battle*, *shortages*, *anxious* and *panic*: these words forged a context in which the voices of officials, themselves discredited because of their poor management of the crisis, appeared weak and powerless. Thus the media had a real impact on Iceland's internal crisis, even though the news was reported by foreign journalists.

The media buzz in the spring of 2008 about a possible conspiracy against Iceland is a good example of the impact that continuous re-

---

18 Hugo Dixon and Edward Hadas, 'Le syndrome islandais guette le Royaume-Uni', Économie, *Le Monde*, November 18, 2008, p. 17. The original quote read: 'Le petit État insulaire s'est écroulé aussitôt que les investisseurs étrangers ont jugé l'État islandais incapable *de secourir* ses banques *écrasées* [...]. La devise nationale *a coulé comme un lingot de plomb*' (italics added).
19 Matthew Hart, 'Iceland's next saga: The wounded tiger's tale', *Globe and Mail*, November 15, 2008, p. F-4 (italics added).
20 Tom Braithwaite, 'Baugur evades Icelandic chill', *Financial Times*, October 4, 2008, p. 19 (italics added).

porting of news—which may not have been news—can have. According to a rumour spread by the newspapers between March 28 and April 9, a group of foreign investors met to plot against Iceland one night in January 2008 at the bar at 101 Hotel in Reykjavík, the haunt of Iceland's financial elite, at the invitation of the American bank Bear Stearns. That bank, which found itself in a perilous situation two months later, reportedly invited the investors to talk about the state of Iceland's economy. According to various sources, the agenda was to topple Iceland's economy in order to profit from it.

In an article published by the *Financial Times* on April 9, David Ibison wrote the following:

> What transpired at this dinner has entered into legend within Iceland's close-knit financial community. ... What started as an alcohol-fuelled evening has become a full-blown investigation by Iceland's Financial Supervisory Authority into an alleged speculative attack by hedge funds on Iceland's currency, banking system and stock market.[21]

The assumption of a conspiracy was based on a series of questions asked by different media, in particular the *Financial Times* beginning on March 28. Comparing Iceland's situation to that of Hong Kong a few years earlier, the newspaper reported suspicions about the specific circumstances of the crisis in Iceland, stating: 'No one denies Iceland faces significant hurdles. But the question remains: to what extent are these economic fissures being widened and exploited by professional speculators?'[22] The persistent doubts indicated that *some people* had an interest in destabilising Iceland's economy, in particular through the inappropriate use of the media, i.e., by circulating un-

---

[21] David Ibison, 'Cool under fire Iceland takes the fight back to finance', *Financial Times*, April 9, 2008, p. 7.
[22] David Ibison, 'To Iceland from Hong Kong', *Financial Times*, March 28, 2008.

founded news: 'via a news hungry media addicted to headlines such as "Iceland melts".'[23]

The newspapers did not let go. The day after the supposed meeting at 101 Hotel, David Ibison reported that the Governor of Iceland's Central Bank, Davið Oddsson, had announced a disastrous hike in the inflation rate and 'claimed that "dishonest brokers" were behind the country's problems'.[24] On March 31, the *Financial Times* indicated that such a theory was plausible in the case of a country as vulnerable as Iceland: 'Vicious rumours recently almost drove a British bank off a cliff. Could that happen to a country? Probably not to the US, the UK or Germany. But it could happen to a small country of which most of us know little.'[25] The allegations of a conspiracy appearing in the newspapers gave rise to an inquiry, which was conducted by Iceland's Financial Supervisory Authority and supported by Kaupþing bank. The telephone calls and emails between Bear Stearns and four investment funds[26] were among the items analysed in an effort to shed light on the matter. Even Prime Minister Haarde was part of the climate of mistrust, sending Bear Stearns a witty remark—'A bear trap needs to be a surprise'[27]—while asserting that he wanted to punish the foreign investment funds ... although he did not specify how.

Shortly after the announcement, news about the inquiry in the foreign media virtually dried up. The severity of Iceland's economic difficulties, as of late September, and the media storm resulting from it—or causing it—relegated the conspiracy theory against Iceland to the shadows—a theory that began with questions in the newspapers,

---

23 Ibid.
24 David Ibison, 'Iceland inflation hits six-year high', *Financial Times*, March 29, 2008, p. 2.
25 Wolfgang Munchau, 'Do not be alarmed by Icelandic whispers', *Financial Times*, March 31, 2008, p. 7.
26 According to David Ibison, the funds were DA Capital Europe, King Street, Merrill Lynch GSRG and Sandelman Partners ('Iceland counters alleged attacks', *Financial Times*, March 31, 2008, p. 6).
27 Geir Haarde, quoted by David Ibison, 'Iceland threatens direct market intervention', *Financial Times*, April 2, 2008, p. 8.

but that will remain in people's minds for a long time to come. At least that is what the *Financial Times* suggested as late as August 2009, when the International Monetary Fund expressed some doubts about the reforms under way in Iceland: 'The view in London is that Iceland has a tendency to imagine a British or Dutch conspiracy behind any bad news.'[28]

Did the media go too far? Was the crisis in Iceland purely a product of media discourse? On the one hand, David Ibison of the *Financial Times* suggested it was, claiming as early as March that the media not only contributed to worsening the climate of panic, but was also partly responsible for the crisis itself: 'Some Iceland watchers argue that while the country undoubtedly faces formidable challenges, ... it is the victim of misinformed rumours, misunderstandings and a vicious whispering campaign.'[29] Victimisation aside, media rumours influence perception: 'The uncomfortable fact for Iceland is that the rumours and talk of a crisis could create the crisis.'[30] Obviously, such dramatisation did not help foreigners gain an adequate understanding of Iceland's situation. To the rest of the world, Iceland looked like a country going down: 'Iceland is burning.'[31]

On the other hand, Tim Harford of the *Financial Times* emphasised that while the situation was reported by the newspapers, it was nonetheless real and a reflection of a deep financial imbalance. He also indicated that if the newspapers had to take any responsibility for the crisis, it was not that they fabricated the crisis, but that they did not warn the public soon enough about the dangers financial analysts had detected:

---

28 George Parker and Andrew Ward, 'IMF plays down rift loan to Iceland', *Financial Times*, August 1, 2009.
29 David Ibison, 'Icelandic whispers shake faith in boom', *Financial Times*, March 25, 2008.
30 Ibid.
31 Íris Erlingsdóttir, 'Iceland is burning', *Huffington Post*, January 20, 2009.

When Iceland's banking system collapsed in October, the problem was not that the media had panicked depositors. On the contrary: even as the money markets utterly lost confidence, British newspapers were claiming that Icesave offered one of the best savings products around.[32]

A media event or not, in hindsight, the coverage of Iceland by the foreign press during 2008 seems excessive, given the size of the country's economy and the crisis experienced at the same time by the Americas, Europe and Asia.

---

32 Tim Harford, 'Shock news? The media didn't get us into this mess', *Financial Times*, December 13, 2008, p. 12.

PART ONE

ASSETS IN JEOPARDY

AN EGALITARIAN, PROGRESSIVE AND PEACEFUL COUNTRY
AN INDEPENDENT UTOPIA

> 'Iceland is *the only* country in the world ... It was *one of the few* countries in the world, *perhaps the only one* ...'
> Financial Times, November 15, 2008[1]

Before the crisis, Iceland enjoyed an excellent reputation in the West, where it was seen as an egalitarian, progressive, peaceful, cultured and ecological society. Prior to and during 2008, all the foreign newspapers published articles and studies ranking Iceland at the top of international wealth, equality and happiness charts. For many foreigners, Iceland represented a model, an ideal, almost a utopia, that seemed unshakeable.

So much has been written about Iceland's qualities—its integrity, openness, prosperity, resilience and balance—that the country enjoyed an embellished reputation. The following description—written by journalist Robert Jackson, who lived in Iceland for several years—provides one example among many of this favourable bias:

> Give it a population of 300,000, about the same as Coventry, 70 per cent of them in the cities of Reykjavik and Akureyri. Ensure they are all related and give the majority the ability to trace their ancestry back to the times of settlement, more than a thousand years earlier. Endow these people with industry and ambition.

---
[1] Robert Jackson, 'Letter from Iceland', *Financial Times*, November 15, 2008 (italics added).

Give them their own language—all but unchanged for a millennium—a literary tradition, three national newspapers, two television channels, free universal healthcare and education and close to zero unemployment. Give this country a consistently high ranking in the world standard-of-living charts and you have the Iceland of the recent past. Not a bad place, all in all.[2]

Like the other Nordic countries, Iceland ranked high on equality, quality of life and progressiveness scales. Foreign newspapers—depending on their own particular values—regularly mentioned these favourable ratings, which supported and affirmed the main characteristics of Iceland's world image. *Le Devoir* emphasized that the northern European countries had closed 'about 80% of the gap between men and women'[3] and that Iceland scored fourth on the equality scale. The *Australian* published one article on life expectancy, in which Iceland topped the life expectancy ladder for men,[4] and another on an international study regarding the quality of childcare services, in which Iceland ranked second.[5]

In early 2008, the newspapers reported the death of American chess player Bobby Fischer, who had been exiled in Iceland since 2005.[6] The fact that Fischer obtained Icelandic citizenship, while detained in Japan awaiting extradition to the United States, was mentioned as an indication of Icelanders' open-mindedness toward outcasts and marginals. This characteristic was seen as an extension of the country's

---

2 Ibid.
3 Agence France-Presse, 'Égalité hommes-femmes: les pays nordiques toujours en tête', *Le Devoir*, November 12, 2008. The original quote read: 'environ 80% de l'écart existant entre les hommes et les femmes'.
4 Stephen Lunn, '"Never say die" trend persists as life expectancies rise', *Australian*, November 26, 2008.
5 Australian Associated Press, 'UN report finds Australia third worst in developed world', *Australian*, December 12, 2008.
6 David Ibison, 'Bobby Fischer: chess genius and estranged American, dies in isolation', *Financial Times*, January 19, 2008, p. 1.

egalitarian values. However, it was the replacement of Iceland's male Prime Minister Geir Haarde, by a woman, Jóhanna Sigurðardóttir, referred to as 'socialism incarnate',[7] that attracted the most foreign commentary: one, because Sigurðardóttir was the first head of state to openly declare she was gay; and two, because her sexual orientation seemed of little importance to Icelanders. That was viewed as yet another indication of Iceland's progressiveness.

Iceland had come by its wealth and social equality relatively recently. Unlike other countries, Iceland had decided to distribute its newfound wealth by investing heavily in health and education. As a result, it has ranked high in wellness studies: 'A 2007 United Nations report measuring life expectancy, real per-capita income and educational levels identified Iceland as the world's best country in which to live.'[8] Iceland's exponential economic growth was seen by many as miraculous: a small country of fishermen—isolated from Europe and the Americas, plagued through history by natural disasters and famines, and afflicted by waves of emigration—became one of the world's richest and most egalitarian societies in just a few decades. Seeking to understand the reasons for this success, the *Australian* wrote:

> Iceland's wealth has long been *a mystery*. ... Even after independence from Denmark in 1944, Iceland remained poor—although laying the basis for future prosperity with an excellent education system, near-universal literacy and a work ethic that drove almost every adult to take two or even three jobs. By the start of the millennium, however, Iceland had become *extraordinarily rich*.[9]

---

[7] 'Fellow MP Agust Einarsson went as far as to call her "socialism incarnate".' Jonas Moody, 'Iceland picks the world's first openly gay PM', *Time*, January 30, 2009.
[8] Sarah Lyall, 'Stunned Icelanders struggle after economy's fall', *New York Times*, November 9, 2008.
[9] *Australian*, 'Iceland's economic collapse could herald a new round of large-scale acquisitions', October 9, 2008 (italics added).

To put the *extraordinary* rise of Iceland in perspective, journalists recalled the deep poverty the island had once known: 'Iceland used to be one of Europe's poorest countries, a bleak place that survived mostly on fishing revenue and the occasional adventurous tourist',[10] 'one of the poorest countries in the Western world',[11] and so on. Iceland is portrayed in foreign media as a country that made up for this lag so quickly, through foreign acquisitions and expansions, infrastructure development and social policies, that by the turn of the century it had become one of the world's richest nations.

Iceland's reputation as a peaceful country is based on facts that are often confirmed by international studies. A global index published in May 2008 found that Iceland is the world's most peaceful country, at the opposite end of the spectrum from major powers Russia and the United States. The index takes both internal and external factors into account: 'Countries are ranked according to how peaceful they are domestically and how they interact with the outside world.'[12] An exceptionally pacifist country, Iceland has a spotless record; as the Czech Minister of Foreign Affairs told the *Financial Times*: 'I think Iceland is the only country that's had no connection with war criminals over the past 100 years—and perhaps Denmark.'[13] The Icelandic government, of course, took advantage of the country's peaceful reputation to promote its role in international diplomacy, seeking a seat on the United Nations Security Council in the summer of 2008. When the May 2008 index was released, the *Guardian* reported that Icelandic Minister of Foreign Affairs, Ingibjörg Sólrún Gísladóttir, called a press conference to emphasize that his country's reputation was 'a driving force in ... [its] first-time candidacy for a non-

---

10 Peter Gumbel, 'Iceland: the country that became a hedge fund', *Fortune*, December 4, 2008, http://www.money.cnn.com/.
11 Élise Vincent, 'Naufragés d'Islande', Horizons, *Le Monde*, October 24, 2008, p. 21. The original quote read: 'l'un des pays les plus pauvres du monde occidental'.
12 Reuters, 'Iceland most peaceful place to live: report', *Australian*, May 21, 2008.
13 Karel Schwarzenberg, quoted by Tony Barber, 'Note to Europe: we are not all saints', *Financial Times*, December 9, 2008, p. 12.

permanent seat on the UN security council'.[14] Unfortunately, the economic crisis and resulting diplomatic tensions with a number of European countries dashed Iceland's hopes and the country did not receive the seat it sought in 2008.

People abroad say that Iceland's culture is a reflection of its landscapes. Thanks to its cultural riches—from the sagas of the Middle Ages to the works of contemporary artists—Iceland holds a surprisingly prominent place in world culture given its size and population. Its reputation as a Mecca for culture has certainly earned it favourable international coverage. A commentary in the *Guardian* suggested that the Icelandic sagas are Europe's most important literary work,[15] ahead of Shakespeare's plays and even Homer's *Iliad*. Comments from readers indicate that Iceland is seen as a literary society: 'Let us begin with a question: which is the best read country in the world? Recent research revealed that in Iceland more books are written, published and sold per person per year than anywhere else on the planet.'[16] Reading became even more important to Icelanders during the crisis. Jill Lawless of the *Detroit News* indicated that she was fascinated by Icelanders' basic need to read: 'Runar Birgisson says sales at his bookstall have doubled since the country's main commercial banks collapsed in early October. "In Iceland, books are not a luxury item", he said. "They are very important for your soul".'[17] Books on the crisis, including *Hvíta bókin* (The White Book) by Einar Már Guðmundsson, were among the bestsellers in 2009.[18]

Iceland is also perceived abroad as a "green" country in the ecological sense, in particular because of its avant-garde use of geothermics and its political will to stop relying on fossil fuels in the medium term.

---

14 Ingibjörg Sólrún Gísladóttir, quoted by Duncan Campbell, 'World "more peaceful" in 2008', *Guardian*, May 20, 2008.
15 *Guardian*, 'The Icelandic sagas: Europe's most important book?', October 3, 2008.
16 Ibid.
17 Jill Lawless, 'Crisis gives Iceland gift of frugality', *Detroit News*, December 25, 2008.
18 *IcelandReview.com*, 'Book on Iceland crisis to be published abroad', July 18, 2009.

With the country's abundant hydroelectric and thermal power, Iceland has a notable green record: as a headline in the *Guardian* says, 'Iceland's energy answer comes naturally'.[19] However, some people question the island's 'natural' image; after seeing the traffic congestion in Reykjavík, David Teather wrote: 'expensive four-wheel drives creep down the narrow main street'.[20] Perhaps such ostentatious signs of wealth flouting fossil fuel waste are more offensive in Iceland than elsewhere because of its green reputation.

Of all the indices that provide for a worldwide comparison of countries, the happiness index is certainly the one that attracts the most interest and the most scepticism. The Scandinavian countries, including Iceland, rank high on this scale: 'We know from the World Database of Happiness that it's usually Denmark, Iceland, Switzerland—they trade places in terms of No. 1.—Um, Iceland? A land of darkness, extreme cold and ice?'[21] The idea of 'happiness' combines Iceland's positive characteristics—egalitarian, progressive, peaceful, cultured and ecological—into a single trait. The ingredients of Icelanders' happiness? One would be strength of character: in spite of the country's extreme climate and geography, Icelanders manage to find contentment. Of course, these are stereotypes and statistics provided by the media to give an overall view of Iceland and Icelanders. Another ingredient, according to American correspondent Eric Weiner, would be naiveté: 'Have you ever met a happy cynic? Among the Icelanders, they sort of embrace naiveté. To do anything really great in this world, you have to be a little bit naive—otherwise you wouldn't do it'.[22] For British journalist Peter Barber, happiness can be contradictory: 'someone can be happily unhappy, which the British, like the Icelanders, know instinctively,[23] Icelanders' happiness

---

19 Jessica Aldred, 'Iceland's energy answer comes naturally', *Guardian*, April 22, 2008.
20 David Teather, 'Iceland first to feel the blast of global cooling', *Guardian*, April 17, 2008.
21 Eric Weiner, interviewed by Julie Traves, 'Happy trails?', *Globe and Mail*, February 23, 2008, p. T-1.
22 Ibid.
23 Peter Barber, 'On the lookout for a happy ending', *Financial Times*, September 29, 2008, p.10.

would also include a measure of insouciance, as British columnist A.A. Gill indicates in his description of a young man walking down a Reykjavík street:

> A young man passing by, dressed in the winter uniform of Icelandic youth—skinny jeans, T-shirt with ironic postmodern slogan, Converses and a bit of a useless scarf, hunched shoulders and a general air of thermometer-denial and hungover insouciance—stops and laughs.[24]

To Iceland's advantage, its reputation as an egalitarian, peaceful and ecological country is so firmly rooted in the discourse that its image partially withstood the media storm unleashed by the crisis. For at least a few months, however, this discourse was drowned out by a tidal wave of more negative images. Some commentators suggest that Iceland's financiers used their country's good reputation to create investor confidence, raise capital, borrow, acquire foreign businesses and control part of the world economy. According to an article appearing in the *Australian*, 'Iceland was not only cool climatically but culturally. ... However, the wealth came not simply from hard work, initiative and valuable catches of cod. It was also built on a massive inflow of funds into the country's banks and highly leveraged raids on the riches of western Europe.'[25]

Despite this bitter analysis, many people continue to see Iceland as a model that inspires and that should guide the action and conduct of other countries. Thus, any tarnishing of its image also affects them, since it is not *only* Iceland that sinks in this crisis, but *also* the hope of a better, fairer and more equitable world.

---

24 A.A. Gill, 'Iceland: frozen assets', *Sunday Times*, December 14, 2008.
25 *Australian*, 'Iceland's economic collapse could herald a new round of large-scale acquisitions', October 9, 2008.

The disappointment of seeing Iceland drawn into a moral, ethical and identity crisis shook those who viewed the country as an ideal of peace, equality and happiness: this disillusionment partially explains the interest of foreign journalists in Iceland throughout 2008, since events on the island are part of a broader issue that affects many.

THE IMPACT OF THE CRISIS ABROAD
A GENERAL DISLIKE OF ICELAND

> 'We have behaved like children and not been able to take care of ourselves and done damage to people in other countries.'
> Thorbjörn Broddason, quoted
> in the *Globe and Mail*, November 15, 2008[1]

For a small country, being in the headlines of world news for several weeks while one of the century's worst global economic crises is unfolding can be quite a shock. Yet, for a number of weeks, the media was abuzz with news about Iceland, urgently releasing information, dwelling on biases and stereotypes, making assumptions and providing interpretations. Then, suddenly, the racket stopped as quickly as it had started. During this time, the small voice of reason—the one conveying facts and corrections—was unable to make itself heard. Having been at the centre of a media storm can forever change how foreigners view a country. In Iceland's case, it also changed Icelanders' own perception of their country. The awakening after the crisis was painful. People realized that actions they thought were strictly domestic in scope had repercussions abroad: 'We were left alone in the middle of the ocean for 1,000 years and nobody paid notice to us,' quipped Icelandic artist Hallgrímur Helgason. 'Now, Iceland can't get out of the spotlight.'[2]

Analyst Chris Giles quantified the repercussions in no uncertain

---

1 Thorbjörn Broddason, quoted by Matthew Hart, 'Iceland's next saga: The wounded tiger's tale', *Globe and Mail*, November 15, 2008, p. F-4.
2 Hallgrímur Helgason, quoted by Christina Talcott, 'Enjoying Iceland's wonders for less', *Washington Post*, December 14, 2008.

terms, in an article in the *Financial Times* on October 8, 2008, stating that:

> For the rest of the world, Iceland's economy is an irrelevance. But for those with money tied up in its banking system—banks owe foreigners $80bn (€59bn, £45bn)—the losses threaten to be large, particularly as the krona depreciates, reducing further the ability to meet its obligations.[3]

Reactions to the events taking place in Iceland were many and varied. Some people feared a domino effect from the North; others viewed Iceland's situation as a warning of what could happen elsewhere. Still others saw it as the spark that could set off an explosion: 'Despite its size, with a population of just 313,000, a financial crisis in Iceland could deliver a further blow to worldwide confidence. Cracks emerging in its economy ... were seen as a lead indicator of the turmoil to follow.'[4] Others managed to laugh about it, but their humour always reflected a new, less positive view of Iceland: 'We aren't as badly off as many', a British jeweller told the *Financial Times*. 'Look at Iceland.'[5]

Be that as it may, depending on the country and the perspective, people were concerned about how the crisis in Iceland would affect their particular interests: in the United Kingdom and Germany, those interests were, first and foremost, economic; in Scotland, the stakes were mainly political; and in the Netherlands, they were both. An unfavourable view of Iceland developed in these countries, straining their relations with the island.

---

3 Chris Giles, 'Topsy-turvy logic leaves an unpalatable choice', *Financial Times*, October 8, 2008, p. 4.
4 David Teather, 'Banking crisis: Iceland takes control of Glitnir', *Guardian*, September 29, 2008.
5 Chris Tighe, 'Shoppers sniff at chancellors' VAT cut', *Financial Times*, November 25, 2008.

One of the big surprises of the crisis, for Iceland, was the realisation that its domestic situation had serious consequences for a number of countries, i.e., that its actions were damaging for people elsewhere in the world and had an economically destabilising impact. That was certainly true for the United Kingdom, where the newspapers followed very closely the spectacular failure of the Icesave bank and the risks associated with Icelandic investments in a number of commercial sectors in Britain. It was also true for Europe in general (especially Germany, the Netherlands, Denmark, Sweden and Finland), as well as for Canada and the United States. The crisis even made waves in the sports world as a result of Icelandic interests in wellknown teams, such as London's West Ham United Football Club,[6] whose fans were worried about its survival.

The mess created by the bankruptcy of the Internet bank Icesave triggered economic destabilisation. The lack of tact with which the bank announced its closing was interpreted as arrogance, and turned public opinion in the United Kingdom, the Netherlands and Germany against Icelandic financiers. Then, the months-long debate over the compensation of depositors (through foreign government loans to the Icelandic government, which the latter initially refused)[7] fuelled resentment both toward Icesave and other Icelandic banks.[8]

London reacted very strongly to the crisis in Iceland, following a series of articles published in the British dailies on the situation; its hostility was shared by a large part of Europe's media. As the *International Herald Tribune* reported, 'Britain may be the biggest and

---

[6] Gary Jacob of the *Times* wrote the following: 'Fears grew yesterday that West Ham United is on the brink of a financial crisis after Bjorgolfur Gudmundsson, the club's owner, was dragged into the global credit crisis.' ('Vultures in the air circling West Ham', from the *Australian*, October 9, 2008.)

[7] After announcing an agreement with the Dutch government, *NRC Handelsblad* reported that Iceland was now refusing the Netherlands' assistance: 'Iceland may reject one billion euro Dutch loan', November 13, 2008.

[8] See, for example, Robert Anderson and Tom Braithwaite, 'Icelandic bank Kaupthing fights for survival', *Financial Times*, October 9, 2008, p. 16.

noisiest claimant, but it is not the only creditor feeling the effects of the collapse of the Icelandic financial system.'[9]

For the United Kingdom, the stakes were high and the British newspapers voiced constant concern about the large number of jobs threatened by Iceland's financial collapse, namely the '55,000 people who work[ed] for Baugur-controlled companies in the UK'.[10] They listed the major British businesses under Icelandic control: 'House of Fraser, Debenhams, Woolworths, Moss Bros, French Connection and the supermarket chain Iceland'.[11] They expressed fears about the sale of these businesses, at the height of the global downturn, stating that 'Icelandic banks have lent money to well-known British retailing and pub groups, raising fears that their collapse could lead to a firesale of British assets.'[12] And they criticized the lack of ethics of Icelandic banks, which artificially inflated the British market, using large easily-obtained loans, claiming that Kaupþing 'was the bank that liked to say yes to some of the UK's most colourful entrepreneurs. ... It played a significant role in the debt-fuelled property boom in the UK'.[13]

In Scotland, Royal Bank of Scotland said it had suffered losses as a result of its ties with Icelandic partners;[14] at the same time, Icelandair suspended flights between Reykajvík and Glasgow, marking an end to the prosperous years in which Icelanders brought business to Scottish boutiques:

> The cancellation of services to the city [by Icelandair] increases the pressure on an already hard-pressed retail

---

9 Eric Pfanner, 'Iceland banks face claims from depositors abroad', *International Herald Tribune*, October 10, 2008.
10 Tom Braithwaite et al., 'Johannesson set to cede Baugur control to Green', *Financial Times*, October 13, 2008, p. 22.
11 *Australian*, 'Iceland bank shares suspended, state takes control, from the *Times*, October 7, 2008.
12 Ibid.
13 *Guardian*, 'Kaupthing. The bank that liked to say yes', October 9, 2008.
14 David Jolly and Julia Werdigier, '2 European banks warn of tougher market conditions ahead', *International Herald Tribune*, November 4, 2008.

sector in Glasgow, spelling the end, for this year at least, of the annual Christmas pilgrimage by hundreds of Icelandic shoppers, with the krona now virtually worthless within the exchange rate and disposable income at a premium against spiralling inflation.[15]

The Isle of Man was hit hard by the Icelandic bankruptcies, as the saver protection system was compromised. The *Financial Times* reported that 'the Isle of Man ... [was] set to spend ... half its disposable reserves and 7.5 per cent of gross domestic product to part-compensate savers in ... a branch of the collapsed Icelandic bank.'[16]

In Germany, where the government had placed a freeze on Kaupþing bank operations, 30,000 account holders faced the risk of losing their savings because of Iceland.[17] The crisis unfolding in Iceland also destabilised the giant Commerzbank, which had already been considerably weakened by its losses in the bankruptcy of Lehman Brothers in the United States.[18]

After seeing Denmark's Sterling Airlines go bankrupt, the Icelandic business community was accused of jeopardizing some of the large institutions of its former colonizer,[19] Denmark, including the major department stores Illum and Magasin du Nord.

In Canada, the newspapers reported that various expansion projects had had to be put on hold because of the collapse of the Icelandic banks. They also published comments reflecting concern about future

---

15 Gerry Braiden, 'Icelandair suspends all Scottish flights amid downturn', *Herald* (Glasgow), October 27, 2008.
16 Andrew Bounds, 'Douglas to spend £150m for Kaupthing savers', *Financial Times*, October 23, 2008.
17 Benoit Bertrand et al., 'Iceland and UK clash on crisis', *Financial Times*, October 10, 2008, p. 1.
18 Michael Prest, 'Commerzbank accepte les remèdes proposés par l'État', Économie, *Le Monde*, November 5, 2008, p. 16.
19 Agence France-Presse, 'L'Islande prend le contrôle d'une quatrième banque', *Le Monde*, March 9, 2009.

trade relations between Canada and Iceland, which had just signed a free trade agreement.[20]

Some people tried to profit from these misfortunes, since the turbulence created opportunities for low-priced acquisitions. That, at least, is what British billionaire Philip Green[21] attempted to do, offering to buy a portion of the debt of Iceland's newly nationalised banks for next to nothing, so he could take control of the Baugur empire. That move, however, did not anticipate the reaction of Icelanders, who were vehemently opposed to it.

Despite Iceland's small size, its financial crisis inevitably had political consequences abroad in addition to economic ones. The Dutch daily *NRC Handelsblad* reported that, as a result of investments linked with Landsbanki bank, the provincial government of North Holland, as well as two members of the town councils in that area, had resigned,[22] acknowledging their responsibility in the matter. Even more symptomatic was the wave of discouragement that washed over the Scottish independence movement because of the failure of Iceland, which constituted a model. For supporters of the movement, Iceland 'represents, in a nutshell, what an independent Scotland might aspire to become.'[23] Opponents of the movement, however, leapt at the opportunity to emphasize that Iceland's failure went to show that the union with the United Kingdom was still beneficial for Scotland: 'When Iceland's biggest banks needed rescue, the UK government practically declared war. ... And when Scotland's biggest banks ran into serious trouble, the UK wrote a £32bn cheque.'[24]

20 See, for example, Paul Waldie, 'Icelandic banking crisis touches Canada', *Globe and Mail*, October 9, 2008, p. B-11.
21 See, for example, Steve Hawkes, 'Failing Iceland calls in the IMF', *Times*, October 15, 2008.
22 *NRC Handelsblad*, 'Provincial government resigns over Icelandic savings scandal', June 11, 2009.
23 *Herald* (Glasgow), 'Our chilling prophecy comes home to roost in Iceland', October 11, 2008.
24 *Financial Times*, 'Smoked Salmond; There is less sense than ever to an independent Scotland', October 18, 2008, p. 6.

Iceland's fall into disfavour was due to the impact of its financial crisis abroad. Its state of disfavour had an immediate effect on its international relations, and worked against it in its request for assistance from the International Monetary Fund—assistance that was initially blocked by the Netherlands and the United Kingdom, as reported by *NRC Handelsblad*:

> Dutch finance minister Wouter Bos and his British colleague Alistair Darling are blocking a loan from the International Monetary Fund (IMF) to Iceland until it agrees to pay back citizens the money they deposited with the bankrupt Icelandic bank Icesave.[25]

In the Netherlands, the resentment and mistrust toward Iceland was so strong that politicians also threatened to block the island's entry into the European Union: 'Dutch foreign minister Maxime Verhagen told his Icelandic counterpart that he could block its bid to join the European Union.'[26] An agreement would ease tensions between the two countries.

So, for the first time in its history, Iceland fell out of favour with its best of friends. A financial analyst with BNP Paribas summarized his colleagues' opinion, stating that 'there is a general dislike of Iceland; every movement in the market gets magnified when it comes to Iceland'.[27]

The radical change in the perception of Iceland abroad, from a strong favourable bias to a strong unfavourable one, has been a disappointment to many. However, for some Icelanders, it is also liberating and

---

[25] Cees Banning and Jan Gerritsen, 'Dutch and British block IMF loan to Iceland', *NRC Handelsblad*, November 7, 2008.
[26] *NRC Handelsblad*, 'The Hague threatens Iceland's EU bid over lost savings', July 22, 2009.
[27] Axel Swenden, quoted by Christopher Brown-Humes et al., 'Credit storm rolls across Icelandic landscape', *Financial Times*, March 4, 2008, p. 29.

a chance for renewal after a period of ostentation. Weary of commentaries from foreign observers, Icelanders have begun looking inward and become less concerned about their country's image abroad. *Iceland Review*—which was nationalistic and even chauvinistic before the crisis—offered words of consolation, indicating that being in the forefront of world news was a way out of the 'small-country complex', suggesting that 'there has been a real shift in the national mentality since the crisis hit in October. For the first time in a long time, Icelanders are not spending as much energy on how they appear to other countries.'[28] Sjón, a writer and lyricist for Björk and the Sugarcubes, agrees with this assessment, but goes one step further:

> The really positive thing that comes out of all this is that people will understand that Icelanders are not so nice. They, too, do stupid things. ... It's very good to be hated a little, to be part of how the world works and not just listen to the grass grow.[29]

Finding the silver lining, with self-examination and detachment, is an Icelandic trait that has survived the crisis. It is certainly one that will help ensure the resilience of a people whose history never ceases to amaze the world.

---

28 Jonas Moody, 'Jóhannarama', *IcelandReview.com*, January 29, 2009.
29 Sjón, quoted by Nicolas Delesalle, 'Les révoltés du geyser', *Télérama*, no. 3086, March 8, 2009. The original quote read: 'La vraie chose positive qui sort de tout ça, c'est que les gens vont comprendre que les Islandais ne sont pas si gentils. Ils font aussi des conneries. [...] C'est très bon d'être un peu haï, de participer à la marche du monde et pas seulement d'écouter l'herbe pousser'.

A CASUALTY OF THE GLOBAL CRISIS
THE FIRST DOMINO TO FALL

'Iceland became a symbol
and casualty of the credit crisis.'
La Presse, December 24, 2008[1]

Iceland was not the only country grappling with the downturn, which was small consolation for a nation hit so hard: as Gérard Bérubé of *Le Devoir* reported, 'the market shakeout was widespread and global'.[2] All market watchers acknowledged that the crisis of 2008 was not like any other. Financial analysts, accustomed to market fluctuations, observed very severe turbulence and 'totally insane movements, with no historical equivalent'.[3] Among the culprits were hedge funds, which have large enough assets to destabilise companies, currencies and governments. In October 2008, hedge funds precipitated the global imbalance when 'they urgently sold their assets, with animal fear'.[4]

The diffuse forces at work in the global economic crisis did not seem to follow any logic, creating cracks that appeared in some cases in large financial centres and in other cases in outlying areas. No country seemed to be sheltered from the random distribution of the effects; the powerful movement driving the crisis was as diffuse and inter-

---

1 Vincent Brousseau-Pouliot, 'Les gagnants et perdants d'une année folle', *La Presse* (Montréal), December 24, 2008. The original quote read: 'Les Islandais sont devenus les victimes et le symbole de la crise du crédit'.
2 Gérard Bérubé, 'Panique sur les places boursières', *Le Devoir*, October 7, 2008. The original quote read: 'la déconfiture boursière a été généralisée, et planétaire'.
3 Éric Galiègue, quoted by Agence France-Presse, 'Marchés boursiers. Nervosité sans précédent des marchés', *Le Devoir*, October 18, 2008.
4 Ibid. The original quote read: 'ils liquident leurs actifs en catastrophe, dans une peur animale'.

connected as the process underlying the spectacular aurora borealis. The geography of the crisis was outlined as follows by the *Financial Times* in October 2008:

> [Italy's Treasury Minister] Giulio Tremonti was almost gloating when he addressed the Italian parliament yesterday. He described the geography of the financial crisis with relish: the northern earthquake, with its epicentre in Iceland, its problematic 'continental dimension', the troubles in the UK, and the fear of a spillover into the Baltics and eastern Europe.[5]

Iceland was at the centre of events, and many images were used by the foreign press in an effort to describe the island's situation and its connection with the global crisis. Iceland became both a symbol and a warning for other countries, as it was the first one to be hit: 'The fate of Iceland', wrote David Teather in an article in the *Guardian*, 'is seen as a warning for the rest of the world'.[6] Many journalists, seeing Iceland's predicament as an indication of what was to come, compared the country to the canary once placed in coal mines as an early warning system for toxic gases:

> In the second half of last year [2007], as the subprime crisis gathered strength in the US, articles appeared in the international press about Iceland as the 'canary in the mine'. They suggested tiny Iceland ... was a leading indicator of how the crisis was mutating into something much bigger, affecting many countries beyond the US.[7]

Updates on Iceland's very uncomfortable position spread rapidly and worried other countries, as they feared becoming the next casualty in

---

5 *Financial Times*, 'Italy's plan', October 10, 2008, p. 16.
6 David Teather, 'Iceland government seizes control of Landsbanki', *Guardian*, October 7, 2008.
7 Robert Wade, 'Iceland pays price for financial excess', *Financial Times*, July 1, 2008.

the crisis. The image of the domino appeared repeatedly in the press: 'The fear', wrote Heather Scoffield of the *Globe and Mail*, 'is that other countries like Iceland that are struggling to deal with large current account deficits will begin to fall like dominoes'.[8] Observers wondered whether Iceland was an isolated case or the first movement of much more widespread turbulence. As with a fast-spreading virus, everyone was concerned about their own fate, wondering whether they would be the next victim, without any real sympathy for those already affected; and no one seemed immune. As Henry Thornton wrote in the *Australian*, '[there is a] lack of trust in the banks by their customers. In Iceland, we hear, the ATMs have no money in them. How do we know this will not happen in ... (fill in your country of choice)?'[9]

Iceland was not the only country to seem to be avoiding taking responsibility by blaming others. British Prime Minister Gordon Brown did likewise by accusing Iceland and the United States of causing the crisis, declaring in October that 'this problem started in America with irresponsible actions.'[10] The successive failings of several other countries gave credence to the idea of a possible domino effect. In November, a commentator for *Le Devoir* wrote: 'Might as well say that half the Old World is now in an urgent situation.'[11]

In a very short time, Iceland became both a *symbol* of the exceptionally severe global crisis and the *face of its first casualty*. Wrestling with problems that extended beyond its borders, the island seemed lost, a fact that drew sympathy and partially explained the extent of the media coverage. David Ibison, Nordic Bureau Chief for the *Financial Times*, declared that:

---

8 Heather Scoffield, 'Three stats you just can't be without on a Saturday: The week in economics', *Globe and Mail*, March 29, 2008, p. B-19.
9 Henry Thornton, 'It's time to restore trust', *Australian*, October 10, 2008.
10 Gordon Brown, quoted by Carter Dougherty and Landon Thomas Jr., 'Britain's bank bailout worth hundreds of billions', *International Herald Tribune*, October 8, 2008.
11 Serge Truffaut, 'Crise financière. Au secours de l'Est', *Le Devoir*, November 3, 2008. The original quote read: 'Autant dire que près de la moitié du Vieux Continent pointe actuellement à l'urgence'.

Sympathy for US investment banks may be hard to find these days but the image of tiny Iceland, with a population of just 313,000, battling to protect its economy against the sharpest minds of global capitalism has captivated the local population and global market practitioners alike.[12]

The sympathy enabled Iceland to take the position of *victim or casualty of the global crisis*, and thus justify its innocence to the rest of the world. In the spring of 2008, the term *casualty* began appearing in the international press; in April, James Surowiecki of the *New Yorker* wrote: 'many people suggest that [Iceland] could become the "first national casualty" of the ongoing credit crunch'.[13] In the fall, the term was used constantly in reference to the island: 'Iceland is the first real casualty of the global crisis.'[14] Iceland was the first to fall in this 'strange war', which certainly drew compassion from abroad: an article in the *Times* stated that 'the credit crunch claimed its first sovereign scalp last night'.[15]

Two parallel strategies contributed to creating the ethos of the country that fell victim to the worldwide crisis. The first was to emphasise the island's *soundness* in a turbulent environment ('Iceland's banks ... bought virtually none of the American mortgage-backed investments that have contaminated the books of U.S. and European banks'[16]). The second was to show its *considerable vulnerability* ('The Icelandic

---

12 David Ibison, 'Cool under fire Iceland takes the fight back to finance', *Financial Times*, April 9, 2008, p. 7.
13 James Surowiecki, 'Iceland's deep freeze', *New Yorker*, April 21, 2008.
14 Jon Danielsson, 'Icesave and the bankruptcy of a country', *Financial Times*, November 12, 2008.
15 *Times*, 'Iceland agrees $US6bn deal with IMF', October 21, 2008.
16 Mark Landler, 'Credit crisis triggers downturn in Iceland', *New York Times*, April 17, 2008.

banks were highly vulnerable';[17] 'Iceland [was] at the mercy of international creditors'[18]).

Not everyone was convinced by the victim discourse. Some people, like Mark Landler of the *New York Times*, thought Iceland got what it deserved ('Iceland was ripe for a correction'[19]) for what it did ('Critics have compared the country to a "toxic hedge fund" built on debt that could be about to go spectacularly wrong'[20]). Michael Stutchbury suggested in an article appearing in the *Australian* that both Iceland's social democratic management and its neo-liberal excesses—stemming from ideas of 'extreme capitalism'[21]—failed. Although more moderate, Jon Danielsson nonetheless believed that observers need not look outside Iceland for the initial cause of the country's difficulties or make Iceland a victim, as it was responsible for the ballooning of its economy: 'the original cause of its problems was inappropriate monetary policy and an outsized banking system'.[22]

Casualty or not, Iceland was certainly a symbol of the global crisis. But the question remains: to what extent should Iceland—and can Iceland, in light of its size—bear the responsibility for what happened?

---

17 Peter Gumbel, 'Iceland: the country that became a hedge fund', *Fortune*, December 4, 2008, http://www.money.cnn.com/.
18 David Jolly, 'Financial tempest spreads to the Gulf states', *International Herald Tribune*, October 26, 2008.
19 Mark Landler, 'Credit crisis triggers downturn in Iceland', *New York Times*, April 17, 2008.
20 David Teather, 'Iceland first to feel the blast of global cooling', *Guardian*, April 17, 2008.
21 Michael Stutchbury, 'Keeping banks afloat our best defence', *Australian*, October 6, 2008.
22 Jon Danielsson, 'Icesave and the bankruptcy of a country', *Financial Times*, November 12, 2008.

COMMUNICATION PROBLEMS
AN ATMOSPHERE OF MISTRUST

'In a small community, much can be left unsaid.'
Financial Times, March 31, 2008[1]

A number of foreign commentators believed that communication problems on the part of the Icelandic government and institutions were, in part, responsible for the crisis that gripped the country. The lack of importance the government placed on good communication affected its relations with both Icelanders and the international community. Sigrún Davíðsdóttir, for example, thought that Geir Haarde was inappropriately nonchalant when he conveyed ambiguous messages at the peak of the crisis. She was amazed that, while Icelanders were panic-stricken and the governments of other countries, including Germany and Denmark, were setting up savings guarantee plans, Geir Haarde would make a statement, reported as follows: 'Iceland's Prime Minister said late last night that no rescue package was necessary for his country's beleaguered banking sector.'[2] According to the *Independent*, what angered the British Cabinet was the fact that the Icelandic government was not forthcoming with information, 'Mr Darling already having complained that the Treasury has found it very difficult to get information from Reykjavik'.[3]

---

1 Sigrún Davíðsdóttir, 'In a small community, much can be left unsaid', *Financial Times*, March 31, 2008, p. 12.
2 Bertrand Benoit and James Wilson, 'Berlin guarantees savings in effort to avoid panic', *Financial Times*, October 6, 2008, p. 1.
3 David Prosser, 'Crisis deepens for Iceland as last of "big three" banks is nationalised', *Independent*, October 10, 2008.

While Iceland was sinking into a crisis and foreign news reports about the country were increasingly worrisome, Icelandic communications did not improve, which created growing apprehension abroad. Jon Danielsson, of the London School of Economics, stated on BBC News that 'the Icelandic authorities do not seem to have appreciated the seriousness of the situation, not communicated appropriately with their international counterparts, leading to an atmosphere of mistrust'.[4] Failure to appreciate the seriousness of the situation, lack of communication, mistrust of its counterparts—it seemed as if Iceland itself was fanning the flames. A report by the Centre for Economic Policy Research found that the Central Bank of Iceland had, under the circumstances, 'display[ed] unusual (and commendable) candour for a central bank'.[5] Yet this created the impression abroad that no one in Iceland was taking the necessary and appropriate decisions: as the report stated: 'unfortunately, it is this inability of the government to control a financial crisis that is likely to cause one'.[6]

An additional problem was the terse nature of the messages issued by Icelandic banks, which worsened the climate of concern and misunderstanding. The Icesave bank, a British subsidiary of Landsbanki, left the following notice on its web site—repeated ad nauseum by the media—when it suspended operations:

> We are not currently processing any deposits or any withdrawal requests through Icesave internet accounts. We apologise for any inconvenience this may cause to our customers. We hope to provide you with more information shortly.[7]

---

4 Jon Danielsson, 'Why raising interest rates won't work', *BBC News*, October 28, 2008.
5 Willem H. Buiter and Anne Sibert, 'The Icelandic banking crisis and what to do about it: The lender of last resort theory of optimal currency areas', *CEPR Policy Insight*, no. 26, October 2008, p. 6.
6 Ibid.
7 Quoted, for example, by Miles Brignall and Hilary Osborne, 'Icesave freezes deposits and withdrawals', *Guardian*, October 7, 2008.

It was the succinct nature of the message that angered depositors, as well as the complete lack of understanding toward them: 'Savers were left bewildered and angry after [the] message',[8] wrote the London *Times*. It was the same soviet style for which the foreign banks criticised the Central Bank of Iceland over a period of months. That, at least, is what Peter Gumbel suggested, writing: 'Officials in Iceland and at central banks elsewhere say that Oddsson's approach was deeply flawed: he penned short notes to other central banks that barely struck them as serious requests for help.'[9]

The brevity of messages and refusal to make information fully public contributed to the tense atmosphere, fraught with uncertainty about the Icelandic government's ability to communicate and its will to do so. Tom Braithwaite of the *Financial Times* also wondered about the control of information by the powerful Baugur conglomerate: 'the company owns a large swathe of the country's broadcast and print media and is accused of undue influence'.[10] The British prime minister, offended, also had doubts about the will of Icelandic authorities to disclose the necessary information: 'We had found it very difficult to get information from them',[11] declared a spokesman for the British prime minister in October. However, for some analysts, it was the whole uncompromising, lofty, even arrogant attitude of Iceland's financial elite that was to be questioned. Rather than attracting sympathy for their difficulties, they managed to unite their allies against them.

The contradictory messages issued by the Icelandic government on numerous matters (the seriousness of the crisis, the reimbursement

---

[8] Andrew Ellson, 'Icelandic savings bank Icesave crashes', *Australian*, from the *Times*, October 9, 2008.

[9] Peter Gumbel, 'Iceland: the country that became a hedge fund', *Fortune*, December 4, 2008, http://www.money.cnn.com/.

[10] Tom Braithwaite, 'The fraud claims that are taking their toll on Baugur', *Financial Times*, March 19, 2008, p. 27.

[11] A spokesman for Gordon Brown, quoted in the *Herald* (Glasgow), 'Treasury officials hold emergency talks on Iceland', October 10, 2008.

of foreign depositors, negotiations with Moscow, etc.) created the impression of confusion, which did not help people outside the country understand what was really going on: 'Mr Haarde ... has a perception challenge on his hands that many investment bankers might recognise.'[12] Indeed, after denying that his country was experiencing any problem, the Prime Minister suddenly and dramatically announced that Iceland was facing the threat of bankruptcy. While he asserted that nothing needed to be done ('no initiative [is] necessary "at this time"'[13]), he still anticipated the worst ('government, companies, households and people have seldom faced such great difficulties'[14]). Such contradictions 'add[ed] to the confusion that ... helped destabilise the country's markets'.[15] All in all, the flaws in communication with the rest of the world were considered to be partially responsible for the abyss into which Iceland so quickly slid.

The Icelandic government admitted, at times, to some of its failings in this respect. In March 2008, Prime Minister Haarde felt the need to initiate an information campaign to communicate the country's position in the crisis more effectively, acknowledging that greater transparency would avoid problems: 'A lot of people don't understand what is going on and that is something we need to work on.'[16] Then, the growing number of misunderstandings and the coverage of confused positions by the foreign media ultimately cast doubt on the will and ability of the Icelandic government to make itself clearly understood. An article appearing in the *Financial Times* suggested the problem was more characteristic of Icelandic culture than the eco-

---

12 David Ibison and Gillian Tett, 'Indignant Iceland faces a problem of perception', *Financial Times*, March 27, 2008, p. 13.
13 Tom Braithwaite, 'Confusion grows over Iceland's rescue plan', *Financial Times*, October 6, 2008.
14 Tom Braithwaite, 'Baugur evades Icelandic chill', *Financial Times*, October 4, 2008, p. 19.
15 Tom Braithwaite, 'Confusion grows over Iceland's rescue plan', *Financial Times*, October 6, 2008.
16 Geir Haarde, quoted by Joanna Chung and Sarah O'Connor, 'Iceland's prime minister calls on its banks to curb expansion plans', *Financial Times*, March 3, 2008, p. 19.

nomic circumstances of the crisis or the government. Citing a report she submitted to the Icelandic Export Council, Sigrún Davíðsdóttir indicated that Iceland's international partners had identified communication as one of the weaknesses of the country's business community: 'Their weak side was a lack of communication within and outside of the companies.'[17] She suggested the following explanation:

> If you come from a very homogenous and small community there is not a lot you need to explain to others—because they will mostly share your experience and outlook. Abroad, where perception is reality, there is a *potentially* dangerous flaw.[18]

The problem for Iceland was that such a *potentially* dangerous flaw can quickly prove to be a *real* one on foreign markets, and the effects can be highly damaging in times of crisis. According to Floyd Norris of the *New York Times*, markets are often more sensitive to perception than fact. Thus, statistics would often be powerless to change a strong impression conveyed by the media—an impression which is spread and influences investors faster. Confidence—conveyed through indirect information—is therefore more important: 'If governments say the deposits are safe and the market believes them, then they don't have to have any money to back up their promises.'[19] Conversely, a lack of confidence in markets can quash any real effort by governments.

In Iceland's case, the first signs of sagging confidence appeared in spring 2008. Standard & Poor's downgraded Iceland's financial rating, primarily because the firm was unable to obtain the desired information from the Icelandic government: 'S&P said that the move "reflects

---

[17] Sigrún Davíðsdóttir, 'In a small community, much can be left unsaid', *Financial Times*, March 31, 2008, p. 12.
[18] Ibid (italics added).
[19] Floyd Norris, 'The world's banks could prove too big to fail', *New York Times*, October 11, 2008.

our lack of information regarding the Icelandic government's official strategy on how to address the country's increasing economic policy issues'.[20] Even worse, one financial analyst felt that it was because he and his colleagues did not have the necessary information to explain the situation that the Icelandic banks experienced such strong market fluctuations: 'Iceland's banks have been punished by credit markets in recent months as investors worry about their reliance'.[21] Had Iceland then changed its approach, would the repercussions on its financial system have been different? Probably not. However, its relations with other countries might not have been so strongly affected and the consequences for Icelanders might not have been so severe.

The ability to communicate, convey information, provide explanations and issue clear, unambiguous messages is crucial in times of crisis. Rumours can spread panic, which is what happened in Iceland in October 2008, when talk about shortages of essential goods shook the country's image. Tom Braithwaite, who was well acquainted with Iceland's situation, wrote in the *Financial Times*: 'Iceland's capital was enduring a psychological battle as talk of food and oil shortages was being dismissed as irresponsible by government ministers, anxious to damp the threat of panic.'[22]

In fact, there never were any shortages and the psychological battle gradually faded. But the impact on Iceland's international image remained: foreigners were left with an impression of chaos, contradiction and confusion that needlessly contributed to spreading doubt, fear, misunderstanding and mistrust. Perhaps in wanting to protect itself, Iceland isolated itself even more.

---

20 Standard & Poor's media release quoted by David Ibison, 'Iceland threatens direct market intervention', *Financial Times*, April 2, 2008, p. 8.
21 Sarah O'Connor, interviewing Simon Adamson, a financial analyst with CreditSights, 'Iceland's banks feel debt costs heat up', *Financial Times*, March 28, 2008, p. 24.
22 Tom Braithwaite, 'Baugur evades Icelandic chill', *Financial Times*, October 4, 2008, p. 19.

ETHICS
IN GREAT DISARRAY

'Iceland is in ethical disarray, stripped by financial catastrophe of its image of itself.'
Globe and Mail, November 15, 2008[1]

Since the Icelandic government had taken over the banks during the crisis and controlled the country's financial system, the foreign newspapers seemed to make little distinction between the island's financial institutions, political parties, politicians and various groups, lumping them all together. From the outside, it was *Iceland* as a whole that refused to compensate modest depositors and assume its responsibilities. The language used by journalists to describe the country's economic straits often reflected moral considerations that had nothing to do with finance. The *Australian*, for example, spoke of 'a morality tale of global concern',[2] while Matthew Hart of the *Globe and Mail* stated that 'today Iceland is in ethical disarray, stripped by financial catastrophe of its image of itself'.[3] Journalists thus referred to the crisis as though it were a tale, using moral vocabulary to tell it, punctuating the narrative with words like *recovery, facility, punition* and *paying the price*. Iceland's role in this tale was that of the culprit, who was caught, trapped, and became an example of what not to do. And the moral of the tale for the *Globe and Mail* was as follows:

---

1 Matthew Hart, 'Iceland's next saga: The wounded tiger's tale', *Globe and Mail*, November 15, 2008, p. F-4.
2 *Australian*, 'Iceland's economic collapse could herald a new round of large-scale acquisitions', October 9, 2008.
3 Matthew Hart, 'Iceland's next saga: The wounded tiger's tale', *Globe and Mail*, November 15, 2008, p. F-4.

> Iceland's *painful experience* serves as a *showcase* of what can happen to a rich country when a population falls in love with *easy* credit and a central bank takes its eye off the inflation meter in a financial system whose rapid growth has been fuelled by low-cost borrowing in foreign currencies.[4]

So Icelanders had to face not only the consequences of the financial crisis, but also the ethical problems that it raised at home and abroad. That meant resolving a question of conscience and coming to terms with what the country represented for the rest of the world—a model that many believed in and that suddenly proved to be a great disappointment. Roger Boyes describes the reversal in Iceland's image, saying:

> Suddenly an island with a population of 300,000—about the same as Canberra—seen for the past decade as the essence of cool, a successful nation where people couldn't stop partying, is on the brink of becoming a failed state. ... But for Icelanders it represents a psychological and moral crisis. Who to blame? How to survive? What did the Icelanders give up when they chased the money, forgot their roots and turned themselves into a Nordic tiger?[5]

The 'Nordic tiger'—which has now become a 'kitten'[6] according to economics professor Oddgeir Ottesen—was quickly updated by Internet encyclopaedias; Wikipedia, for example, redefined the expression in late 2008 as follows:

---

4 Robert Jackson and Brian Milner, 'Iceland's meltdown', *Globe and Mail*, June 3, 2008, p. B-1 (italics added).
5 Roger Boyes, 'Skating on thin ice', *Australian*, October 10, 2008.
6 Oddgeir Ottesen, quoted by Keith B. Richburg, '"Nordic Tiger" Iceland finds itself in meltdown', *Washington Post*, October 10, 2008, p. A-1.

'Nordic Tiger' was a term used to refer to the period of economic prosperity in Iceland that began in the post-Cold War 1990s and ended in a national financial crisis in 2008, when the country's major banks failed and were taken over by the country's government.[7]

There are other examples of the effects the crisis has had on Iceland's ethical image, as portrayed by the media. However, it should be noted that financiers throughout the world are often considered to demonstrate questionable morality. That is what Yves Mamou refers to as 'moral hazard', 'i.e., the temptation of financial players to take risks for which they know the cost of failure would be assumed by society',[8] a concept that could easily apply to Iceland's case. For the British, however, Iceland's case was more serious as its bankers were accused of not keeping their word. And, as Prime Minister Gordon Brown declared, 'They have failed not only the people of Iceland, they have failed people in Britain'.[9] The *Australian* goes even farther, suggesting that Iceland, along with the United States, is the most immoral country: 'in all the rest of the world', it stated, 'only Iceland is comparably immoral'.[10]

British journalists believed that Iceland's entire approach was harmful to others, because it unduly favoured its own interests by initially refusing to compensate foreign savers—an unethical and thoughtless move. The *Financial Times* felt that Iceland was being unfair, treating foreigners differently from its own citizens:

---

7 http://en.wikipedia.org/wiki/Nordic_Tiger, consulted in January 2009.
8 Yves Mamou, 'De la difficulté d'anticiper les crises', Économie, *Le Monde*, October 9, 2008, p. 3. The original quote read: 'hasard moral', 'soit la tentation des acteurs de la finance à prendre des risques dont ils savent que le coût en cas d'échec sera pris en charge par la collectivité'.
9 Gordon Brown, quoted in Associated Free Press, 'Iceland acting illegally in freezing accounts—UK PM', *Australian*, October 10, 2008.
10 Frank Devine, 'Upstart Yanks aren't bowing out', *Australian*, October 24, 2008.

The government reiterated it was prioritising Icelandic savers above shareholders, directors and overseas operations as the financial regulator took control. UK depositors in the bank's Icesave accounts were frozen out of its website and unable to make withdrawals while branches in Iceland were open as usual.[11]

Iceland's financial ethics were thus seen to be lacking. So, too, were its social ethics, since the victims of its financial difficulties were primarily modest savers, small groups and charitable organisations who risked losing all their assets because of Iceland: 'By far the greatest rancor', wrote Eric Pfanner, 'has surrounded ordinary bank deposits taken out by individuals, government organizations and charities.'[12] Iceland's entire financial community was discredited because of this issue, which affected international trade. The *Globe and Mail* believed that the country earned a bad reputation, which hurt its business people, stating that 'they're increasingly being seen abroad as unreliable partners'.[13] While Iceland had been previously considered a green, egalitarian, rich and technologically-advanced country, liked by almost everyone, its image was deeply affected throughout 2008 by the spill-over from its financial turmoil.

In the media's amalgamated portrayal of the crisis—its management, and the ethics of its financiers and men in positions of power—there was also the question of Icelanders' lifestyle. The beginning of the 21st century seemed to mark a glorious period of unprecedented prosperity for the country, which ended abruptly in autumn 2008. The international media spoke harshly of the lavishness and excessiveness of that time: 'Iceland enjoyed a fantastic party. Now it is having a huge

---

11 Tom Braithwaite, 'Reykjavik steps in with new powers', *Financial Times*, October 8, 2008, p. 4.
12 Eric Pfanner, 'Iceland banks face claims from depositors abroad', *International Herald Tribune*, October 10, 2008.
13 Ómar Valdimarsson and Toni Vorobyova, 'Iceland seeks Russian, Nordic help as shares fall', *Globe and Mail*, October 15, 2008, p. B-14.

hangover',[14] wrote the *Guardian*. A number of articles indicated, in a bitter and even vengeful tone, that Icelanders would have to pay the price for such frivolous times, that they would no longer be able to go to Glasgow or elsewhere on shopping sprees, now that they were ruined.[15]

Some journalists judged Icelanders' relationship with credit and the irresponsibility that stemmed from it. They felt that Icelanders' actions were thoughtless and should be considered as a betrayal of themselves, their culture and their history. The *Globe and Mail* referred to the morality of the sagas in striving to understand recent events: 'the sagas describe a people vitally concerned with how to conduct themselves, with what is proper and ethical in relations between people who had to regulate themselves in a society without rulers'.[16]

According to Gérard Lemarquis, a journalist with *Le Monde*, Icelanders' obsessive relationship with credit did not suddenly appear in 2008, it was generations-old:

> First of all, there is a domestic problem that is not new: Icelanders have, for several generations, been living beyond their means on credit. Several generations have done so since the war, it's their culture, and they have always paid their debts by working a second or even a third job. They felt that they were living when they had money, i.e., when they no longer had time.[17]

---

14 Gwladys Fouché, 'Iceland is in the heart of the economic storm', *Guardian*, October 6, 2008.
15 Gerry Braiden, 'Icelandair suspends all Scottish flights amid downturn', *Herald* (Glasgow), October 27, 2008.
16 Matthew Hart, 'Iceland's next saga: The wounded tiger's tale', *Globe and Mail*, November 15, 2008, p. F-4.
17 Gérard Lemarquis, 'L'Islande au bord du gouffre', *Le Monde*, October 9, 2008, p. 3. The original quote read: 'Il y a d'abord un problème intérieur qui n'est pas nouveau : les Islandais, depuis plusieurs générations, vivent à crédit, au-dessus de leurs moyens. Plusieurs générations l'ont fait depuis la guerre, c'est leur culture, et ils ont toujours payé leurs dettes au prix d'un deuxième, voire d'un troisième boulot. On a ici le sentiment de vivre quand on a de l'argent, c'est-à-dire quand on n'en a plus le temps'.

Analysts strove to evaluate Iceland's real wealth at the peak of the boom and wondered whether its prosperity was not an organized system of poverty hidden by excessive prices. After a stay in Iceland, Alastair Begg wrote an article for the *Herald* in which he stated that 'the cost of living and property was so high that families were obliged to have two substantial salaries coming in to maintain any standard of living'.[18] Thus, the easily obtained credit and the widespread mortgage culture would inevitably lead to an economic, social and moral crisis. In her article entitled 'Iceland's stranded', Élise Vincent wrote:

> Credit was almost a religion in Iceland, all the way down to bankruptcy. A loan for the 4 x 4, a loan for the kitchen, television. When the children wanted to buy a house, they mortgaged their parents'. All credit cards were deferred debit and everything was paid for using them: cigarettes and even bread.[19]

Journalists then went on to ask what lessons should be learned from this obsession with money? Novelist Arnaldur Indriðason mentioned the fragility that comes with such an obsession: 'I don't think Iceland realized where the money was really coming from ... or how fragile it all was.'[20] Insouciance, fragility, impression of a world fading away: 'The financial crisis', wrote John Lloyd in a *Financial Times* article, 'carries whispers of vulnerability, global and personal.'[21] The moral of this failure has been reflected in the regrets expressed by Icelanders themselves now that the strange 'party' is over. A feeling of incred-

---

18 Alastair Begg, 'Problem of "hidden poverty" in Iceland', *Herald* (Glasgow), October 22, 2008.
19 Élise Vincent, 'Naufragés d'Islande', Horizons, *Le Monde*, October 24, 2008, p. 21.
The original quote read: 'Jusqu'à la banqueroute, le crédit était presque une religion, en Islande. Prêt pour le 4 x 4, prêt pour la cuisine, la télévision. Quand les enfants voulaient acheter une maison, ils hypothéquaient celle des parents. Toutes les cartes de crédit étaient à débit différé et tout se payait avec : les cigarettes comme le pain'.
20 Arnaldur Indriðason, quoted by Peter Gumbel, 'Iceland: the country that became a hedge fund', *Fortune*, December 4, 2008, http://www.money.cnn.com/.
21 John Lloyd, 'How to survive the end of "civilisation"', *Financial Times*, November 29, 2008.

ible fragility can be perceived their testimonials, which refer to the excesses of a period that quickly disappeared. One Icelander told the *Guardian* that 'It is just unimaginable. ... We've all been living ahead of ourselves, so in many ways this was inevitable. People here have been so obsessed with money. Iceland is like a nouveau riche country'.[22] At the end of the day, the crisis was not only financial: it shook Icelanders' values and social fabric, affecting their moral and even spiritual fibre. It has certainly had an impact on islanders' identity and has prompted them to question their aspirations for happiness and ways of achieving it.

---

[22] Sigriður Dögg Audunsðottir, quoted by David Teather, 'Icelandic government battles to save the economy', *Guardian*, October 6, 2008.

FREE-THINKING ARTISTS
BJÖRK AND OLAFUR ELIASSON

'Any colonisation isn't a good idea.'
Björk, quoted in the *Australian*, January 10, 2008[1]

Many foreign journalists are familiar with Iceland primarily through its artists, Björk being perhaps the best known. During 2008, the singer's statements to the media reflected her country's disarray, as her discourse changed from universal considerations to an appeal for national assistance. There are other major Icelandic artists as well, be they from the music world, such as Sigur Rós, Múm, GusGus and Emilíana Torrini, or the visual arts, such as well-known sculptor Olafur Eliasson who, according to the *Australian*, 'has joined singer Björk as his nation's most famous export'.[2]

Icelandic artists are happy to play the game of Nordic exoticism—much to the delight of the foreign newspapers, which lap it up. And there is no shortage of examples. An article in *Le Devoir*, entitled 'Iceland, a veritable musical geyser',[3] refers to the landscapes, volcanoes and fjords as sources of inspiration for Icelandic musicians. It mentions a conversation with Lárus Jóhannesson, an important figure in Iceland's music scene, stating that 'you have to spend the winter [up there] to understand why ... people commonly start playing music in

---

[1] Björk, quoted by Matthew Westwood, 'Made to mingle with electricity', *Australian*, January 10, 2008.
[2] Rachel Campbell-Johnston, 'Wrys and falls of a natural showman', *Australian*, May 1, 2008.
[3] Agence France-Presse, 'L'Islande, véritable geyser musical', *Le Devoir*, June 16, 2008.

childhood',[4] as if the long dark winter nights in Iceland could create callings. Such references to the Nordic imaginary are often part of performances by Icelandic artists. In describing Sigur Rós's tour, the *Globe and Mail* wrote that the band 'performed free shows across the Nordic country—on fields and in caves, in deserted fish plants and far-flung community halls'.[5] A review of an exhibit by Icelandic Love Corporation—which plays with arctic elements—described a video sequence in which 'three women dressed themselves in furs and jewels to imagine a world where cold had become so rare that Arctic landscapes [are] now only playgounds for the rich'.[6] These types of references, full of clichés, commonplaces and phrases about the North and its impact on its inhabitants, are alluded to by ecological artist Olafur Eliasson, whose relationship with the land is presented as a natural link with the Nordic idiosyncrasies of Iceland, in harmony with the climate and landscape, in perfect artistic symbiosis: 'It's not esoteric or spiritual or particularly existential. It's pretty physical, actually'.[7] The artist complains about the limitations a Nordic interpretation place, on an understanding of his work, ironically declaring that 'you can barely talk about the Nordic landscape without the ministry of culture launching a campaign'.[8]

During 2008, as the crisis deepened and drew attention, the foreign media shifted its focus from the natural and Nordic nature of Icelandic art to more political issues. The national identity—formerly disparaged by artists as being passé and needing to give way to a universalism nurtured by social and environmental concerns—reappeared with a vengeance in their discourse. Up until July 2008, state-

---

4 Ibid. The original quote read: 'il faut passer l'hiver [là-bas] pour comprendre pourquoi [...] la pratique de la musique [y] est courante dès l'enfance'.
5 Jennifer van Evra, 'Seven days: Your guide to the week's entertainment', *Globe and Mail*, April 14, 2008, p. R-5.
6 Kate Taylor, 'An art collective's SOS', *Globe and Mail*, April 22, 2008, p. R-2.
7 Olafur Eliasson, quoted by Rachel Campbell-Johnston, 'Wrys and falls of a natural showman', *Australian*, May 1, 2008.
8 Ibid.

ments often appeared in foreign newspapers, such as those by Lárus Jóhannesson, to the effect that Iceland was a unique artistic breeding ground in light of its size and geographic location, 'both inside and outside Europe',[9] in a sort of flexible no man's land. There were also announcements of environmentally-oriented concerts such as 'Náttúra' organised by Björk in collaboration with the National Geographic Society, and, of course, claims by Björk of being a citizen of the world before being an Icelander. In January, she told a journalist with the *Australian* that 'with globalisation and everything, being from one country and having that particular one sound of whatever your nation represents is not true. There's no such thing any more'.[10]

The period before the crisis was also one in which Icelandic artists, seen abroad as ecologists, inspired by nature and aspiring to live in harmony with their environment, adopted bold positions that sometimes raised eyebrows. That's what happened when Björk declared that 'a lot of Icelanders feel we should bypass the industrial age and go straight into the 21st century'[11]. Olafur Eliasson, for his part, criticises the Scandinavian sense of consensus that jeopardises individual critical thinking, saying 'that's what's so worrying about Scandinavia: that people are all the same and they are not worried about it'.[12] In March, *Le Monde* reported that Björk had created diplomatic waves between China and Iceland when she dedicated her song *Declare Independence* to Tibet at a concert in Shanghai, although the lyrics were originally dedicated to Greenland and the Faeroe Islands.[13] That was not the first time the singer had denounced colonialism, including

---

9   Lárus Jóhannesson, quoted in Agence France-Presse, 'L'Islande, véritable geyser musical', *Le Devoir*, June 16, 2008. The original quote read: 'à la fois à l'intérieur et à l'extérieur de l'Europe'.
10 Björk, quoted by Matthew Westwood, 'Made to mingle with electricity', *Australian*, January 10, 2008.
11 Björk, quoted by Tony Naylor, 'Is this it?', *Guardian*, July 5, 2008.
12 Olafur Eliasson, quoted by Rachel Campbell-Johnston, 'Wrys and falls of a natural showman', *Australian*, May 1, 2008.
13 Agence France-Presse, 'L'ambassade de Chine en Islande proteste contre la chanteuse Björk', Culture, *Le Monde*, March 8, 2008, p. 24.

Denmark's long occupation of her country:[14] 'Any colonisation isn't a good idea, it doesn't matter which nationality.'[15] She believes that colonisation always leaves traces, like the ones that still permeate Icelandic culture and society: 'it's a lack of confidence. When you're a colony for so long, you feel like a second-class citizen'.[16]

Despite all that, Björk returned to help her country during the crisis. In December, newspapers around the world reported that the singer wanted 'to take part in healing the Icelandic economy'[17] by promoting a return to its 'green roots'[18] through the creation of an investment fund. That move reflected a shift in the artist's attitude, from universal considerations at the beginning of the year to a deep attachment to Iceland during the crisis. Some foreign journalists viewed her about-face with derision. Owen Thomas, a reporter for *Gawker*, revealed in an article entitled 'Can Björk save a ruined Iceland?' that the idea for the fund had been supported by a former Kaupþing bank executive; 'Björk will offer startups', said Thomas, 'they invest in "emotional capital". Couldn't they get the same benefit by just playing her CDs nonstop?'[19] However others were delighted by statements made by the artist during the crisis. The French media saw beneficial effects, stating that 'the crisis ... woke up its [Iceland's] placid inhabitants! And specifically its artists, who spearheaded an unusual protest on the island'.[20]

Far from stock exchanges and bank offices, Iceland's artists offer a complex image of a country well known and liked. The collapse of

---

14 Iceland was under Danish domination for six centuries, until 1944.
15 Björk, quoted by Matthew Westwood, 'Made to mingle with electricity', *Australian*, January 10, 2008.
16 Ibid.
17 Agence France-Presse, 'La chanteuse Björk crée un fonds pour "guérir l'économie islandaise"', Économie, *Le Monde*, December 20, 2008, p. 15. The original quote read: 'participer à la guérison de l'économie islandaise'.
18 Ibid.
19 Owen Thomas, 'Can Björk save a ruined Iceland?', *Gawker*, December 24, 2008.
20 Nicolas Delesalle, 'Les révoltés du geyser', *Télérama*, no. 3086, March 8, 2009. The original quote read: '[la crise] a réveillé ses placides habitants! Et plus particulièrement les artistes, qui se sont lancés dans une contestation inédite sur l'île'.

the island's economy, however, changed their discourse; their openness to universal concerns gave way to introspection about national identity, which seems inevitable in times of crisis.

HUMOUR
'CTRL-ALT-DEL. WELCOME TO ICELAND 2.0'

'Icelanders collapse in laughter.'
Financial Times, November 28, 2008[1]

Humour, with all the truths and revelations it conveys, fortunately made its way into some foreign media discourse on Iceland during the crisis. Humour offered a way of reporting on the turmoil, while taking a distance from it and providing a point of view that would have otherwise been unacceptable. British, Icelandic, American, German and other journalists made light of the events taking place in Iceland, often to reassure readers about their own situation. For example, after deploring the state of Britain's economy, the popular newspaper the *Daily Mail* asked: 'Are you depressed by the financial meltdown? ... things could be worse—we could be in Iceland.'[2] Comparing your own situation to that of someone less fortunate can really lighten the load. As Michael Lewis pointed out in 'Wall Street on the tundra', published by *Vanity Fair*, 'Iceland instantly became the only nation on earth that Americans could point to and say, 'well, at least we didn't do *that*.'[3] But, then, sometimes comparisons were turned around. For example, the *Financial Times* made light of the recent collapse of the British bank Northern Rock, stating it hoped along with Icelanders that 'this northern rock [Iceland] will be more resistant to the credit crunch than the UK bank.'[4]

---

1 David Ibison, 'Icelanders collapse in laughter', *Financial Times*, November 28, 2008.
2 *The Daily Mail*, quoted in the *Guardian*, 'It could be worse—you could be in Iceland', October 8, 2008.
3 Michael Lewis, 'Wall Street on the tundra', *Vanity Fair*, April, 2009.
4 Tom Braithwaite, 'Falling krona exposes consumer debt', *Financial Times*, October 7, 2008, p. 5.

Jokes about Iceland did not necessarily convey false information: they exaggerated the country's plight and highlighted the absurdity of it, but did so in many cases with a keen knowledge of the issues. Here are a few of the best examples found in the articles surveyed; Iceland was not necessarily the main topic of these stories, further indicating that the country's predicament had become part of common discourse:

> What is the capital of Iceland? About five euros.[5]

> The 2009 Mercedes-Benz SL63 [is] a car for performance nuts whose bank accounts are filled to overflowing. You can safely assume those bank accounts aren't in Iceland.[6]

> Record unemployment levels have been announced today as the Credit Crunch tightens its grip. Worst hit sectors are the construction trade and the Icelandic bank robbers.[7]

> An Icelander asks a Swiss official why a landlocked country needs a Minister of Fisheries. The Swiss official looks at the Icelander and asks: 'Why do you have a Minister of Finance?'[8]

---

5   Or $3.50 as other authors wrote. Quoted here by Ralph Atkins, 'Germans take the credit for crisis jokes', *Financial Times*, December 24, 2008, p. 3.
6   Jeremy Cato and Michael Vaughan, 'Luxury cars', *Globe and Mail*, November 25, 2008, p. F-8.
7   Quoted on http://listverse.com/2008/10/16/20-hilarious-credit-crunch-jokes, consulted in July 2009.
8   Greg Burns, 'Financial fiasco fires up Iceland's ire, civic unrest', *Chicago Tribune*, January 2, 2009.

In addition to these jokes, many plays on words, featuring vocabulary related to the North, Arctic and cold, were used in the titles and texts of the articles. For example, the *Sunday Times* printed a column, 'Iceland: frozen assets', in which A.A. Gill wrote: '[Iceland is] the first victim of the economic ice age'.[9] Iceland's geographic situation and economic position were sometimes superimposed, such as in an article by the *Australian*, declaring that 'Iceland is melting down, but it has nothing to do with global warming'.[10] Through such superimposition of the geographic and economic, Icelanders became 'the punch line in jokes about credit freezes, economies on ice and financiers being thrown into "the cooler"'.[11]

Then there was the famous auctioning of Iceland by a British joker on the eBay auction site, with a starting price of 99 pence and bidding that went up to ten million pounds. Advertised as a unique opportunity to buy a Northern European country, the joke was reported by newspapers around the world. Some Internet users made humoristic comments on the bid, saying for example: at that price it would still be a bargain except 'Björk isn't included'; 'Question—Do you have it in any other colours than white? Answer—How did you want it: in the red?'[12]

While humour offered a way of lightening the mood, some articles were cruel and opened old wounds. The harshest example of British humour on the crisis was the following satirical piece, entitled 'Saving Iceland', written by Robert Shrimsley for the Notebook section of the *Financial Times*:

> The ECB [European Central Bank] therefore opened its discount window to Iceland, allowing it to borrow

---

9   A.A. Gill, 'Iceland: frozen assets', *Sunday Times*, December 14, 2008.
10 Christian Kerr, 'Signs of success are sunk in mire', *Australian*, October 9, 2008.
11 Greg Burns, 'Financial fiasco fires up Iceland's ire, civic unrest', *Chicago Tribune*, January 2, 2009.
12 Quoted in *Daily Telegraph*, 'Iceland for sale on eBay for 99p', October 10, 2008.

funds posted against German collateral. As part of the deal Germany gets to annex Iceland for the knockdown price of 2 krona a share—giving it an equity value of $250m—and all but wiping out the country's shareholders. Investors are said to be furious, claiming that Reykjavik alone is worth $10bn. The deal is an attractive one for Germany, which has long wanted its own pure fish play and now acquires Iceland's prime fisheries unit for next to nothing. However, the move has enraged Denmark, which claims pre-emption rights over the Iceland fund it ran until 1944. It has threatened legal action unless it is given first refusal over the isle. Officials are now trying to broker a sale and leaseback arrangement under which Denmark leases Iceland to Germany for a nominal sum while retaining its claim.[13]

While there was jeering in foreign media discourse on Iceland, there was also a certain fascination about the ability of Icelanders to laugh at themselves and to demonstrate resilience in the face of adversity. In a *Financial Times* article, 'Icelanders collapse in laughter', David Ibison stated: 'there may not seem much to laugh about in Iceland. But Icelanders take pride in their darkly ironic sense of humour'.[14] A journalist for the *Chicago Tribune* was also of the opinion that, despite everything going on around them, 'Icelanders still indulge in dark humor about their plight'.[15] The examples of their sense of humour abound: in one article, an Icelandic Porsche dealer, upset about the drop in sales, said his only comfort was that he also owns a Chevrolet dealership;[16] in another, an unemployed electrician said that 'when he has finished here, he is going abroad to find work—

---

13 Robert Shrimsley, 'Saving Iceland', *Financial Times*, March 27, 2008, p. 14.
14 David Ibison, 'Icelanders collapse in laughter', *Financial Times*, November 28, 2008.
15 Greg Burns, 'Financial fiasco fires up Iceland's ire, civic unrest', *Chicago Tribune*, January 2, 2009.
16 Reported by Mark Landler, 'Credit crisis triggers downturn in Iceland', *New York Times*, April 17, 2008.

"Poland, probably"—and he smiles a crooked Icelandic smile';[17] and in yet another, a banker, imagining that in future Iceland will be like Cuba today, said 'in 30 years' time, there will be 30-year-old Range Rovers driving around'.[18]

Humour did not ease the crisis, but it did make it easier to accept. As a demonstrator from Reykjavík indicated with the line, 'Ctrl-Alt-Del. Welcome to Iceland 2.0',[19] many people would have liked to delete the recent years of excesses and start again, as if they had never happened. At least the gibing enabled people to forget the dejection for the span of a laugh.

---

17 A.A. Gill, 'Iceland: frozen assets', *Sunday Times*, December 14, 2008.
18 David Ibison, 'Icelanders see Icarus-like plunge of greed', *Financial Times*, October 23, 2008.
19 Reported by Jonas Moody, 'The Republic is dead. Long live the Republic!', *Iceland Review*, vol. 47, no. 1, 2009.

PART TWO

BANKRUPTCY

NUMEROUS WARNINGS
A FORESEEABLE COLLAPSE

'Warnings about this sorry end had been coming from many different sources for months.'

Iceland Review, spring 2009[1]

During the crisis in 2008, a number of journalists emphasized the sudden and unforeseeable nature of what happened in Iceland. A brief look back, however, will show that warnings had been coming from many different sources for months. Early in the year, the financial rating agencies issued the first warnings about Iceland by downgrading the country's ratings. In January, Moody's announced that the rating it had assigned Iceland—up until then an excellent triple A—was at a crossroads 'because of the perceived fragility of the country's banks'.[2] In February, the agency reiterated that Iceland's banks were in a challenging situation. Then, in March, it downgraded its outlook for the entire country, which, according to David Ibison, indicated that Moody's was 'gradually losing confidence in the ability of the nation to avoid a banking crisis'.[3] Several newspapers then expressed serious concern. *Le Monde* warned that excessiveness threatened Iceland's financial equilibrium since 'the country's banks held assets eight times greater than its GDP'.[4] An article by Simon Watkins in the *Financial Mail* (South Africa) stated that 'these banks [Lands-

---

1 Bjarni Brynjólfsson, 'The pots and pans revolution', *Iceland Review*, vol. 47, no. 1, 2009.
2 David Ibison, 'Moody's blows hot and cold on Iceland', *Financial Times*, January 29, 2008, p. 41.
3 David Ibison, 'Moody's poised to downgrade Iceland', *Financial Times*, March 6, 2008, p. 27.
4 George Hay, 'L'Islande, victime du "credit crunch"', Économie, *Le Monde*, March 8, 2008, p. 18. The original quote read: 'le secteur bancaire local détient désormais des actifs représentant huit fois le produit intérieur brut de l'Islande'.

banki, Kaupþing] are now seen as the most unsafe in the developed world'.[5] In April, Standard & Poor's indicated that Iceland, Estonia and Latvia were 'the most vulnerable European countries to a global slowdown',[6] while Fitch Ratings agency expressed serious doubts about the stability of the Icelandic banking system; as a result, 'investors panicked, and the currency and the stock market both plunged 25% in a matter of days'.[7]

In a matter-of-fact article for the *Guardian*, David Teather provided the following bleak picture of Iceland's economy:

> Risk-averse investors have begun pulling out. Since the beginning of the year, the Icelandic krona, the smallest independent currency in the world, has fallen by 25%. The main stockmarket index has fallen by about 40% from its peak last summer, inflation in the overheated economy is running at 6.8% and interest rates reached 15.5% last week. The country has also been running a large trade deficit, partly because of rampant consumer spending.[8]

It is difficult not to grasp, from this message, a certain sense of urgency and the risk of more serious deterioration. The *New Yorker*, for its part, indicated that concern was mounting: 'many people suggest that [Iceland] could become the "first national casualty" of the ongoing credit crunch'.[9] In June, the *Financial Times* reported, in one of its many articles on Iceland, 'growing fears that its overheating econ-

---

5 Simon Watkins, 'Iceland's banks top "riskiness league"', *Financial Mail*, March 16, 2008.
6 Robert Anderson, 'Fears grow of Baltic states' addiction to external capital', *Financial Times*, April 18, 2008, p. 25.
7 Peter Gumbel, 'Iceland: the country that became a hedge fund', *Fortune*, December 4, 2008, http://www.money.cnn.com/.
8 David Teather, 'Iceland first to feel the blast of global cooling', *Guardian*, April 17, 2008.
9 James Surowiecki, 'Iceland's deep freeze', *New Yorker*, April 21, 2008.

omy ... [was] about to slip into recession'.[10] By mid-summer, experts had started to worry: 'Analysts said there were reasons to be nervous about the health of the country's large banks.'[11]

The financial rating agencies were not the only ones to issue early warnings. Highly regarded economists had asserted before the crisis that the situation would become unbearable for Iceland if a major crisis occurred. In 2006, Frederic S. Mishkin, Columbia University professor and former economist with the U.S. Federal Reserve, published a report entitled *Financial Stability in Iceland* for the Iceland Chamber of Commerce. Although the Icelandic government and banks used the report to convince foreign investors that their assets were stable, Mishkin's findings were not as optimistic as they might have liked to claim. He indicated, for example, that a crisis in investor confidence was all it would take for everything to crumble, stating that traders 'could create a self-fulfilling prophecy by massively pulling out of Icelandic assets'.[12] (The 'prophecy just came true',[13] wrote *BusinessWeek* in October 2008.) Then, in 2007, economist Robert Wade gave a speech in Reykjavík in which he warned about the weaknesses in Iceland's financial structure. Willem H. Buiter and Anne Sibert similarly claimed in their April 2008 report—not made public until October 2008—that 'it was not the drama and mismanagement ... that brought down Iceland's banks. Instead it was absolutely obvious ... that its banking model was not viable'.[14] American economist Robert Aliber gave a speech in Reykjavík in May 2008 in which he warned his audience about the urgency of the country's situation. In his own colourful language, he said: 'I give you nine months. Your

---

10 David Ibison et al., 'Rise in CDS spreads fuels Iceland fears', *Financial Times*, June 26, 2008, p. 25.
11 Sarah O'Connor, 'Icelandic banks' 1,000bp CDS', *Financial Times*, July 22, 2008, p. 39.
12 Frederic S. Mishkin, quoted by Kerry Capell, 'The stunning collapse of Iceland', *BusinessWeek*, October 9, 2008.
13 Kerry Capell, 'The stunning collapse of Iceland', *BusinessWeek*, October 9, 2008.
14 Willem H. Buiter and Anne Sibert, 'The Icelandic banking crisis and what to do about it. The lender of last resort theory of optimal currency areas', *CEPR Policy Insight*, no. 26, October 2008.

banks are dead. Your bankers are either stupid or greedy. And I'll bet they are on planes trying to sell their assets right now.'[15]

With all the enthusiasm generated by Iceland's economic expansion, the question arises as to whether warnings about a crisis could really be heard, before the banks' problems became full blown. Some journalists questioned the will of Icelandic authorities to disclose—or even become aware of—the real risks threatening the country's financial system, for fear that such information would definitively weaken the markets. In May 2008, Cliff Tan wrote an article for the *Financial Times* entitled and conveying the message that 'Nordic banks must not mistake camouflage for cover'.[16] After the crisis, Peter Gumbel recalled how the chief of Iceland's Financial Supervisory Authority had described the situation in August: '"The banks are solid and can withstand considerable financial shocks", [Jónas] Jónsson noted enthusiastically. Less than six weeks later all three banks were defunct.'[17] In October, Willem H. Buiter and Anne Sibert revealed that they had not disclosed their analysis of the weaknesses in Iceland's financial system earlier at the request of their Icelandic colleagues, admitting that 'in April and July 2008, our Icelandic interlocutors considered our paper to be too market-sensitive to be put in the public domain and we agreed to keep it confidential'.[18] These examples indicate that the country's real situation was camouflaged or that, at least, there was no *will to become aware of it*.

In retrospect, it is easy to see signs that should have alerted governors, bankers and the public. Even the Central Bank of Iceland, at the

---

15 Robert Aliber, quoted by Michael Lewis, 'Wall Street on the tundra', *Vanity Fair*, April 2009.
16 Cliff Tan, 'Nordic banks must not mistake camouflage for cover', *Financial Times*, May 30, 2008, p. 8.
17 Peter Gumbel, 'Iceland: the country that became a hedge fund', *Fortune*, December 4, 2008, http://www.money.cnn.com/.
18 Willem H. Buiter and Anne Sibert, 'The Icelandic banking crisis and what to do about it. The lender of last resort theory of optimal currency areas', *CEPR Policy Insight*, no. 26, October 2008.

centre of the fiasco, admitted as much in February 2009 in a report entitled 'The banking crisis in Iceland in 2008', going so far as to identify warning signs that existed three years earlier:

> The banks attracted international attention late in 2005 and early in 2006. ... The criticism was wide ranging, targeting the banks' growth pace, risk appetite, low deposit ratios and high dependence on borrowed funds, as well as cross ownership, lack of transparency, and so on.[19]

Such a defense by the Central Bank might be right, but it does not solve the problems of the past weeks. In an article printed in spring 2009, *Iceland Review* also pointed a finger at the institutions it had applauded a year earlier. In an article printed in spring 2009, Bjarni Brynjólfsson cites a Finnish expert, stating that 'our banks were bound to fail and ... our bankers broke almost every rule in the book about sound and careful banking. The large owners of the banks were obviously totally unfit to run them.'[20] But in the national euphoria arising from the words and deeds of the new Vikings, who, like Willem H. Buiter and Anne Sibert suggest, could have expressed opposition without being accused of harmful pessimism?

---

19 Ingimundur Friðriksson, 'The banking crisis in Iceland in 2008', *Sedlabanki.is*, February 6, 2009.
20 Bjarni Brynjólfsson, 'The pots and pans revolution', *Iceland Review*, vol. 47, no. 1, 2009.

BANKRUPTCY
ICELAND BECAME SYNONYMOUS WITH *CRISIS*

'Iceland will go down in history as a textbook example of how excess credit can derail an economy.'
Financial Times, October 8, 2008[1]

'Countries don't go bankrupt', declared a U.S. Citibank executive in the 1980s,[2] referring to emerging markets whose financial difficulties were undermining his institution. During 2008, journalists and financial analysts repeatedly stated that the sources—and consequences—of the crisis went beyond finance. They believed that a crisis of confidence was eroding the global economy. The public's confidence in its institutions became shakier as certain wellknown, reputable banks buckled under the weight of the crisis, then crumbled. Confidence deteriorated all the more rapidly as the countries that were to regulate and guarantee deposits and savings showed signs of weakness. As one economist told the *International Herald Tribune* in October 2008, 'There is no such thing as a safe bank now. They are only as safe as the authorities make them.'[3] The crisis hoever, brought down more than financial institutions: it threatened to topple governments and entire countries.

The tragedy of Iceland's 'bankruptcy' was that it stemmed from an emotional statement made by the country's Prime Minister, Geir

---

1 Julian Callow, quoted by Chris Giles, 'Topsy-turvy logic leaves an unpalatable choice', *Financial Times*, October 8, 2008, p. 4.
2 Walter Wriston, quoted by Harry Koza, 'Citigroup's toxic assets should prolong any rescue attempt', *Globe and Mail*, November 28, 2008.
3 Willem H. Buiter, quoted by Carter Dougherty and Landon Thomas Jr., 'Britain earmarks $87 billion to bail out banks', *International Herald Tribune*, October 8, 2008.

Haarde, on national television on the evening of Monday, October 6, 2008. Intending to explain the situation that forced his government to give the Icelandic Financial Supervisory Authority control of the banks, Haarde said: 'We were faced with the real possibility that the national economy would be sucked into the global banking swell *and end in national bankruptcy.*'[4] Haarde had wanted to reassure Icelanders, bankers and the rest of the world, but his statement set off a chain reaction with serious consequences. He then tried to clarify his remarks, but it was too late. The idea that Iceland was on the verge of bankruptcy—even though technically a country cannot go bankrupt—was reported by media around the world. The night after he made the statement, the British media, followed by American and European, broke the news: the crisis had brought down the first country and Iceland was in national bankruptcy.

Once the announcement appeared in the media, all qualifying information rapidly disappeared. Iceland *became* a bankrupt country, so much so that the expression 'Iceland-like bankruptcy' was used to describe other economies known to be precarious. Iceland was referred to as a bankrupt country (without any qualification) on numerous occasions by the foreign media in late 2008. Here are a few examples:

> Now bankrupt Iceland.[5] (October 8)

> As a result, in Iceland today, it is the entire country that is in bankruptcy.[6] (October 9)

---

4 Geir Haarde, quoted by Tom Braithwaite, 'Iceland takes emergency action', *Financial Times*, October 6, 2008 (italics added).
5 Frances Williams, 'US retains top competitiveness ranking', *Financial Times*, October 8, 2008.
6 Yves Mamou, 'De la difficulté d'anticiper les crises', Économie, *Le Monde*, October 9, 2008, p. 3. The original quote read: 'Du coup, en Islande aujourd'hui, c'est le pays tout entier qui est en faillite'.

> In the past few weeks, Iceland has gone bankrupt.[7]
> (October 22)
>
> [Iceland] went bankrupt, Monopoly style, with accounts frozen, credit blocked, and savings up in smoke.[8]
> (October 24)
>
> After Iceland's bankruptcy, will the Baltics follow?[9]
> (November 6)

The Icelandic government tried—completely in vain—to convince the media that, despite the Prime Minister's statement, the island was still a responsible, viable and solvent country. News bearing Geir Haarde's unfortunate choice of words continued to spread and raised concern in other countries. Here, for example, is what a commentator for *Le Monde* wrote a week after the incident in an article entitled 'The solvency of states starts to concern traders':

> 'The country is not bankrupt for the moment; it is not forsaking its obligations', clarified Geir Haarde, the Prime Minister of Iceland, more seriously on Friday, October 10. Why would the Icelandic government be more solvent than the collapsing Icelandic banks it just urgently nationalised? By acquiring rotten banks and toxic assets, doesn't it become rotten and toxic itself? The question applies, even if to a lesser degree, to all large countries.[10]

---

7 Doug Saunders, 'Market meltdown teaches Europe that size matters', *Globe and Mail*, October 22, 2008, p. A-19.
8 Élise Vincent, 'Naufragés d'Islande', Horizons, *Le Monde*, October 24, 2008, p. 21. The original quote read: '[L'Islande] a fait banqueroute, façon Monopoly, avec comptes gelés, crédits bloqués, épargne partie en fumée'.
9 Olivier Truc, 'L'Estonie, la Lettonie et la Lituanie redoutent une "faillite à l'islandaise"', *Le Monde*, November 6, 2008, p. 15. The original quote read: 'Après la faillite de l'Islande, celle des pays baltes'.
10 Pierre-Antoine Delhommais, 'La solvabilité des États commence à préoccuper les opérateurs', Économie, *Le Monde*, October 13, 2008, p. 12. The original quote read: '"Le pays

As the global financial crisis deepened in 2008, a new term, complementary to *bankruptcy*, began appearing frequently in the newspapers: *bailout*. According to the *Globe and Mail*, "'bailout" is a pretty general term that can involve many different actions. Essentially, it means helping out a company or other entity that is in danger of collapse, usually with government money'.[11] It thus entails outside support, imminent difficulty and the ethics associated with public funds. The article went on to provide examples of recent bailouts of countries, including the United States, Britain and Iceland. In Iceland's case, help would come from outside: from international organizations (such as the International Monetary Fund), friends (Scandinavia, the United States and even the United Kingdom) or countries with a political or financial interest in assisting (Russia or China).

Along with *bankruptcy* and *bailout*, the term *financial collapse* was used in reference to Iceland. Throughout 2008, the country was viewed as a small, high-risk nation whose situation was desperate: its government was unable to manage the crisis, and foreign loans—through a bailout—seemed the only way of avoiding collapse. The growing number of high-impact phrases, disaster scenarios and dramatisations appearing in the media created an ethos of seriousness and urgency: 'Iceland seized control of its second-largest bank yesterday, pumped capital into its largest bank and lined up an emergency infusion of cash from Russia in an increasingly desperate attempt to avoid financial collapse.'[12] According to Eric Pfanner, Iceland was clearly about to go bankrupt:

---

pour le moment n'est pas en faillite, il ne renonce pas à ses obligations", a tenu à préciser, plus sérieusement, vendredi 10 octobre, Geir Haarde, le premier ministre islandais. Pourquoi l'État islandais serait-il plus solvable que les banques islandaises en déroute qu'il vient de nationaliser dans l'urgence? En rachetant les banques pourries et leurs actifs toxiques, ne devient-il pas lui-même pourri et toxique? La question se pose, même si c'est de façon moins aiguë, pour tous les grands pays'.

11 *Globe and Mail*, 'Mortgages, capital and that darn TED spread', October 10, 2008, p. B-3.
12 Brian Milner, 'Iceland at the brink', *Globe and Mail*, October 8, 2008, p. B-1.

> People go bankrupt all the time. Companies do, too. But countries? Iceland was on the verge of doing exactly that on Tuesday. ... As the meltdown in the Icelandic financial system quickened, with the government seemingly powerless to do anything about it, analysts said there was probably only one realistic option left: for Iceland to be bailed out. ... 'Iceland is bankrupt', said Arsaell Valfells, a professor at the University of Iceland. 'The Icelandic krona is history'.[13]

The idea that the country was bankrupt would follow Iceland like a millstone around its neck, being so closely associated with its image abroad that, for people who knew little about the country, it was the only image they had—that of a casualty of the global crisis, a rich country suddenly ruined by debt, a country whose sovereignty was threatened, but most importantly a people humiliated in the eyes of the world.

With time, however, commentators had to face the obvious: Iceland *was not* bankrupt; the country continued to function despite its difficulties; the disaster scenarios imagined in October did not happen. But that did not require the newspapers to set the record straight. The information conveyed by the media makes up a narrative that can be read diachronically, but the narrative does not necessarily have to meet any plausibility requirement. News that is exaggerated or even inaccurate is rarely contradicted once it has been released, unless there is a complaint. National images projected by the media are generally formed by a combination of approximations, true and false news, but most importantly by the continuous accumulation of discourse which is differentiated through a competitive process. What emerges from the accumulation is an image that is constantly renewed and nurtured by true, false, plausible and implausible infor-

---

[13] Eric Pfanner, 'Iceland is all but officially bankrupt', *International Herald Tribune*, October 9, 2008.

mation. In that respect, Iceland's case is not so different from that of other countries, with one exception: it is a *small country*, thus a country that is determined more by the discourse of others than by its own. Moreover, what was said outside of Iceland ultimately had an impact on the people who live there. In December 2008, Jim Landers wrote that 'Icelanders hide their face when you ask about the economy. "The only thing most people have ever heard about Iceland is that it went bankrupt," said political scientist Gunnar Helgi Kristinsson'.[14]

That is indeed a sad way to increase one's renown in the world, and it will certainly take several years for that image of Iceland to improve. While the country was not technically bankrupt, its reputation was definitely ruined, no longer being based on its best qualities. Icelandic journalist Sigríður Vigdís Jónsdóttir tells how she felt about the transformation when, on a trip abroad, she saw her country in the headlines for the first time:

> It wasn't so much the financial meltdown that intrigued me, but the fact that my country was getting attention. What had happened to the good old days when Icelanders were praised for electing the first female president in the world? Or when Surtsey Island appeared from the ocean in a volcanic eruption and cute stories about the sweet, little country made it around the globe? After each of those events, the foreign media packed its bags and left. Now, with the story of the financial collapse, there was neither a clear end, nor could we control the narrative. Foreigners were talking and writing about us, and there was nothing we could do about it. I should have seen it coming. Already before, living in Britain, I had noticed that my usual answers to the usual questions—northern lights, geothermal energy, the

---
[14] Jim Landers, 'Iceland's road to bankruptcy was paved with U.S. ways', *Dallas Morning News*, December 10, 2008.

singer Bjork (was she an Eskimo? Was I?)—no longer worked.[15]

Perhaps Icelanders have chosen not to forget the causes and effects of the crisis and to keep the memory of them alive so that future generations will not be taken in by anyone who comes along brandishing illusions like the new Vikings. The rest of the world will shift its focus to other events, but will remember what was said during the worst days of Iceland's crisis: of course, getting back to normal never makes news. While the word *Iceland* may no longer be synonymous with *crisis*, 'for the time being, as Julian Callow, of Barclays Capital, says "Iceland will go down in history as a textbook example of how excess credit can derail an economy"'.[16]

---

[15] Sigríður Vigdís Jónsdóttir, 'Iceland! Read all about it!', *International Herald Tribune*, May 13, 2008.
[16] Chris Giles, 'Topsy-turvy logic leaves an unpalatable choice', *Financial Times*, October 8, 2008, p. 4.

SOCIAL AND ECONOMIC INCEST
A CLOSELY-KNIT ECONOMY

> 'Note that, for Freudians, Icelandic entrepreneurs are either brothers or father-son partnerships.'
> *Le Monde*, October 9, 2008[1]

In all economies, social networks create confidence and encourage trading and dealing. However, in Iceland's case, the question arises as to whether the overly close ties between politicians, some entrepreneurs and managers ultimately eroded the foundations of its 'economic miracle'. Iceland's financial community was described by the London and New York newspapers as one big family—'the country's closely knit financial sector'[2]—which allowed extraordinary financial fluidity and led to a laissez-faire type of society coupled with a system of political favours that posed a risk for the entire country. As Robert Anderson wrote in an article for the *Financial Times*, 'the interconnectedness and indebtedness of the island's financial sector [was] particularly damaging.'[3] Overly tight relations are said to have gradually developed between political and economic players, and specifically between bankers and those responsible for regulating their activity. On this sparsely populated island, where financial activities are concentrated in a single city, family, friendly, political and social relations inevitably converge. That can lead to the risk of straying from an

---

1 Gérard Lemarquis, 'L'Islande au bord du gouffre', *Le Monde*, October 9, 2008, p. 3. The original quote read: 'Notons, pour les freudiens, que les entrepreneurs islandais sont soit des frères, soit une association père-fils'.
2 Chris Hugues and Sarah O'Connor, 'Icelandic krona suffers amid turmoil', *Financial Times*, March 20, 2008, p. 27.
3 Robert Anderson, 'Glitnir funds fail to stop fear', *Financial Times*, September 30, 2008, p. 8.

ethical standpoint, and create the impression of complicity, collusion and laxity. That, at least, was the perception that developed abroad and drew attention to 'Iceland's incestuous economy',[4] with all the inherent pitfalls:

> One of the reasons they say the financial risk was so precipitous was that the entrepreneurial pool is so small. The bankers and the regulators, the ministers and the judges are all the same people—they've known each other all their lives, their wives and their children are friends, and nobody wanted to be the one who said no.[5]

The risk and appearance of complicity between different powers, laxity in the application of rules, and collusion among entrepreneurs, bankers and financiers tend to increase in a society where family and social ties are closely knit and highly valued. Those ties create new ones that should normally be characterized by opposition or competition. In Iceland, 'entrepreneurs [are] often the main shareholders of the banks'[6]—a fact that worried foreign financial communities because of concerns about economies in which 'financial institutions and companies are closely linked through shared holdings and loans'.[7]

'David Friedman—Milton's son—once wrote that about one thousand years ago', recalls Henri Thornton in an article for the *Australian*, 'individuals could buy a seat in the Icelandic parliament'.[8] The situation in 2008 was reminiscent of that time, since prominent political and financial figures still seemed to be in a league, which sparked consid-

---

4 *Financial Times*, 'Icelandic banks', February 1, 2008, p. 14.
5 A.A. Gill, 'Iceland: frozen assets', *Sunday Times*, December 14, 2008.
6 Gérard Lemarquis, 'Happés par la tourmente, les Islandais lorgnent sur l'Union européenne', Économie, *Le Monde*, October 8, 2008, p. 11. The original quote read: 'les entrepreneurs [sont] aussi souvent les principaux actionnaires des banques'.
7 Robert Anderson and David Oakley, 'Icelandic bank shares and the krona remain in front line of turmoil', *Financial Times*, October 1, 2008, p. 27.
8 Henry Thornton, 'Vexed questions', *Australian*, October 27, 2008.

erable unrest: 'Protest demonstrations mostly have targeted a small group of "financial vikings" who turned the banking system into a big hedge fund—with government complicity, of course.'[9] The members of the same elite controlled the country's economic and political levers, exchanging favours in the process: 'since the beginning of the 21st century, banks and government have worked hand in glove.'[10] Such familiarity seemed so natural that it was exposed without precaution at an event in New York in March 2008,[11] when the head of Baugur, Jón Ásgeir Jóhannesson, extolled the virtues of his businesses on the same platform as the Prime Minister, Geir Haarde, who was there to reassure investors about Iceland's financial soundness.

Clearly, Iceland cannot be criticised for being too sparsely populated, and its small population cannot be considered the only cause of the crisis: other small countries manage to avoid collusion and abuses of power. However, certain events in Iceland's recent financial history raise troubling ethical questions. Britain-based professor Robert Wade considered the exchange of favours between those who privatised the banks and those who took control of them as reprehensible back-scratching:

> The banks were privatised around 2000 in a hasty and politically driven process. Ownership went to people with close connections to the parties in the conservative coalition government, which had scant experience in modern banking. The central bank and the finance ministry were staffed at the top by people who preferred as light a regulatory touch as possible.[12]

---

[9] Greg Burns, 'Financial fiasco fires up Iceland's ire, civic unrest', *Chicago Tribune*, January 2, 2009.
[10] Roger Boyes, 'Skating on thin ice', *Australian*, October 10, 2008.
[11] Tom Braithwaite, 'The fraud claims that are taking their toll on Baugur', *Financial Times*, March 19, 2008, p. 27.
[12] Robert Wade, 'Iceland pays price for financial excess', *Financial Times*, July 1, 2008.

Journalists from all over—the United Kingdom, France and the United States—denounced this incestuous climate, pointing to a 'conflict of interest'[13] and 'guilty gifts',[14] and voiced suspicions of political favouritism: 'David Oddsson privatised Iceland's banks, and in exchange the newly-rich owners of these banks ensured that Oddsson's party remained in power. Even after he stepped down, he had himself appointed as head of Iceland's Central Bank.'[15]

Even within financial groups, similar incestuous movements controlled changes in the leadership of affiliated companies and gave preference to members of certain families, in a game of musical chairs that puzzled analysts, but did not fool them. Tom Braithwaite described the effects of such close ties and the interest in subsidiaries of Icelandic conglomerates as follows: '[It] sounds complicated, [and] it is. The network of cross-shareholdings in Iceland, many of them held through traditionally secretive private holding entities, makes it impossible to pin down the ownership of companies.'[16] In a letter printed in the large European dailies, Norwegian-French judge Eva Joly spoke of 'false pretenses' and 'clan-like operation of institutions [that were] the cause of all the ills'.[17] This situation bred mistrust toward the country's leaders: 'Iceland's largely homemade crisis was created by a small group of powerful political and financial figures who literally have looted the nation's treasury.'[18]

When people spoke out against questionable ties between powerful players, they were silenced through the sudden control of informa-

---

13 Gérard Lemarquis, 'L'Islande au bord du gouffre', *Le Monde*, October 9, 2008, p. 3. The original expression was 'conflit d'intérêt'.
14 Ibid. The original expression was 'coupable libéralité'.
15 Íris Erlingsdóttir, 'Iceland is burning', *Huffington Post*, January 20, 2009.
16 Tom Braithwaite, 'Baugur evades Icelandic chill', *Financial Times*, October 4, 2008, p. 19.
17 Eva Joly, 'L'Islande ou les faux semblants de la régulation de l'après-crise', *Le Monde*, August 1, 2009. The original quotes read: 'faux semblants' and 'fonctionnement clanique des institutions, cause de tous [l]es maux'.
18 Íris Erlingsdóttir, 'Iceland—The Nordic Zimbabwe', *Huffington Post*, January 5, 2009.

tion; for example, in the summer of 2009, lawyers for Kaupþing bank sent Wikileaks[19] a letter demanding it remove from its web site the list of recipients of loans granted by the bank in the days preceding its filing for bankruptcy protection in 2008. The bank also ordered Icelandic national radio and television (RUV) to hush the matter. Once again, the appearance of collusion raised doubts about the integrity of the institutions, as indicated by *Le Monde* journalist Hélène Bekmezian, who talked about a 'bank scandal':

> The order [to RUV] was given by the Reykjavik District Commissioner, Rúnar Guðjónsson, whose son, Guðjón Rúnarsson, is head of the Icelandic Financial Services Association and spokesperson for the country's failed banks. One more point: the Commissioner's other son, Frosti Reyr Rúnarsson, was head of Kaupthing's securities brokerage division.[20]

This incestuous climate in Iceland's spheres of power weakened the country's economy and society by undermining the checks and balances: 'it means any contagion can spread rapidly through the system'.[21] That is what happened in 2008, with unfortunate consequences that Icelanders hoped to reduce through changes at the top of their institutions and government. However, when new revelations came to light in the following months, Icelandic analysts wearily wondered whether anything had really changed; as Hélène Bekmezian asked, 'Have they taken the same ones and started over again?'[22]

---

19 *Wikileaks*, 'Financial collapse: Confidential exposure analysis of 205 companies each owing above €45M to Icelandic bank Kaupthing, 26 Sep 2008', July 26, 2009.
20 Hélène Bekmezian, 'L'Islande face à un scandale bancaire de plusieurs milliards d'euros', *Le Monde*, August 4, 2009. The original quote read: 'L'ordre [à la RUV] a été donné par le commissaire de Reykjavik, Rúnar Guðjónsson, dont le fils, Guðjón Rúnarsson, dirige l'Association islandaise des services financiers et joue le rôle de porte-parole des banques en faillite du pays. Détail : l'autre fils du commissaire, Frosti Reyr Rúnarsson, a dirigé le département de courtage de Kaupthing'.
21 Tom Braithwaite, 'Baugur evades Icelandic chill', *Financial Times*, October 4, 2008, p. 19.
22 Hélène Bekmezian, 'L'Islande face à un scandale bancaire de plusieurs milliards d'euros', *Le Monde*, August 4, 2009. The original quote read: 'On prend les mêmes et on recommence?'

DAVIÐ ODDSSON AND THE CENTRAL BANK OF ICELAND
POLITICAL INTERVENTION IN ECONOMICS

'His decision[s] reflected politics, technical incompetence and ignorance of markets, and his comments thereafter were highly destabilising.'
Financial Times, October 13, 2008[1]

On February 9, 2009, Davið Oddsson, the Chairman of the Board of Governors of the Central Bank of Iceland and former Prime Minister, published—on the Bank's official web site—his personal response to a letter from the government asking him to resign. That move was one of many condemned by the public and financial analysts alike. According to comments published in foreign media, including those of David Ibison, Stefán Kristinsson, Willem H. Buiter, Anne Sibert, Peter Gumbel, Brian Milner, and Richard Portes, his action needlessly delayed a return to some sort of normality in the country's economic management. Be that as it may, according to the articles in the foreign media that reflect the changing image of Iceland's Central Bank and its chairman, it is clear that this episode was only the latest in an unfortunate series that tarnished Iceland's reputation.

Throughout the crisis, statements by Davið Oddsson, appearing in the foreign press, were said to fuel discontent, hinder attempts to settle the crisis and hamper Iceland´s reputation. In late October, he

---

1 Richard Portes, 'The shocking errors behind Iceland's meltdown', *Financial Times*, October 13, 2008, p. 13.

claimed that he had attempted to prevent the banks from failing, but that people had turned a deaf ear: 'he [said he had] repeatedly warned the heads of the banks that they were in danger but was ignored'.[2]

In the spring, Oddsson blamed foreigners for the turmoil and claimed that the rest of the world did not understand Iceland's economic issues. The *New York Times* quoted Oddsson as saying that 'much of the dialogue about Iceland is based on a misunderstanding about our economy'.[3] The *Financial Times* quoted numerous statements of this nature in which Oddsson asserted that '[some] "dishonest brokers" were behind the country's problems'[4] and that 'Iceland was the victim of an assault, ... "a final attempt to tear the Icelandic financial system down"'.[5] At the peak of the crisis, Oddsson accused his counterparts at other central banks—themselves grappling with problems due to the shaky global economy—of refusing to do more for Iceland: 'Mr Oddsson believes their refusal contributed to the collapse'.[6] In a speech he gave to the Iceland Chamber of Commerce, reported in *Wall Street Journal*[7] and severely commented by Peter Gumbel[8], Oddsson made statements that jeopardized, according to *Financial Times*' journalist David Ibison, action by his country to pull out of crisis: 'The comments by Mr Oddsson ... could undermine planned legal action by Reykjavik against the UK government'.[9] Finally, Oddsson accused the country's bankers of having acted without due consideration and warned them that the State would never come to their aid. Unfortu-

---

[2] David Ibison, 'Oddsson defends role in Iceland's collapse', *Financial Times*, October 23, 2008.
[3] Davið Oddsson, quoted by Mark Landler, 'Credit crisis triggers downturn in Iceland', *New York Times*, April 17, 2008.
[4] David Ibison, 'Iceland inflation hits six-year high', *Financial Times*, March 29, 2008, p. 2.
[5] David Ibison, 'Iceland counters alleged attacks', *Financial Times*, March 31, 2008, p. 6.
[6] David Ibison, 'Oddsson defends role in Iceland's collapse', *Financial Times*, October 23, 2008.
[7] Davið Oddsson, quoted in *Wall Street Journal*, 'Excerpts: Iceland's Oddsson', October 17, 2008.
[8] Peter Gumbel, 'Iceland: the country that became a hedge fund', *Fortune*, December 4, 2008, http://www.money.cnn.com/.
[9] David Ibison, 'Iceland thaws over clash with UK', *Financial Times*, November 23, 2008.

nately for him—and for Iceland—a week later, the *Wall Street Journal* translated his comments—'we do not intend to pay the debts of the banks'[10]—which sent shock waves.

The foreign media criticised Oddsson on a number of occasions for his conduct during the crisis, some journalists even accusing him of having worsened Iceland's economic predicament as a result of his rash actions. In their report on the banking crisis, Willem H. Buiter and Anne Sibert accused him of being irresponsible, stating that 'a number of policy mistakes were made by the Icelandic authorities, especially by the governor of the Central Bank of Iceland, David Oddsson'.[11] According to *Agence France-Presse*, the hasty nationalisation of the banks, led by Oddsson, was one of the errors that precipitated the crisis.[12] Peter Gumbel commented on his conduct in dealings with the United Kingdom, stating that 'Oddsson's erratic behavior ... compounded Iceland's financial and diplomatic problems. ... Oddsson continued to flip-flop'.[13]

The controversial Davið Oddsson—who is a lawyer by training—has always attracted the attention of the foreign press. Peter Gumbel recalls the career path that Oddsson chose and that made him one of the most important public figures in Iceland: 'A one-time actor and producer of radio comedy shows, Oddsson, 60, was elected mayor of Reykjavik while in his early 30s and went on to become Iceland's longest-serving Prime Minister, in office from 1991 to 2004.'[14] The neo-liberal policies he implemented—'model[ling] himself on Brit-

---

10 Davið Oddsson, quoted in *Wall Street Journal*, 'Excerpts: Iceland's Oddsson', October 17, 2008.
11 Willem H. Buiter and Anne Sibert, 'The Icelandic banking crisis and what to do about it. The lender of last resort theory of optimal currency areas', *CEPR Policy Insight*, no. 26, October 2008.
12 Agence France-Presse, 'Crise. L'Islande nationalise ses banques à marche forcée', *Le Devoir*, October 10, 2008.
13 Peter Gumbel, 'Iceland: the country that became a hedge fund', *Fortune*, December 4, 2008, http://www.money.cnn.com/.
14 Ibid.

ain's Margaret Thatcher'[15]—signalled a disengagement of the State and paved the way for an increase in Iceland's standard of living. The country's situation prior to his time in office was described as being particularly drab: 'Iceland used to be one of Europe's poorest countries, a bleak place that survived mostly on fishing revenue and the occasional adventurous tourist who came to bathe in the natural hot springs or explore the moonlike lava fields'.[16]

However, the apparent wealth that seemed to stem, according to the foreign media, from his reforms proved to be illusory, because it was sustained by excessive borrowing by businesses and the banks, as the *Globe and Mail* pointed out: 'during his long tenure as Prime Minister ... the government privatized the banks, slashed taxes and introduced radical free-market reforms, setting the stage for an economic boom and explosive, debt-fuelled expansion of the financial sector'.[17] In addition, Oddsson's ties with the new Vikings raised suspicion. It is is seen as if the new Vikings became rich thanks to the privatisation of the banks and the financial deregulation that Oddsson introduced. Some people even saw it as back-scratching: 'David Oddsson privatized Iceland's banks, and in exchange the newly-rich owners of these banks ensured that Oddsson's party remained in power'.[18] The *BBC* believed that the political appointment of the Central Bank governors greatly hurt Iceland, affirming that 'by choosing governors based on their political background rather than economic or financial expertise, the central bank may be perceived to be ill-equipped to deal with an economy in crisis'.[19] This opinion was shared by the *Globe and Mail*, which maintained that the events of October 2008 reflected the incompetence of the governors of the Central Bank, stating 'how ineptly the central bank, Sedlabanki, and the chairman of its board of

---

15 Ibid.
16 Ibid.
17 Brian Milner, 'IMF demand forces Iceland to raise rates', *Globe and Mail*, October 29, 2008, p. B-14.
18 Íris Erlingsdóttir, 'Iceland is burning', *Huffington Post*, January 20, 2009.
19 Jon Danielsson, 'Why raising interest rates won't work', *BBC News*, October 28, 2008.

governors, David Oddsson, have handled the banking crisis'.[20]

Davið Oddsson was criticised not only by financial analysts and foreign journalists, but by Icelanders themselves. In October, *Le Monde* reported that Icelanders—more than 4,000 of whom had held demonstrations in Reykjavík calling for his resignation—had 'made David Oddsson ... a scapegoat. ... They blamed him for being one of the main people responsible for the country's bankruptcy'.[21] British economist Richard Portes shared that view, asserting that 'Mr Oddsson is part of the problem, not of any solution, and should resign immediately'.[22] According to an article appearing in the *Economist*, even bankers no longer trusted him: '[they] blame him for almost everything'.[23] He no longer had any friends among his counterparts at the other central banks, who, according to Peter Gumbel, believed 'that Oddsson's approach was deeply flawed'.[24]

For Icelanders, who found the economic crisis difficult and saw the spotlight of the international media trained on their insular life, the disrepute into which their central bank governor fell was very discouraging. The vast majority of media reports about the country focused specifically on its financial system. According to many of those reports, it was an important aspect of Iceland's credibility and ability to govern itself that took a hard blow because of Davið Oddsson.

---

20 Brian Milner, 'IMF demand forces Iceland to raise rates', *Globe and Mail*, October 29, 2008, p. B-14.
21 Jean-Pierre Stroobants and Élise Vincent, 'La crise islandaise inquiète de nombreux épargnants du Benelux', Économie, *Le Monde*, October 21, 2008, p. 14. The original quote read: 'transformé David Oddsson [...] en bouc émissaire. [...] Ils lui reprochent d'être l'un des principaux responsables de la faillite du pays'.
22 Richard Portes, 'The shocking errors behind Iceland's meltdown', *Financial Times*, October 13, 2008, p. 13.
23 *Economist*, 'Cracks in the crust', December 11, 2008.
24 Peter Gumbel, 'Iceland: the country that became a hedge fund', *Fortune*, December 4, 2008, http://www.money.cnn.com/.

ARROGANCE
EXCESSIVE CONFIDENCE

'It's hard to understand how they could still believe they are in a position to negotiate.'
Globe and Mail, October 21, 2008[1]

In reaction to the concerns raised abroad by warnings from the financial rating agencies and newspapers about the fragility of Iceland's economy, Geir Haarde and the Icelandic banks adopted a hostile attitude. Haarde rejected judgements about Iceland's economy, declaring in March that 'the movements in credit markets "are totally out of line and not justified"'.[2] In a *Financial Times* article entitled 'Indignant Iceland faces a problem of perception', David Ibison and Gillian Tett indicated that such arrogance was not new in the financial world, but was inexcusable given the country's situation: 'a cynic might suggest that such comments have a familiar ring. Over the past year, numerous hedge funds caught up in the global financial turmoil have also complained about "irrational" or "unfair" investor behaviour'.[3] Representatives of Glitnir, convinced that their institution was stable, ridiculed the warnings issued by London and New York. A manager with the bank claimed that the ratings did not devalue Iceland or its institutions, which were above all suspicion, but certainly eroded confidence in the parties that provided them: 'This harsh criticism ... [has] caused Moody's credibility to suffer significantly for the past

---

1   A financial analyst, quoted by Brian Milner, 'Out of options, Iceland leans on IMF', *Globe and Mail*, October 21, 2008, p. B-3.
2   Geir Haarde, quoted by David Ibison and Gillian Tett, 'Indignant Iceland faces a problem of perception', *Financial Times*, March 27, 2008, p. 13.
3   David Ibison and Gillian Tett, 'Indignant Iceland faces a problem of perception', *Financial Times*, March 27, 2008, p. 13.

year'.[4] The President of Landsbanki, Björgólfur Guðmundsson, arrogantly declared in April—only months before his bank ended up in a precarious situation—that the doubts expressed abroad were completely unfounded, saying 'it is an absurd discussion because it is almost unthinkable to us that we would default'.[5]

At the peak of the turmoil in the fall, Iceland's prime minister *demanded* considerable economic aid from the West. That Iceland so enjoined foreign countries to come to its assistance may reveal a certain malaise, as suggested in the Globe and Mail: "It's hard to understand how they could still believe they are in a position to negociate."[6] Prime Minister Haarde faulted his partners for being slow to act, as reported on October 8 in the *Guardian*: 'Geir H. Haarde publicly criticised the lack of assistance the country had received from Europe'.[7] Furthermore, according to the Danish daily, *Politiken*, in November President Ólafur Ragnar Grímsson shocked diplomats when he said that Iceland's relations with its traditional allies, including Denmark, seemed compromised because of their lack of support. *Politiken* reported the incident as follows:

> Iceland's President Olafur Ragnar Grimsson has accused Sweden, Denmark and Great Britain of turning their backs on Iceland in its battle to survive the financial crisis. During a luncheon with foreign diplomats in Reykjavik last week, Grimsson threatened to seek new allies as his country's former allies have failed his crisis-ridden country. According to the Norwegian news agency NTB, shocked diplomats could hardly believe

---

4   A Glitnir manager, quoted by David Ibison, 'Moody's poised to downgrade Iceland', *Financial Times*, March 6, 2008, p. 27.
5   Björgólfur Guðmundsson, quoted by Mark Landler, 'Credit crisis triggers downturn in Iceland', *New York Times*, April 17, 2008.
6   A financial analyst, quoted by Brian Milner, 'Out of options, Iceland leans on IMF', *Globe and Mail*, October 21, 2008, p. B-3.
7   Angela Balakrishnan, 'U.K. to sue Iceland over any lost bank savings', *Guardian*, October 8, 2008.

their own ears, according to a memorandum from the Norwegian embassy.[8]

Then, according to the *Globe and Mail*, after receiving a promise of assistance from the International Monetary Fund (IMF), the Icelandic government announced on October 28 that the $2 billion from the IMF was insufficient and that it needed an additional $4 billion: 'Crisis-hit Iceland said yesterday it needed another $4-billion (U.S.) in loans on top of the $2-billion it wants from the International Monetary Fund.'[9] In November, when the United Kingdom asked for assurance of compensation for its savers and the IMF had still not confirmed its assistance, Haarde urged the IMF's board to act without delay, saying, 'I hope that the executive board of the IMF will put our economic plan on the agenda as soon as possible'.[10]

Viewed from abroad, the weakening of Iceland's economy due to the crisis seems to have had a bearing on such exaggerated confidence, as indicated by the title of an article by Matthew Hart, 'Iceland's next saga: The wounded tiger's tale'.[11] In the article, Hart suggests that the crisis nonetheless changed Iceland's general attitude, quoting writer Bragi Ólafsson as follows:

> What people are mostly saying is that there will be a very dramatic change in our way of thinking. We have been very greedy—a very rude society. You know—people in Range Rovers talking on their phones and honking horns. But almost overnight this has changed.[12]

---

8   *Politiken*, 'Iceland: Denmark has turned its back', November 12, 2008.
9   Patrick Lannin and Sakari Suoninen, 'Iceland seeks $4-billion more in aid', *Globe and Mail*, October 28, 2008, p. B-18.
10 Geir Haarde, quoted by David Jolly, '$6 billion rescue for Iceland put on hold', *International Herald Tribune*, November 12, 2008.
11 Matthew Hart, 'Iceland's next saga: The wounded tiger's tale', *Globe and Mail*, November 15, 2008, p. F-4.
12 Bragi Ólafsson, quoted in ibid.

Perceived abroad as signs of arrogance, these reactions by Iceland gave the impression that the country had excessive expectations of the rest of the world, expressed through an attitude that was overbearing and out of place.

ICELAND'S VERY LOYAL FRIEND
RICHARD PORTES

'Prof Portes stands by his views.'
Financial Times, October 9, 2008[1]

Not many foreign commentators can claim to be experts on Iceland. A few academics and journalists—including David Ibison of the *Financial Times*—take an interest in the country, mostly through their field of expertise: economics, social issues, literature, film, tourism or sports. There are two economists, however, who have made Iceland one of their focuses: Richard Portes and Robert Wade, both London-based researchers and key people in the media on Iceland. Richard Portes' name comes up often in the foreign newspapers, because of the analyses he publishes or his often controversial comments reported by financial journalists. His opinions, favourable toward the financiers, are sometimes challenged by other experts, such as Robert Wade. Both men played an important role in the media storm that swamped Iceland in 2008; they deserve specific attention because of their involvement.

A professor of economics at the London Business School, Richard Portes is the founder and director of the Centre for Economic Policy Research. His profile does not specifically mention Iceland, but defines his areas of expertise as follows: 'He has written extensively on sovereign debt, European monetary and financial issues, international capital flows, centrally planned economies and transition, macr-

---

[1] Emiliya Mychasuk and Emiko Terazono, 'Viking saga', *Financial Times*, October 9, 2008, p. 20.

oeconomic disequilibrium, and European integration'.[2] In November 2007, he published a 60-page report, entitled *The Internationalisation of Iceland's Financial Sector*, together with his colleague Friðrik Már Baldursson from the University of Reykjavík. The study, carried out for the Iceland Chamber of Commerce, analysed the effects of foreign expansion by Iceland's banks.

In the spring of 2008, Portes remained optimistic and reassuring when the first warnings were issued about Iceland's situation. He encouraged people to remain calm and 'urged investors to pay more attention to the data'.[3] He insisted that the banks were stable and that there was no cause for concern, maintaining that 'these banks are strong, they have no noxious paper. ... The short-term movements are not indicative of anything but speculation'.[4]

Portes' position, as reported by the London and New York newspapers, could be summarized in two phrases: *the financial markets were exaggerating the seriousness* of Iceland's situation and *their reaction was unjust*. In March 2008, Portes told the *Financial Times* that Iceland was facing, first and foremost, a problem of perception. According to him, the country's banking system was not in any danger:

> Prof Portes, for his part, insists that the answer to this question is actually very reassuring: if Iceland's banking system faced a crisis, the government could either use its existing resources to rescue the banks or borrow more funds from the markets.[5]

---

2   http://faculty.london.edu/rportes/shortbio.htm, consulted in October 2009.
3   David Ibison, 'Iceland pushes rates to 15% as turmoil bites', *Financial Times*, March 26, 2008, p. 1.
4   Richard Portes, quoted by Chris Hugues and Sarah O'Connor, 'Icelandic krona suffers amid turmoil', *Financial Times*, March 20, 2008, p. 27.
5   David Ibison and Gillian Tett, 'Indignant Iceland faces a problem of perception', *Financial Times*, March 27, 2008, p. 13.

In a letter to the editor in July, Portes maintained his position and said he found the reaction of analysts to be exaggerated, including that of his colleague Robert Wade who believed that Icelanders had borrowed 'as though there ... [were] no tomorrow'.[6] For Portes, such an opinion was unjustified: 'That sounds more like the Americans or indeed the British than the Icelanders'.[7] When Iceland's economy finally showed serious signs of weakness in October, Portes stayed the course and claimed that Iceland's banks, which had been unfairly targeted, remained cautious and well managed:

> The Iceland problem was immediately vastly exaggerated. ... The world is a little unjust. ... They have been prudently managed and haven't been excessively dependent on the wholesale money markets compared to anyone else.[8]

Portes was usually in agreement with the views of Icelandic top-ranking businessmen and some of the actions taken by the government. For example, when Iceland undertook its controversial negotiations with Russia, Portes supported Reykjavík's initiative, stating that 'it ... [was] rather imaginative of the Russians and the Icelanders. They should have done it earlier'.[9] According to the *Financial Times*, Portes criticised the Central Bank's decision to invest in Glitnir at the same time as Jón Ásgeir Jóhannesson (of Baugur).[10] Moreover, Portes was one of the harsh critics of the Central Bank chairman and former prime minister Davíð Oddsson. In a bitter attack appearing in the

---

6 Robert Wade, quoted by Friðrik Már Baldursson and Richard Portes, 'Criticism of Icelandic economy does not square with the facts', *Financial Times*, July 4, 2008, p. 14.
7 Friðrik Már Baldursson and Richard Portes, 'Criticism of Icelandic economy does not square with the facts', *Financial Times*, July 4, 2008, p. 14.
8 Richard Portes, quoted by David Teather, 'Icelandic government battles to save the economy', *Guardian*, October 6, 2008.
9 Richard Portes, quoted by Brian Milner, 'Russia's "imaginative" Icelandic rescue', *Globe and Mail*, October 8, 2008, p. B-10.
10 Tom Braithwaite, 'Confusion grows over Iceland's rescue plan', *Financial Times*, October 6, 2008.

Financial Times on October 13, 2008, Portes declared that 'politicians should not become central bank governors. Mr Oddsson is part of the problem, not of any solution, and should resign immediately'.[11] He said that Oddsson's decisions were biased. In his opinion, Oddsson's actions 'reflected politics, technical incompetence and ignorance of the markets, and his comments thereafter were highly destabilising'.[12]

Portes' views clashed with those of another well-known London-based economist, Robert Wade, with whom he maintained a debate through the newspapers. Wade, a professor of political economy at the London School of Economics, received the Leontief Prize from Tufts University in 2008. In a press release announcing the award, the University described Professor Wade's contribution as follows: 'Robert Wade has really been a champion of studying the role of government in promoting economic development in developing countries and challenging the wisdom that free trade is the way countries develop'.[13] The views of these two men on the economy and consequently on Iceland's financial situation were conflicting. Wade wanted to see the economy take precedence over finance again. Portes and his co-researcher Friðrik Már Baldursson criticised that position, maintaining that 'Robert Wade gets Iceland very wrong. ... Prof Wade's comments are political, including rumour-mongering. This and his carelessness with the data are regrettable in the fragile conditions of today's international financial markets'.[14] Robert Wade responded to the attack by referring to an International Monetary Fund report and stressing that Portes refused to see the situation as it was. He indicated that Portes was unable to foresee the crisis for which

---

11 Richard Portes, 'The shocking errors behind Iceland's meltdown', *Financial Times*, October 13, 2008, p. 13.
12 Ibid.
13 http://ase.tufts.edu/gdae/about_us/leontief/TuftsDailyFeb08.pdf, consulted in October 2009.
14 Friðrik Már Baldursson and Richard Portes, 'Criticism of Icelandic economy does not square with the facts', *Financial Times*, July 4, 2008, p. 14.

Iceland was heading because his analyses were overly optimistic, describing Portes' view as a 'rosy account'.[15]

The debate between these two men seemed to start with a speech—entitled 'New Vikings'—given by Robert Wade in Reykjavík a few months prior to the crisis of 2008. In that speech, he issued a stern warning about the risks the country could be facing. During that glorious period, Wade's pessimism was at odds with the somewhat triumphant tone of the report published by Portes and his associate on the success of Iceland's financial sector. A few months later, at the peak of the crisis, an article published by the *Financial Times* stated that the two men had maintained their positions: '[Wade] having rung alarm bells about Iceland's banks'[16] and 'Prof Portes stands by his views, and says the Icelandic banks' portfolios were sound'.[17] Which of the two, the optimist or the pessimist, will have best served Iceland's greater interests? The fallout from the crisis would tend to suggest that friends can sometimes make strange advisers.

---

15 Robert Wade, 'IMF reports uncertain outlook for Iceland', *Financial Times*, July 15, 2008, p. 14.
16 Emiliya Mychasuk and Emiko Terazono, 'Viking saga', *Financial Times*, October 9, 2008, p. 20.
17 Ibid.

THE NEW VIKINGS
YESTERDAY'S HEROES, TODAY'S VILLAINS

> 'The Viking financiers have sought refuge abroad. Their public relations experts say rehabilitating their images will have to wait until the financial blood-letting stops.'
> *Dallas Morning News*, December 10, 2008[1]

Iceland, the land of the sagas and homeland of the Vikings, has, in part, enjoyed a dual and contradictory reputation: that of giving the Western world the most accomplished literary texts of the Middle Ages; and that of being the descendants of people who, through their aggressive warlike ways, terrorised towns and villages from Paris to Constantinople. Dominated by the Danish for over five centuries and afflicted by calamities of all sorts, Iceland attained independence in 1944; then, in the 20th century, the country achieved unprecedented prosperity, propelling it to the top of wealth indices. According to the foreign press it owed that extraordinary growth to the liberalisation of global trade, from which a group of young entrepreneurs profited so skilfully that foreign journalists quickly associated them with the Vikings. Here is how Jim Landers, for example, described that new generation of financial warrior in the *Dallas Morning News*:

> Over the last six years, a group of about two dozen young, U.S.-educated financiers took Iceland on a Viking voyage of acquisitions, grabbing airlines, banks, mortgage lenders and securities traders from Texas to Hong Kong.[2]

---

1 Jim Landers, 'Iceland's road to bankruptcy was paved with U.S. ways', *Dallas Morning News*, December 10, 2008.
2 Ibid.

The term *new Vikings* (*Viking entrepreneurs, Viking financiers*) first appeared during the prosperous years preceding the crisis of 2008; it generally refers to a group of young businessmen who controlled Iceland's economy and extended their power abroad, taking advantage of the liberalisation of global trade and the privatisation of Iceland's banks at the turn of the 21st century. In 2007, professor Robert Wade used the term in a controversial speech he gave in Reykjavík, entitled 'New Vikings',[3] in which he cautioned against the excesses of those financiers and the risks they were incurring. The term quickly acquired pejorative and ironic connotations as the empire built by the new Vikings collapsed. Sarah Lyall looks back at those businessmen after the fall, stating that 'like the Vikings of old, Icelandic bankers were roaming the world and aggressively seizing business, pumping debt into a soufflé of a system'.[4] Roger Boyes described them as a generation who adapted the pillaging of Vikings to our own time: 'If there are still Vikings in this Iceland, they are the financial marauders setting out for Britain or mainland Europe, not to pillage and plunder but to snap up a chunk of fashion house'.[5]

As the term *new Vikings* entered the language, warlike vocabulary started to appear in official discourse. Prime Minister Geir Haarde was said to have responded to negative comments from foreign financiers about Iceland, making it 'clear he would *defend* the financial system *with all the tools in his armoury*'.[6] Similarly, the Chairman of Landsbanki, Björgólfur Guðmundsson, declared that 'the island needed *a war chest to "protect* the economy and economic management from setbacks"'.[7]

---

[3] Emiliya Mychasuk and Emiko Terazono, 'Viking saga', *Financial Times*, October 9, 2008, p. 20.
[4] Sarah Lyall, 'Stunned Icelanders struggle after economy's fall', *New York Times*, November 9, 2008.
[5] Roger Boyes, 'Skating on thin ice', *Australian*, October 10, 2008.
[6] David Ibison, 'Iceland fends off hedge fund attack', *Financial Times*, April 18, 2008, p. 6 (italics added).
[7] Björgólfur Guðmundsson, quoted by David Ibison, 'Iceland wealth fund is proposed', *Financial Times*, April 25, 2008, p. 2 (italics added).

These nouveau riche Vikings awakened an atavistic interest in victory, the traces of which had long disappeared from the island. This inclination reappeared in a new form, which was alluring despite its pitfalls: 'tales of fast cars, yachts and penthouses, accounting scandals and Russian money did not seem to hamper the country's love affair with its self-made men'.[8] The new Vikings led an openly flashy lifestyle, which Icelanders were not accustomed to, but which had its appeal. Such extravagance was both mind-boggling and fascinating for Icelanders and foreigners because of its scale: 'The bankers partied by flying in Elton John for a Reykjavik birthday bash. They dined at Nordic/Asian fusion restaurants where entrees started at $50. They danced at Reykjavik clubs where bottle service tabs ran to hundreds of dollars'.[9] Above the rules that apply to ordinary people, this generation often appeared arrogant and self-assured, generating fear, loathing, pride and admiration. With it, delusions of grandeur swept over Reykjavík, where luxury buildings were quickly erected as though the city were the metropolis of an empire. Luxury office towers went up, along with ultra-modern apartments costing close to a million euros, and a boutique hotel that would become the new Vikings' haunt—101 Hotel (101 for the postage code of downtown Reykjavík), The construction of the Reykjavík concert hall, a titanic and megalomaniac project, was budgeted at two per cent of the country's gross domestic product, which would be equal to a $250 billion project in the United States.[10] In the new Viking era, Icelanders had the impression that they were living in another world, that the crisis would somehow turn out to be crazy talk and illusions: 'The oxygen Iceland was breathing was foreign money. ... Investors borrowed massively in countries with cheap money and

---

8 Rowena Mason, 'Iceland falls out of love with its billionaires', *Telegraph*, October 19, 2008.
9 Jim Landers, 'Iceland's road to bankruptcy was paved with U.S. ways', *Dallas Morning News*, December 10, 2008.
10 Ben Holland, 'Iceland "like Chernobyl" as meltdown shows anger can boil over', *Bloomberg*, December 23, 2008.

parked it in Iceland, raking in the difference'.[11] While analysts and the general public were aware of the source of such borrowing, in that boom time, people preferred to keep the magnitude and potential risks quiet. However, once the dust had settled after the worst fallout from the crisis in the autumn of 2008, accountants set to work to calculate the cost of the new Vikings' huge neo-liberal binge: a year later, the Icelandic daily, *Morgunbladid*, reported that the claims against Landsbanki alone totalled 35 billion euros.[12] Thus, a handful of men boosted the country's economy and sense of patriotic pride for a few years, modelling themselves on a revitalized and modernized version of the Viking conqueror. The country's fall was as steep as the risks those men took. In Robert Jackson's view, they destroyed Iceland's international reputation:

> This is a man-made disaster and worse still, one made by a small group of Icelanders who set off to conquer the financial world, only to return defeated and humiliated. The country is on the verge of bankruptcy and, even more important for those of Viking stock, its international reputation is in tatters. It hurts.[13]

The profile sketched by the foreign press attributes to the new Vikings a virile personality, resembling all the male stereotypes that Scandinavia had seemed to get away from as far as the Western world could see: '[those] bonus-chasing, testosterone-fuelled bankers'[14] '[with] flamboyant personalities'[15] 'have developed a reputation for bold and

---

11 Matthew Hart, 'Iceland's next saga: The wounded tiger's tale', *Globe and Mail*, November 15, 2008, p. F-4.
12 *Morgunbladid*, quoted in IcelandReview.com, 'Highest claim to Landsbanki ISK 925 billion', November 18, 2009.
13 Robert Jackson, 'Letter from Iceland', *Financial Times*, November 15, 2008.
14 Sarah O'Connor, 'Glitnir chief rolls up her sleeves for mammoth task', *Financial Times*, October 19, 2008.
15 Bill Bailey, 'Icelandic bank collapse raises questions for UK', *Financial Times*, October 9, 2008, p. 10.

highly leveraged aggressiveness',[16] 'risk taking, decisiveness, and swiftness in their investments'.[17]

The Viking entrepreneurs who dominated Icelandic finance are often described in few words: a handful of men controlling a few empires, made up of various conglomerates and supported by accommodating banks whose strings they pulled. Three families stand out among them: 'shipping and brewing moguls Bjorgolfur Gudmundsson and his son, Thor Bjorgolfsson; retail magnates Johannes Jonsson and his son, Jon Asgeir Johannesson; and frozen food entrepreneurs Lydur Gudmundsson and his brother, Agust Gudmundsson'.[18] The foreign press considered Jóhannes Jónsson's son, Jón Ásgeir Jóhannesson, typical of the new Viking personality, as he best embodied the conquering—and for a time victorious—mega business hero, through his flamboyance, skilful handling of power and arrogance.

Born in 1968, Jón Ásgeir Jóhannesson founded at age 21, with his father, a chain of discount food stores, called Bonus, which were highly successful in Iceland. The family business quickly grew, and Jóhannesson rose to the top of the conglomerate, despite his gaffes and public statements which made him a colourful media character. Arrogant, sometimes crude and contemptuous, he liked show, and inspired both admiration and aversion: '[he] has been likened to a rock star for his long hair and rebellious streak'.[19] Financial journalists referred to him as a money and power-hungry visionary: 'A long-haired 40-year-old grocery magnate'[20] 'described by colleagues as the company's visionary. From a young age he expressed a desire to make money—one that he has achieved via a sprawling retail portfolio.'[21]

---

16 David Ibison, 'Icelandic whispers shake faith in boom', *Financial Times*, March 25, 2008.
17 Reuters, 'How times changed', *Globe and Mail*, October 10, 2008, p. B-11.
18 Rowena Mason, 'Iceland falls out of love with its billionaires', *Telegraph*, October 19, 2008.
19 Tom Braithwaite, 'The fraud claims that are taking their toll on Baugur', *Financial Times*, March 19, 2008, p. 27.
20 Peter Gumbel, 'Iceland: the country that became a hedge fund', *Fortune*, December 4, 2008, http://www.money.cnn.com/.
21 Tom Braithwaite and Lucy Killgren, 'The men behind the invasion into Britain's retail domain', *Financial Times*, October 4, 2008, p. 19.

The Baugur group which he headed owned big names abroad: House of Fraser in the United Kingdom, Magasin du Nord in Denmark, and an interest in Saks in the United States. Charged with fraud, he scorned the legal proceedings initiated against him and accused the Icelandic government of having political motivations. Contemptuous of the justice system, he vowed in 2005 'that there was "no chance in hell" he would go to jail'.[22]

Björgólfur Guðmundsson and his son Thor (Björgólfur Thor Björgólfsson), presented by the *Guardian* in 2008 as the richest men in Iceland,[23] exercised considerable power and influence, but were less in the limelight. Both billionaires, their empire collapsed during the crisis. The fall of Björgólfur Guðmundsson was certainly the most spectacular: *Forbes* magazine evaluated his assets at more than a billion dollars at the beginning of 2008, then ... at zero at the end of the year.[24] Likening him to the character Monte Cristo, Gérard Lemarquis described him as an entrepreneur who quickly adapted to situations and seized the opportunities created by the opening of Eastern European markets:

> Businessman Björgolfur Gudmundsson, who just lost tens of billions of kronur in three days, had attempted to open maritime freight transport to competition in Iceland. Forced into bankruptcy, he emigrated to England. A reformed alcoholic, but confident in the future of alcohol consumption in Russia, he set up a brewery there and introduced vodka-soda breezers in Saint Petersburg. Well managed, the business prospered and was sold to Heineken. 'Gudmundsson Monte Cristo', once back in Iceland, had the means to acquire the Lands-

---

22 Jón Ásgeir Jóhannesson, quoted by Tom Braithwaite, 'The fraud claims that are taking their toll on Baugur', *Financial Times*, March 19, 2008, p. 27.
23 Mikey Stafford, 'West Ham deny crisis after Icelandic bank folds', *Guardian*, October 8, 2008.
24 Luisa Kroll, 'Billionaire blowups of 2008', *Forbes*, December 23, 2008.

banki bank with Russian money. But father and son went into the pharmacy and telephone sectors in Eastern Europe, then made a wide variety of investments, not always successful, in Great Britain. The father, like a Russian oligarch, acquired a British first division football club, West Ham, a kid's dream.[25]

Not as well known abroad, the brothers Ágúst and Lýður Guðmundsson have an American-like career path: '[they] founded Bakkavor in Iceland in 1986 [when] they were just 21 and 19 years old and had no capital. With the confidence of youth they starting up a fish processing business'.[26] They were considered 'self-made men', started with nothing, then managing to build a powerful agri-food group, with large branches abroad.

The new Vikings, booed and blamed for all the problems during and after the crisis, were seen as heroes in Iceland, and even elsewhere in the West, during their period of glory. In fact, relatively recent articles in the media include testimonials by Icelanders—financiers, artists and ordinary people—who were proud of these men and their conquests. While their reputation has undergone a reversal with the crisis, it should not be forgotten that these men were backed and supported by their country, before they came to be despised and accused of treachery. They were part of a certain social, cultural and economic renaissance. During their heyday, 'Iceland was not only

---

25 Gérard Lemarquis, 'L'Islande au bord du gouffre', *Le Monde*, October 9, 2008, p. 3. The original quote read: 'L'homme d'affaires Björgolfur Gudmundsson, qui vient de perdre des dizaines de milliards de couronnes en trois jours, avait tenté d'ouvrir à la concurrence le transport de fret maritime en Islande. Acculé à la faillite, il émigra en Angleterre. Alcoolique repenti mais confiant dans l'avenir de la consommation d'alcool en Russie, il y créa une brasserie et introduisit à Saint-Pétersbourg la consommation des mélanges "breezers" vodka-soda. Bien gérée, l'entreprise prospéra et fut revendue à Heineken. "Gudmundsson Monte-Cristo", de retour en Islande, avait les moyens d'acquérir la Landsbanki avec l'argent russe. Mais le père et le fils se lancèrent dans la pharmacie et le téléphone en Europe de l'Est, puis dans une grande variété d'investissements pas toujours heureux en Grande-Bretagne. Le père, tel un oligarque russe, s'offrit un club de foot de première division britannique, West Ham, un rêve de gosse'.
26 Maggie Urry, 'A case of sink or swim', *Financial Times*, September 2, 2008, p. 19.

cool climatically but culturally—quirky pop music, zany fashions and cutting-edge research into genetics accompanied the emergence of its billionaires in the oligarchs' league'.[27] Postcolonial revenge, a nationalistic surge and patriotic pride all came together and fuelled a feeling shared by many Icelanders of having entered a sort of golden age: 'Icelanders could hold their heads high before the rest of the world'.[28]

Although the critics targeted primarily the politicians, entrepreneurs and financiers, they were not the only ones to maintain the pipedream. Writers and artists were also involved in the popular new 'Viking conquest' movement, from which they benefited as well. In March, Georg 'Goggi' Hólm, bass player for the Sigur Rós band, used the then fashionable warlike vocabulary, likening the launch of the band's latest DVD to a new form of conquest: 'It is in our Viking blood to want to conquer nations and peoples, but our longboat was in the repair shop having the barnacles removed, so we just made a film to send out into the world on our behalf instead'.[29]

During the crisis, in a letter published from Iceland and picked up by the *Financial Times*, novelist Hallgrímur Helgason, author of the novel *101 Reykjavík*, said he hoped his people would not forget the pride that inspired those daring young men, even though they failed:

> Deep down inside we idolised these titans, these money pop-stars. Awestruck we watched their adventures and admired them when they supported the arts and charities. We never had clever businessmen, not for a thousand years, not to mention men who had won battles in other countries.[30]

---

27 Robert Jackson, 'Letter from Iceland', *Financial Times*, November 15, 2008.
28 Ibid.
29 Georg 'Goggi' Hólm, quoted in *Guardian*, 'Catch of the day: Sigur Ros take charge', March 7, 2008.
30 Hallgrímur Helgason, quoted by Robert Jackson, 'Letter from Iceland', *Financial Times*, November 15, 2008.

The new Viking adventure surprised a lot of people, mainly because of the aggressiveness of Icelandic entrepreneurs, who seemed to have endless capital reserves: 'Helped by ample supplies of cash and cheap credit, Iceland's entrepreneurs have spent the past few years cultivating a reputation for risk-taking and assertiveness',[31] wrote Robert Anderson. Iceland's partners were disconcerted by the new Vikings' insatiable appetite for power and conquest, as it was at odds with the self-restraint normally associated with Scandinavians. The new Vikings were set on risk-taking and acquisition. According to David Ibison, Nordic Bureau Chief for the *Financial Times*, the successes arising from that drive comforted a people bruised by years of colonial domination: 'For a country that was more than 500 years under the control of Denmark, these developments have unleashed a dormant sense of national pride'.[32]

Yet, the collapse of the Icelandic banking system brought this period of glory to an abrupt end. With the fall of Iceland's economy, the new Vikings lost their fellow countrymen's respect. Foreign journalists generally believe that Icelanders approached the crisis with composure and discernment. But, in reaction to it, they quickly identified scapegoats: 'The "new Vikings", a handful of formerly admired men in suits and ties, are now despised'.[33] According to Jonas Moody, the vestiges of their excessiveness in the capital are now seen as ridiculous: '[they] have become the object of derision and national shame—there is ridicule over the airfields crammed with private jets; people cringe at the thought of shipping container after shipping container full of French wine arriving at the harbor'.[34]

---

[31] Robert Anderson, 'Elisa board survives attack', *Financial Times*, January 22, 2008, p. 18.
[32] David Ibison, 'Cool under fire Iceland takes the fight back to finance', *Financial Times*, April 9, 2008, p. 7.
[33] Nicolas Delesalle, 'Les révoltés du geyser', *Télérama*, no. 3086, March 8, 2009. The original quote read: 'Les "nouveaux Vikings", poignée de costards-cravate autrefois admirés, sont aujourd'hui conspués'.
[34] Jonas Moody, 'The Republic is dead. Long live the Republic!', *Iceland Review*, vol. 47, no. 1, 2009.

As for the new Vikings themselves, their defeat did not compel them to act with more humility; on the contrary. Jón Ásgeir Jóhannesson greeted the news of Iceland's spectacular financial collapse with a crude remark: 'the banks collapsed in succession. And we were sitting there thinking "Jesus Christ, there is no money here"'.[35] He refused to take any responsibility for the crisis. 'We did it in the same way that many other people in other countries were doing.'[36] According to the *Financial Times*, when asked what he would do with his property, he refused to comment: 'In aggressive questioning on TV yesterday, Mr Johannesson was asked whether he would be selling his private jet or a multi-million dollar apartment in New York. He declined to answer'.[37] Not particularly disconcerted by events, he was convinced that he could easily earn Icelanders' trust back: 'We just have to do good. And earn our respect back'.[38] But with the pressure mounting, Jóhannesson fled Iceland. Like the people banished in the sagas of old, the new Viking had to leave his country in disgrace. According to Robert Jackson, this episode marked the end of an era:

> One of the most telling images was the departure of Jon Asgeir's private jet on news that the government had nationalised Glitnir bank ... wiping out his ... Baugur business empire. Painted black and as sleek as a Stealth bomber, the aircraft was photographed taxiing from its hangar. ... Like the last helicopter out of Saigon, the departure of Asgeir's jet symbolised the end of an era, the last act of Iceland's debt-fuelled spending spree.[39]

The successive departures of the new Vikings were likened to acts of treason toward Iceland, a sentiment reflected in the remarks of an

---

35 Jón Ásgeir Jóhannesson, quoted by Tom Braithwaite, 'Chastened Baugur hopes to navigate debt crisis', *Financial Times*, October 31, 2008.
36 Ibid.
37 Tom Braithwaite et al., 'Johannesson set to cede Baugur control to Green', *Financial Times*, October 13, 2008, p. 22.
38 Ibid.
39 Robert Jackson, 'Letter from Iceland', *Financial Times*, November 15, 2008.

Icelander who said: 'they've all taken flight, run away to the Cayman Islands'.[40] Commentators for the *Financial Times* were of a similar mind and harshly judged these men for their lack of courage in fleeing their country when it was facing serious difficulties: 'In the past few days most of the private jet flights have been out of Iceland as the country's wealthy entrepreneurs fled the country's financial collapse'.[41] This reaction would go hand in hand with an attempt to rebud their image in the media; as the *Dallas Morning News* reported, 'the Viking financiers have sought refuge abroad. Their public relations experts say rehabilitating their images will have to wait until the financial blood-letting stops'.[42]

Once the new Vikings had fled, what happened in Iceland? According to foreign media, a dynamic, new group—of women, this time—emerged and exercised economic and politic power differently. A leader in the *Financial Times* asked weather the male model had run its course. Saying that the authorities had put into practice one of the Icelandic values most highly respected abroad—gender equality—Iceland hopes to clean up the disaster created by yesterday's heroes. The appointments of these women 'are an immediate and highly visible rejection of the testosterone-fuelled risk-taking that is the popular villain of the piece'.[43]

---

40 An Icelander, quoted by Roger Boyes, 'Skating on thin ice', *Australian,* October 10, 2008.
41 Tom Braithwaite and Elizabeth Rigby, 'BHS chief touches down on mission to Iceland', *Financial Times,* October 11, 2008, p. 15.
42 Jim Landers, 'Iceland's road to bankruptcy was paved with U.S. ways', *Dallas Morning News,* December 10, 2008.
43 *Financial Times,* 'A woman's work?', October 14, 2008.

GENDER ISSUES
WOMEN: THE ANTIDOTE TO THE CRISIS

> 'Icelandic women will clean up
> the young men's mess.'
> *Financial Times*, October 14, 2008[1]

As the first signs of the crisis appeared, the dominant nationalistic discourse of the new Vikings gave way to the voices of Icelandic women, who are represented in the media as those who had come to the aid of their country and its economy. Iceland is known for its egalitarian values, and the crisis was an opportunity for the country to reveal the scope of its convictions; yet, at the same time, a deep gender divide in its society came to light. According to reports by foreign newspapers, the women who emerged were not looking to follow in the footsteps of their male predecessors. On the contrary, they are shown as having made a clean sweep, completely replacing the male-dominated culture with one defined as female. These issues were of very keen interest to the French and Québec press, much to the delight of the women's movement in Iceland. The English-language press, however, took a more divided stance, with some media finding gender issues out of place in a context of financial turbulence affecting society as a whole.

The crisis was both an awakening and an opportunity for Icelandic feminists. After interviewing former journalist Björg Björnsdóttir, Nicolas Delesalle of *Télérama* describes the revelation that the events of fall 2008 prompted:

> On the morning of the crisis, Björg woke up a feminist:
> 'It was men who brought this country to its knees. Now

---

[1] Sarah O'Connor, 'Icelandic women will clean up the "young men's mess"', *Financial Times*, October 14, 2008, p. 6.

it's time for women. They're more aware of the risks and take more time to think; these are the values that must guide us'.²

Her statement reflects the sentiments of other feminists elsewhere in the world. In a letter to the editor of the *Financial Times*, Lamia Walker, Director of the London Centre for Women in Business, stated that the crisis in Iceland has enabled women to attain certain key positions for the first time and has potentially meant significant strides for them: 'organisations have an opportunity right now to capture the movement in social change by appointing qualified women to key positions'.³

A number of women now hold high-ranking positions in the country. The appointments of Birna Einarsdóttir to the new Glitnir bank (renamed Íslandsbanki on February 20, 2009), of Elín Sigfúsdóttir to the new administration of Landsbanki and of Lára V. Júlíusdóttir as chair of the board of the Central Bank of Iceland, as well as the election of Jóhanna Sigurðardóttir as Prime Minister, have signalled a significant change in Iceland's leadership. For Sarah O'Connor of the *Financial Times*, this change represents a huge clean-up after the disaster created by men. In October 2008, she wrote:

> Many have also criticised the young and predominantly male bankers whose 'eyes became bigger than their stomachs'. 'Now the women are taking over', said one government official. 'It's typical, the men make the mess and the women clean it up.'⁴

---

2 Björg Björnsdóttir, quoted by Nicolas Delesalle, 'Les révoltés du geyser', *Télérama*, no. 3086, March 8, 2009. The original quote read: 'Au matin de la crise, Björg s'est réveillée féministe : « Ce sont les hommes qui ont mis ce pays à genoux. Maintenant, c'est l'heure des femmes. Elles ont une plus grande conscience des risques, réfléchissent davantage, ce sont ces valeurs-là qui doivent nous guider'.
3 Lamia Walker, 'Crisis gives women a shot at top corporate jobs', *Financial Times*, October 18, 2008, p. 6.
4 Sarah O'Connor, 'Icelandic women will clean up the "young men's mess"', *Financial Times*, October 14, 2008, p. 6.

For many, the time had come to reject the values that had guided the new Vikings (and men in general) and to adopt a new, more sensible and balanced approach to management. Men were harshly criticised from all quarters. A member of the Reykjavík City Council, who found the country's former male role model worrisome and inappropriate, was quoted by the *Globe and Mail* as follows: "'They talk about the Viking model,' Ms. Sturludottir says of the aggressive business climate that reigned in Iceland. "What is the Viking model? Rapists and robbers!'"[5] A piece appearing in the *Financial Times* indicated that it would have been impossible to get Iceland back on an even keel without a gender change in management; it stated in reference to the women recently chosen to lead the banks: 'they signal a shift in banking culture that could not have been achieved by the appointment of any of their male colleagues, no matter how wise and sensible'.[6]

There is a widely-accepted assumption, presented, for example, in the economy section of *Le Monde* and based on a study carried out in France, that 'the more women a business has in its workforce—and women managers in particular—the less its stock price has dropped since the beginning of [the global crisis]',[7] and the less it will be affected by the crisis. According to journalist Kiran Stacey, that assumption would be pure myth. In an article for the *Financial Times*, he strongly rejected the idea of a female economic culture different from that of a male:

> Some are murmuring that more women at the top is what we need. ... Yet, according to analysis of British companies carried out by the *Financial Times*, troubled companies would be misguided to rely on female chief

---

[5] Oddný Sturludóttir, quoted by Matthew Hart, 'Iceland's next saga: The wounded tiger's tale', *Globe and Mail*, November 15, 2008, p. F-4.
[6] *Financial Times*, 'A woman's work?', October 14, 2008.
[7] Annie Kahn, 'Les femmes, antidote à la crise boursière', Économie, *Le Monde*, October 16, 2008, p. 20. The original quote read: '[p]lus une entreprise compte de femmes—et de femmes cadres en particulier—dans ses effectifs, moins son cours de bourse a baissé depuis le début de [la crise]'.

executives derisking their operations after male misadventures. If anything, *the research suggests that companies with female CEOs tend to be even more aggressive—* with many pursuing ambitious expansion strategies and borrowing large amounts.[8]

Be that as it may, during the crisis, Iceland became part of a global debate on feminism and the place of women in spheres of power. Iceland is used by the feminists as a example of a country that continues to uphold the values for which it is known by making a radical change toward a more female-oriented approach. In so doing, it offers others hope of a shift in social and financial culture. It was in this context that unexpected news was announced in late 2009: that Björk would be creating a business start-up fund. The world-renowned Icelandic singer wants to convey a message through this fund that is both global and feminist. She believes it is necessary to invest in 'sustainable activities that emphasize Iceland's natural and cultural resources' and 'to participate in the healing of its economy'.[9] To achieve this, she maintains that female values must be incorporated into the world of finance.[10] With a modest capital outlay (100 million kronur, i.e., about 500,000 euros), the initiative has important symbolic value: that of reminding the world and especially Iceland that gender equality is a guarantee of wellness.

That is what one of the very rare pieces of good news about Iceland to appear in the foreign press supported in mid-November 2008: at that time, Iceland was ranked fourth in the world for its egalitarian

---

8 Kiran Stacey, 'Recession dents image of macho management', *Financial Times*, November 5, 2008 (italics added).
9 Björk, quoted by Agence France-Presse, 'Björk donne son nom à un fonds d'investissement islandais', *Cyberpresse*, December 18, 2008. The original quotes read: 'des activités durables qui mettent en valeur les ressources naturelles et culturelles de l'Islande' and 'participer à la guérison de l'économie islandaise'.
10 Ibid. The original quote read: '[d']introduire les valeurs féminines dans le monde de la finance'.

policies and conduct.[11] Suddenly, despite the financial disaster into which the country had sunk, at least one of the most appreciated aspects of its reputation in the West had been maintained and even strengthened.

---

11 Annie Kahn, 'Les disparités entre hommes et femmes s'atténuent', Environnement et sciences, *Le Monde,* November 13, 2008, p. 4.

PART THREE

THE REST OF THE WORLD

SCANDINAVIA
OUR NORDIC FRIENDS

'Nordic support group is making excuses.'
Financial Times, October 7, 2008[1]

Unlike Iceland's highly strategic relations with Russia, its friendship with the other Scandinavian countries—based on a shared cultural and linguistic background—was marked by constraint and guilt during the crisis; yet, in the end, the friendship served the island's interests well. Iceland's ties with Denmark, Sweden, Norway and the Faeroe Islands—the first state to come to its assistance—define Iceland's first perimeter of international influence, a sort of original family circle, a transition zone between the country's interior and the outside world. For lack of other support, Reykjavík has often relied on the assistance of its Nordic 'friends' to show the rest of the world that it benefits from the solidarity of other nations. Thus, when the first signs of Scandinavian aid appeared in spring 2008, Davið Oddsson, Chairman of the Central Bank of Iceland, told foreign journalists that 'the joint action [of the Nordic countries] sent out a strong message that Iceland no longer stood alone'.[2] John Zhu of *Le Monde* interpreted those signs in the same way, stating that 'Iceland ... [was] no longer alone'.[3]

The support from Iceland's Nordic 'brother countries' was a boost to the island's image at a time when it desperately needed it: 'Any

---

1 *Financial Times*, 'Iceland', October 7, 2008.
2 Davið Oddsson, quoted by David Ibison, 'Nordic central banks step in to back Iceland', *Financial Times*, May 17, 2008, p. 2.
3 John Zhu, 'Un tournant majeur dans la crise qui sévit en Islande', Économie, *Le Monde*, May 21, 2008, p. 14. The original quote read: 'l'Islande n'est plus seule'.

demonstration of co-ordinated Nordic support', wrote David Ibison of the *Financial Times,* 'would represent a significant step forward for Iceland as it seeks to restore its international credibility'.[4] Reykjavík acknowledged that this friendship had saved it from greater peril in a Central Bank news release, which stated in early 2009 that its neighbours were the only ones to respond to its calls for help:

> No other central banks apart from the Nordic ones were prepared to lend their support in 2008, in spite of the Central Bank's requests and in spite of the public declarations from the international community.[5]

The foreign newspapers portrayed the relationship between the Nordic countries as constrained and capable of causing disappointment. That was the case in October 2008, when the crisis in Iceland worsened very significantly. The Prime Minister's political call for help through the media—'In this time of crisis, we are convinced ... we can count on our fellow Nordic friends'[6]—brought only disappointment: 'We have not received the kind of support that we were requesting from our friends'.[7] As Gérard Lemarquis remarked, 'Reykjavík asked the Nordic central banks to make an effort, but the Scandinavian ministers ... waited to respond'.[8] A loan came later and from an unexpected source—the Faeroe Islands, the tiny, often forgotten nation in the Nordic group—followed by incredibly wealthy Norway; Sweden was still considering the request at the end of November. The hesita-

---

4 David Ibison, 'Iceland puts hope in its neighbours', *Financial Times,* October 26, 2008.
5 Ingimundur Friðriksson, 'The banking crisis in Iceland in 2008', *Sedlabanki.is,* February 6, 2009.
6 Geir Haarde, quoted in the *Herald* (Glasgow), 'Call for Nordic countries to help', October 28, 2008.
7 Geir Haarde, quoted by Tom Braithwaite, 'Iceland attacks "friends" for lack of support', *Financial Times,* October 7, 2008.
8 Gérard Lemarquis, 'Accablés par la crise, les Islandais rêvent de l'euro', Économie, *Le Monde,* October 29, 2008, p. 13. The original quote read: 'Reykjavik a demandé aux banques centrales nordiques de faire un effort, mais les ministres scandinaves [...] ont réservé leur réponse'.

tion from some of the countries made it clear that Iceland could not fully count on the Nordic world, which would have saved it the humiliation of having to go to the International Monetary Fund (IMF); it was forced to accept the fact that aid from these countries was *subject to* the IMF's conditions. At least that was how the *Financial Times* interpreted the situation: 'The four [*sic*, excluding the Faeroes, but including Finland] Nordic nations have said they are willing to support Iceland *but only after it [has] agreed to design and implement an economic stabilisation plan in association with the IMF*'.[9] In short, the Nordic countries took a cautious approach to Iceland, which was a hard blow to their friendship.

Thus, the relationship between Iceland and the other Scandinavian countries, as depicted by the media, was characterised by constraint and uneasiness. While necessary, cooperation among these countries was also based on vested interests that were not always readily apparent. In that respect, assistance seemed to stem more from a compromise than a natural inclination, be it before, during or after the crisis. In May 2008, the Governor of the Central Bank of Sweden, Stefan Ingves, declared that 'co-operation was *necessary* in times of difficulty'.[10] In October 2008, during the most difficult time for Iceland, Reykjavík nonetheless had to do a lot of arm-twisting to get its partners to intervene on its behalf. The Icelandic government initially asked them 'to make an effort'[11] (which they waited to do), prompting the *Financial Times* to declare that the 'Nordic support group is making excuses'.[12] It was not until Reykjavík had done some diplomatic sidestepping and solicited Moscow's help—much to its partners' dismay—that Iceland was able to force the hand of the other

---

9   David Ibison, 'Nordic nations work on Iceland bail-out', *Financial Times*, November 5, 2008 (italics added).
10 Stefan Ingves, quoted by Paul J. Davies and Peter Garnham, 'Iceland agrees 1.5bn swap scheme with neighbours', *Financial Times*, May 16, 2008 (italics added).
11 Gérard Lemarquis, 'Accablés par la crise, les Islandais rêvent de l'euro', Économie, *Le Monde*, October 29, 2008, p. 13. The original quote read: 'faire un effort'.
12 *Financial Times*, 'Iceland', October 7, 2008.

Nordic countries. Even then, the examples of cooperation reported by the newspapers were not without vested interests: that was true of the assistance offered by SAS airlines to Sterling passengers in distress[13] (Sterling was a Danish airline that Icelanders had acquired, then said to have contributed to its failure); and that provided by Sweden, which granted Iceland a loan to protect its own depositors, whose funds were at risk due to the collapse of Iceland's Kaupþing bank.[14] The Netherlands, as well as the United Kingdom, would similarly grant Reykjavík disputed loans to protect the interests of their own citizens. All in all, the relationship between the Nordic countries was more like a blend of pious wishes and guilt, never as strong as one might like to believe. Norway was aware of this and stated that 'it ... [was] essential to strengthen cooperation between Nordic authorities'.[15]

The media often came back to the idea that the Nordic world shares a common culture, based on the strong solidarity among the Nordic states and the people who live there. The newspapers also referred to Scandinavian economists as being among the strongest supporters of neoliberalism and globalisation. In April 2008, the *Financial Times* wrote that 'Nordic states stay hot on globalisation'.[16] The Swedish Prime Minister, Fredrik Reinfeldt, was quoted by the newspaper as saying, 'there is a Nordic sense of being. ... It is not just about institutions. There are many optimists in this, all in terms of globalisation. It is good that we are optimists'.[17] Yet, that optimism was shaken after the large Icelandic banks filed for bankruptcy protection: they had invested in the other Nordic countries and elsewhere in the world, and they thus upset the economies of their friends. Iceland's Glitnir bank,

---

13 See, for example, Laura Dixon, 'Iceland's Sterling airline collapses', *Australian*, October 30, 2008.
14 Tom Braithwaite, 'Iceland's biggest bank gets Swedish loan', *Financial Times*, October 8, 2008.
15 Central Bank of Norway press release, quoted by David Ibison, 'Norway's central bank warns on stability', *Financial Times*, December 2, 2008.
16 Quentin Peel, 'Nordic states stay hot on globalisation', *Financial Times*, April 11, 2008, p. 4.
17 Fredrik Reinfeldt, quoted in ibid.

for example, had acquired two Norwegian banks (Kreditbanken Retail Bank and Bnbank) and a securities brokerage (Norse Securities), as well as two large management firms: one in Sweden (Fischer Partners) and the other in Finland (FIM Asset Management). The collapse of Glitnir had unfortunate consequences for Norway, Sweden and Finland.[18] While globalisation enabled Iceland to enjoy unprecedented economic growth and prosperity, it also led to its meteoric fall; that was a hard blow to Scandinavia's reputation, as its social democratic model then came under a great deal of criticism. An article in the *Herald*, for example, suggested that advocates of the model lived in a counterfactual economic world, refusing to see the risks inherent in the 'high-cost-of-living economies of Iceland and Scandinavia'.[19]

Generally speaking, Iceland attracted sympathy from the rest of the world, which enabled it to avoid the usually harsher conditions imposed on countries facing a similar crisis. As Matthew Hart indicated in a *Globe and Mail* article, 'it is impossible not to feel sympathy for Icelanders as they face a desperate future'.[20] Aid from the Nordic world was also provided out of concern, with, however, a few seemingly colonial-tinged gestures. That, at least, is how Norway's aid was presented: as *Afterposten* reported, 'the Norwegian government sent a delegation of officials from various state ministries to Iceland on Wednesday. They're charged with trying to help their financially strapped Nordic neighbour'.[21] This *technical* aid was reminiscent in many respects of that given by a metropolis to one of its protégés. *Le Monde* shared this view and was even more direct in its description

---

18 As reported, for example, by Robert Anderson, 'Big banks break up in effort to restore confidence', *Financial Times*, October 8, 2008, p. 4.
19 Alastair Begg, 'The real facts', *Herald* (Glasgow), November 5, 2008.
20 Matthew Hart, 'Iceland's next saga: The wounded tiger's tale', *Globe and Mail*, November 15, 2008, p. F-4.
21 Nina Berglund, 'Norway sends aid team to crisis-hit Iceland', *Afterposten*, October 22, 2008.

of the relationship: 'Sweden, Denmark and Norway', wrote John Zhu, 'have flown to the rescue of their little brother, Iceland'.[22]

Be that as it may, Scandinavian solidarity is a serious matter for Iceland: although slow in coming, help from the Nordic countries was real and indicated that those nations are, despite everything, able to show solidarity in times of crisis. When the difficulties first began, this solidarity was reflected in unified support, the terms of which were flexible: 'Iceland can also rely on support from other Nordic governments *under a loose but significant memorandum of understanding*'.[23] At the peak of the crisis, after some hesitation, these countries coordinated their efforts by providing aid that was complementary to that from other sources: 'The finance ministers of Denmark, Finland, Norway and Sweden said in a joint statement that the funds would help Iceland stabilize its economy'.[24]

Iceland, finding itself in a desperate situation, thus benefited from being part of Scandinavia. Although the supposedly natural friendship between the countries in this group showed limits when tested by the crisis and certain Nordic states helped the island out of self-interest, the ties uniting the five countries enabled Iceland to catch its breath. In the end, it was the image of an overbearing, yet quite united Scandinavia that emerged in the eyes of the world.

---

22 John Zhu, 'Un tournant majeur dans la crise qui sévit en Islande', Économie, *Le Monde*, May 21, 2008, p. 14. The original quote read: 'La Suède, le Danemark et la Norvège, écrit John Zhu, ont volé au secours de leur petit frère islandais'.
23 David Ibison, 'System crisis rated as "low probability"', *Financial Times*, March 25, 2008 (italics added).
24 David Jolly, 'Iceland gets its IMF loan, Turkey awaits its own', *International Herald Tribune*, November 20, 2008.

RUSSIA
OUR NEW FRIEND

'So in a situation like that, one has to look for new friends.'
Geir Haarde, October 2008[1]

The statement by Iceland's Prime Minister that the country was turning to Russia because it had not obtained the help requested from its traditional allies caused surprise, fear, scepticism and anger as soon as it appeared in the foreign media. Whether actual fact or mere strategy, it shook the Western world given the seriousness of the potential consequences. If Reykjavík's goal was to stage a huge media stunt, it was successful. As one Icelandic diplomat later admitted, 'we knew that talking to them would create a shock, and that was partly the point'.[2]

Knowing the fear that Russia inspires in the West, Iceland sought to force its partners, namely the Nordic countries, to grant the loans requested. 'The Norwegians do not want to see the Russians extend their influence over the Arctic,'[3] asserted Þorbjörn Broddason, a professor at the University of Iceland. The Icelandic government hoped that the veiled threat would 'stimulate Nordic generosity'.[4] *BBC News* agreed, reporting that according to analysts 'the Icelandic govern-

---
[1] Geir Haarde, quoted by Tom Braithwaite, 'Iceland attacks "friends" for lack of support', *Financial Times*, October 7, 2008.
[2] An Icelandic diplomat, quoted by Peter Gumbel, 'Iceland: the country that became a hedge fund', *Fortune*, December 4, 2008, http://www.money.cnn.com/.
[3] Þorbjörn Broddason, quoted by Gérard Lemarquis, 'Accablés par la crise, les Islandais rêvent de l'euro', Économie, *Le Monde*, October 29, 2008, p. 13. The original quote read: 'Les Norvégiens ne veulent pas voir les Russes étendre leur influence sur l'Arctique'.
[4] Ibid. The original quote read: 'stimulera la générosité nordique'.

ment never seriously considered taking money from Russia—it was simply a strategy to secure help from Western Europe and the US'.[5]

Almost all foreign journalists judged Iceland's initiative harshly. Brian Milner of the *Globe and Mail* did not hide his surprise about the source of the aid requested by Reykjavík, which he called 'a most unlikely source'.[6] Serge Truffaut of *Le Devoir* stated that 'Iceland's Prime Minister ha[d] signed an agreement [that] chilled the blood of more than one European leader'.[7] John Vinocur wrote in a piece for the *International Herald Tribune* that the move by Reykjavík stirred the memory of the threat looming over the world in the latter half of the 20th century: 'Of course, there is no New Cold War, and that is fine. The problem is that what has replaced it, while no replica, feels familiar'.[8] Icelandic specialist Richard Portes was the only one amid such widespread disapproval who believed that it was clever and the best possible manoeuvre, stating: 'It's rather imaginative of the Russians and the Icelanders. They should have done it earlier.'[9]

Iceland's request for assistance from Russia was presented with skilful verbal vacillation, enabling it not to commit itself too deeply to the process. First announced as a fact, the loan became a mere request for aid the next day, in a 'media to and fro' by the two countries that their respective allies followed with considerable interest. The *International Herald Tribune* reported two news items on the loan in one day: the first identified a discrepancy between the versions of Reykjavík and

---

5 Konstantin Rozhnov, 'Russia's role in rescuing Iceland', *BBC News*, November 13, 2008.
6 Brian Milner, 'Russia's "imaginative" Icelandic rescue', *Globe and Mail*, October 8, 2008, p. B-10.
7 Serge Truffaut, 'Crise financière. Au secours de l'Est', *Le Devoir*, November 3, 2008. The original quote read: 'le premier ministre islandais a signé une intervention [qui a] glacé le sang de plus d'un dirigeant européen'.
8 John Vinocur, 'Europe's unlikely attempt to renew a "partnership" with Russia', *International Herald Tribune*, April 21, 2008.
9 Richard Portes, quoted by Brian Milner, 'Russia's "imaginative" Icelandic rescue', *Globe and Mail*, October 8, 2008, p. B-10.

Moscow; the second provided essentially a retraction by Iceland:

> Details of the loan discussions remained unclear on Tuesday as Iceland's Central Bank said it had a confirmation from Prime Minister Vladimir Putin of Russia that a loan would be granted, while the deputy finance minister Dmitry Pankin told the Interfax agency that no decision had been made.[10]

> Iceland later acknowledged that it had been premature, saying it had contacted the Russians but had not yet reached an agreement.[11]

This announcement—and its retraction—was accompanied by a statement by Iceland, claiming to be laying all its cards on the table. Prime Minister Haarde held a number of press briefings in which he vowed that the potential agreement with Russia would have no political repercussions: 'We look at this as a non-political deal, if there is to be a deal, which we don't know yet. I don't know of any particular political strings that the Russians would want to attach to this.'[12] The Russian ambassador to the United Kingdom, Yuri Fedotov, also maintained that the assistance his country was offering Iceland was 'natural', but some foreign commentators were sceptical. The *Financial Times* quoted Fedotov as saying, 'our offer is nothing other than *the natural gesture of support* that you would expect to see from one country to another in an interdependent world'.[13]

Many observers, however, saw political designs in Moscow's aid. Fears

---

10 Julia Werdigier, 'Iceland takes extreme steps to save its finance system', *International Herald Tribune*, October 7, 2008.
11 Eric Pfanner and Julia Werdigier, 'Caught in financial crisis, Iceland tries to tap Russia', *International Herald Tribune*, October 7, 2008.
12 Geir Haarde, quoted by Ómar Valdimarsson and Toni Vorobyova, 'Iceland seeks Russian, Nordic help', *Globe and Mail*, October 15, 2008, p. B-14.
13 Yuri Fedotov, quoted by James Blitz, 'British corporate leaders to visit Russia', *Financial Times*, October 20, 2008 (italics added).

were expressed, in particular by the British, Australian and Canadian newspapers, that the 'friendship' between Iceland and Russia could have repercussions that went beyond the economic crisis and concerned the geopolitical balance of the West. Russia's solicitude toward Iceland was, according to *Le Devoir*, an opportunity for Moscow 'to infiltrate into the old Soviet hunting ground'[14] and extend its influence. Eric Pfanner and Julia Werdigier were also of this opinion. They indicated in a text for the *International Herald Tribune* that Moscow's goal was to recover lost prestige, stating that 'for Russia, the loan would be a way to show its financial power and willingness to help distressed economies'.[15] According to the *Financial Times*, 'the loan would be the first time in Russian history that it … granted foreign aid to a state outside its normal sphere of influence'.[16] That certainly overlooked the fact that Soviet Union had sided with the Spanish republicans and supported African and South American countries. In any event, the move by Reykjavík was viewed as creating the real possibility of a Russian foothold in the West.

Gérard Lemarquis of *Le Monde* suggested that Western countries may have brought about the situation by neglecting Iceland, stating sardonically: 'The return of the Russians brings a smile to the faces of those [among the Icelanders] who remember the cold war. At that time, the Americans had a base with 4,000 soldiers which they have since deserted for warmer destinations.'[17] Alex Barker of the *Financial Times* believed that Reykjavík was only pretending to be innocent in the negotiations, stating that 'Iceland has told NATO allies its puta-

---

14 Serge Truffaut, 'Crise financière. Au secours de l'Est', *Le Devoir*, November 3, 2008. The original quote read: 's'infiltrer dans l'ancienne chasse gardée soviétique'.
15 Eric Pfanner and Julia Werdigier, 'Caught in financial crisis, Iceland tries to tap Russia', *International Herald Tribune*, October 7, 2008.
16 Catherine Belton and Tom Braithwaite, 'Iceland asks Russia for €4bn after West refuses to help', *Financial Times*, October 8, 2008, p. 4.
17 Gérard Lemarquis, 'L'Islande au bord du gouffre', *Le Monde*, October 9, 2008, p. 3. The original read: 'Ce retour des Russes fait sourire ceux [parmi les Islandais] qui se souviennent de la guerre froide, écrit-il. Les Américains avaient alors une base de 4 000 soldats qu'ils ont désertée depuis pour des destinations plus chaudes'.

tive deal with Russia will not influence foreign policy. Rumours in Reykjavik had suggested Russia might use a base vacated by the US Air Force in 2006.[18] Whether mere rumour or actual agreement, the potential alliance raised fears and fuelled anger toward Reykjavík, which appeared to be unaware of Moscow's manipulation.

Iceland's overture toward Moscow surprised NATO's military partners: as recently as April 2008, the *International Herald Tribune* had reported that four French Mirage fighter planes were flying over Iceland to discourage Russian bombers from trespassing into its air space. The bombers had started venturing along a route that Soviet planes used to use during the Cold War. Iceland's Minister of Justice and Defence, Björn Bjarnason, had counted 13 of those provocative Russian flights into Icelandic air space since 2006. Reykjavík's complaints were not taken seriously by Moscow: 'The response was Russia resurgent to the core: Get used to them. Then, Bjarnason said, the ambassador directed his hosts to read a related statement made in August by Vladimir Putin. End discussion.'[19] In light of the tense climate in the spring, Reykjavík's turnaround a few months later was all the more surprising for its partners.

Some foreign newspaper reports bordered on paranoia about Russia. According to the *Financial Times*, for example, Reykjavík's request for help would lead to the gradual financial 'Finlandisation' of Western Europe: 'Russia's aim is the re-creation of a "lite" version of the Soviet empire.'[20] Russia's new economic strength, stemming from petroleum, raised fears in this time of global crisis: 'If the West is not careful', warned the *Australian*, 'Iceland will signal the ominous start of a new round of mergers and acquisitions—not of companies,

---

18 Alex Barker et al., 'Iceland frosty as London gets tough', *Financial Times*, October 9, 2008, p. 5.
19 John Vinocur, 'Europe's unlikely attempt to renew a "partnership" with Russia', *International Herald Tribune*, April 21, 2008.
20 Edward Lucas, 'Do not let Russia "finlandise" Western Europe', *Financial Times*, October 9, 2008, p. 11.

but of whole countries.'[21] According to Frank Ching of the *Globe and Mail*, this episode with Russia was only the first in an economic war to come, which would lead to Chinese domination: 'Already, Iceland, which didn't get the help it needed from its European friends, has turned to Russia for a $5.3-billion loan. It is entirely conceivable that other countries could tap China for similar assistance.'[22] In the *International Herald Tribune*, Samuel Charap and Andrew Kuchins took a more moderate stance on the negociations: 'the loan … appears to be a gesture of cooperation,, a demonstration that Russia wants to be a responsible stakeholder in the international economic system'.[23] This opinion, however, seemed to stand alone amid the general denunciation of the Icelandic-Russian 'friendship'.

In the media coverage of this aspect of the Icelandic crisis, the Russians had the upper hand and took advantage of it: 'The negotiations are a creative process',[24] said one official spokesperson. The Moscow media, for its part, viewed Iceland's request with a mix of mockery and coldness. *Moscow News* felt that Iceland was merely a tool for enhancing Russian political prestige: 'Moscow needs political heavyweights as friends, not an island state with a population of 310,000. But Iceland is a perfect instrument to demonstrate Russia's goodwill to the rest of the developed world at very little cost'.[25] For the news agency Novosti, which supported the idea of helping Iceland, the loan was a means of extending Russian influence to larger countries:

> There are several reasons why Russia should agree to issue the loan to Iceland. The first and overwhelming

---

21 *Australian*, 'Iceland's economic collapse could herald a new round of large-scale acquisitions', October 9, 2008.
22 Frank Ching, 'It's in China's own interest to extend a helping hand', *Globe and Mail*, October 15, 2008, p. A-25.
23 Samuel Charap and Andrew Kuchins, 'Russia's peace offensive', *International Herald Tribune*, October 13, 2008.
24 An official spokesperson, quoted by Charles Clover et al., 'Iceland works on Russian deal', *Financial Times*, October 15, 2008, p. 9.
25 Marina Pustilnik, 'Iceland seeks Russian comfort', *Moscow News*, October 10, 2008.

one is geo-economic. ... Crises come and go, but allies (sometimes) remain. Iceland ... is certain to remember this gesture and take more kindly to Russian investments in the future. ... Besides, it makes a good starting post for flights to Latin America.[26]

Contrary to the Icelandic leaders' claims that Russia's assistance was strictly economic, with no political strings attached, *Moscow News* reported that it would mean important political advantages for Russia: '[it] is purely political, there is nothing economic in it.'[27] That was also how the *BBC* viewed the issue—it deemed that 'all connections to Russia are political',[28]—as well as *Le Monde*, which saw the loan as leading to a shift in the political and military balance of Europe. George Hay judged Reykjavík harshly, asserting that approaching the Russians was 'not as wise'[29] as going to the International Monetary Fund:

A 4 billion euro loan from Russia ... would upset the geopolitical order. Iceland is a member of NATO, and it is to be expected that Russia will demand something in return for a loan to a small country equal to one third of its GDP. ... The Russian assumption would lead onto strategic and military terrain.[30]

---

26 Yelena Zagorodnyaya, 'Iceland turns to Russia for bailout', *RIA Novosti*, October 10, 2008.
27 Marina Pustilnik, 'Iceland seeks Russian comfort', *Moscow News*, October 10, 2008.
28 Jón Ólafsson, quoted by Konstantin Rozhnov, 'Russia's role in rescuing Iceland', *BBC News*, November 13, 2008.
29 George Hay, 'Pour l'Islande, mieux vaut le FMI que les Russes', Économie, *Le Monde*, October 10, 2008, p. 15. The original expression was 'moins avisé'.
30 Ibid. The original quote read: 'Un prêt russe de 4 milliards d'euros [...] viendrait bouleverser la donne géopolitique. L'Islande est membre de l'OTAN, et on peut s'attendre à ce que la Russie exige une récompense pour avoir prêté au petit pays l'équivalent d'un tiers de son PNB. [...] L'hypothèse russe entraînerait plutôt sur le terrain militaire et stratégique'.

Most journalists covered the advantages the loan could give Russia in its conquest of the Arctic, over which it claims sovereignty. For the *Australian*, the refusal to grant Iceland an emergency loan was a strategic error on the part of the United States and the European Union: 'it is a false economy that will prove diplomatically expensive'.[31] For this newspaper, Iceland represents an outpost for the Russians and its support would enable Russia to justify its advance toward the North Pole:

> It doesn't take much to work out what Russia is thinking. A former superpower, in search of territory and allies, which planted its own flag on the seabed of the North Pole last year—what better prize could it want than a NATO member that has just been rebuffed by its Western allies?'[32]

A *Financial Times* article entitled 'Iceland attacks "friends" for lack of support' quoted a financial strategist as saying that Russia's goodwill toward Iceland 'could be helpful when it gets into difficult negotiations over territorial rights in the Arctic'.[33] *Le Monde* also expressed concern about Russia's Arctic ambitions: 'Iceland lost its geopolitical importance, but could become of interest again if the melting of the polar ice were to transform the northern shores of Siberia into a marine highway'.[34] The *Australian* shared these apprehensions, stating that 'Iceland's mid-Atlantic location makes it a hugely desirable ally for Russia, which has its eye on oil and gas below the North Pole'.[35]

---

31 Bronwen Maddox, 'Snub to Iceland will be costly blunder', *Australian*, October 11, 2008.
32 Ibid.
33 Chris Weafer, quoted by Tom Braithwaite, 'Iceland attacks "friends" for lack of support', *Financial Times*, October 7, 2008.
34 Gérard Lemarquis, 'L'Islande au bord du gouffre', *Le Monde*, October 9, 2008, p. 3. The original quote read: 'L'Islande a perdu de son importance géopolitique, mais pourrait redevenir intéressante si la fonte des glaces polaires devait transformer le nord des côtes de la Sibérie en autoroute maritime'.
35 Bronwen Maddox, 'Snub to Iceland will be costly blunder', *Australian*, October 11, 2008.

Thus, for these analysts, Russia's 'fraternal' aid raised a great deal of suspicion. It also prompted a number of unfavourable commentaries concerning Iceland. However, the Icelandic government can be satisfied that its diplomatic/media strategy, if there was one, was completely successful. On the one hand, Iceland stepped up pressure to obtain aid quickly from its traditional partners, the Scandinavian countries, and the IMF, which, with Washington and London's agreement, seemed more readily inclined to take action. That, at least, is what the *Globe and Mail* reported: 'the Russian offer sped up the efforts of other international lenders owing to worries over what Russia may ask in return'.[36] On the other hand, the pressure created by the strategy contributed to lightening the conditions imposed by the IMF. As the *Financial Times* stated, 'although the slow pace of those talks [with Russia] ultimately resulted in Iceland agreeing a package led by the IMF, it is noteworthy that those loans came with fewer conditions than the Fund has imposed in the past'.[37] Obtaining urgent aid from its partners, with fewer conditions imposed by the IMF: that was a skilful diplomatic feat by Iceland. The country thus emerged a winner from this risky venture, which unexpectedly changed European alliances. According to *Time* magazine, Moscow's arrival on the scene ironically served… the British government. In the heart of the crisis, the United Kingdom saw a new enemy emerge: Iceland, a Russian ally who had infiltrated the British economy. Did that threat frighten the British enough to make them forget the effects of the crisis in their own country? As Catherine Mayer wrote, 'That won't worry the British government at all. In times of crisis, it's good to have friends, but it's even more useful to have enemies.'[38]

---

36 Reuters, 'It could take $24-billion to fix Iceland', *Globe and Mail*, November 18, 2008, p. B-11.
37 David Rothkopf, 'The Fund faces up to competition', *Financial Times*, October 21, 2008.
38 Catherine Mayer, 'Iceland: Britain's credit crunch scapegoat', *Time*, October 10, 2008.

THE CONFLICT WITH THE UNITED KINGDOM
ONE OF US, NOT ONE OF THEM

'The crisis sparked a furious war of words between London and Reykjavik.'
Herald (Glasgow), October 10, 2008[1]

Relations between Iceland and the United Kingdom have sometimes been strained. Both insular and claiming to be very different from other countries, they have long had a love-hate relationship which has fluctuated back and both through history. Icelanders seem cyclically compelled to confront the British, to the point where it is almost as though the British had colonised their country instead of the Danish. There is a very distant Viking link between the two islands, but the rivalry has arisen more in modern times. In a text for the *Financial Times*, Brian Groom wondered what had caused the tension between the two countries: 'We always seem to be at odds with this independent-minded nation. Britain violated Iceland's neutrality by occupying it in 1940 and tussled with it over fishing rights in the 1950s and 1970s cod wars.'[2] The 'cod wars'—or more specifically, diplomatic conflicts in which the United Kingdom tried to intimidate Iceland by deploying military vessels—are indicative of their difficult relations. In these wars, the United Kingdom contested Iceland's maritime limits and, by extension, its sovereignty, over the issue of fishing rights. The small island's victory over the large has come to look like post-colonial revenge in Icelandic history.

---

1 *Herald* (Glasgow), 'Treasury officials hold emergency talks on Iceland', October 10, 2008.
2 Brian Groom, 'Back to the future. A leader for today', *Financial Times*, October 13, 2008.

During the crisis in the fall of 2008, the 'war' between the two nations was waged on two fronts: on the one hand, the United Kingdom invoked anti-terrorism legislation to freeze Icelandic assets in its territory; on the other hand, London and Reykjavík entered into a legal battle, threatening each other with legal action. On both fronts, the battle took place through the media, fuelling disagreement over the interpretation of statements made by each party, which David Ibison called 'a war of words'.[3] The rapid verbal escalation between the two capitals was all the more surprising given the composure characteristic of both the British and the Icelanders. Journalists, themselves, used heated vocabulary to report on the conflict, making statements like 'the UK authorities *exasperated* with responses from Iceland seem to have *overreacted*'.[4]

The conflict seemed to have been caused by a series of misunderstandings. According to a *Guardian* report on October 8, 2008, 'the chancellor, Alistair Darling, told the BBC that ... "The Icelandic government, believe it or not, ... told me yesterday they have no intention of honouring their obligations here"'.[5] A few hours later, Prime Minister Gordon Brown came on strong and condemned the freezing of British bank accounts in Icelandic banks, supposedly ordered by Reykjavík; 'What happened in Iceland is completely unacceptable,' Brown told BBC television. 'I've been in touch with the Icelandic prime minister (Geir Haarde), I've said that this is effectively illegal action that they've taken'.[6] It was on the basis of these statements that the British government announced tough measures against Iceland. However, the subsequent transcript of the conversation between

---

[3] David Ibison, 'UK dispute with Iceland escalates', *Financial Times*, October 24, 2008.
[4] Jon Danielsson, 'Why raising interest rates won't work', *BBC News*, October 28, 2008 (italics added).
[5] Alistair Darling, quoted in *Guardian*, 'Darling vows to help Icesave savers', October 8, 2008.
[6] Gordon Brown, quoted in Agence France-Presse, 'Iceland acting illegally in freezing accounts—UK PM', *Australian*, October 10, 2008.

Darling and his Icelandic counterpart would indicate that it was a misunderstanding: 'a transcript ... appears to question the British government's claim',[7] wrote David Ibison. A few days later, another transcript, this one of an interview with the Governor of the Central Bank of Iceland, Davið Oddsson, on Icelandic television, indicated that the British were right. The same day as the telephone conversation between Darling and his Icelandic counterpart, '[Oddsson] made unfortunate comments aimed at local audiences that "we will not pay for irresponsible debtors and ... not for banks who have behaved irresponsibly"'.[8]

On October 7, London announced an immediate freeze on all Landsbanki assets in Britain: 'in a statement, the Treasury said it was taking the action "to protect the retail depositors [and] ensure the stability of the UK financial system"'.[9] To do so, the United Kingdom used anti-terrorism legislation adopted in the wake of the September 11, 2001 terrorist attacks in New York. At that point, the tension between the two countries reached a peak: 'Iceland's relations with the UK threatened to fall to the lows of the 1970s "cod wars" yesterday as anti-terrorism powers were used in an effort to recoup money owed to UK depositors in a failed Icelandic bank'.[10] The British government's response angered Icelanders. The first official reactions were somewhat ironic: Prime Minister Geir Haarde was quoted by journalist Eric Pfanner as saying, 'we did not consider this to be a particularly friendly act'.[11] Then, the exasperation of Icelanders themselves was reported by the media: 'It was a move viewed in Iceland as hateful and unnecessary'[12] (the *Financial Times*); 'Mr Brown is clearly public enemy No 1 in Ice-

---

7 David Ibison, 'Transcript challenges UK position on Iceland savings', *Financial Times*, October 23, 2008.
8 Arsaell Valfells, 'Gordon Brown killed Iceland', *Forbes*, October 16, 2008.
9 Tom Braithwaite, 'Kaupthing goes into administration in UK', *Financial Times*, October 8, 2008.
10 Alex Barker et al., 'Iceland frosty as London gets tough', *Financial Times*, October 9, 2008, p. 5.
11 Geir Haarde, quoted by Eric Pfanner, 'Iceland is all but officially bankrupt', *International Herald Tribune*, October 9, 2008.
12 Robert Jackson, 'Letter from Iceland', *Financial Times*, November 15, 2008.

land'[13] (the *Independent*); 'Gordon Brown killed Iceland. [It] looks like an act of revenge'[14] (*Forbes*). Icelanders were extremely upset to be labelled 'terrorists' by a country they considered an ally: 'How can you compare my grandmother's bank to al-Qaeda?'[15] asked novelist Andri Snær Magnason. They accused the British both of holding Iceland in a financial siege,[16] and of delivering the fatal blow, without which the country could have got back on its feet. As Jonas Moody stated in a text for *Time* magazine, 'some Icelandic economists say the terrorist appellation provided the extra push that sent Iceland's already reeling financial system over the ledge into complete failure.'[17]

There was a series of legal threats in addition to these actual shows of strength: first from London on October 8 ('the British government planned to sue Iceland to recover the deposits'[18]); then from Reykjavík a few days later ('Geir Haarde is threatening to take legal action in response over funds frozen'[19]). These statements jeopardised the equilibrium and reputation of both former allies, according to the *Financial Times* editorial team, who pointed up the potential consequences of the escalation. *Financial Times* journalists Alex Barker, Tom Braithwaite, Sarah O'Connor, Jim Pickard and Nicholas Timmins wrote the following in a joint article appearing on October 17:

> London and Reykjavik have appointed lawyers as the NATO allies threaten to sue each other over Iceland's banking collapse. ... Lawyers say the two countries are

---

13 Claire Soares, 'Who are you calling terrorists, Mr Brown?', *Independent*, October 24, 2008.
14 Arsaell Valfells, 'Gordon Brown killed Iceland', *Forbes*, October 16, 2008.
15 Andri Snær Magnason, quoted by David Ibison, 'Icelanders see Icarus-like plunge of greed', *Financial Times*, October 23, 2008.
16 Sarah O'Connor, 'Iceland accuses UK of financial "siege"', *Financial Times*, October 16, 2008.
17 Jonas Moody, 'Iceland to Britain: "We're no terrorists"', *Time*, November 3, 2008.
18 Angela Balakrishnan, 'U.K. to sue Iceland over any lost bank savings', *Guardian*, October 8, 2008.
19 Agence France-Presse, 'Iceland PM says could sue Britain over savings row', *Australian*, October 13, 2008.

more likely to reach a political settlement than to take each other on in the courts. It is rare for historically friendly countries to clash in court, partly because of the diplomatic and reputational damage they risk as they trade allegations and disclose potentially embarrassing evidence.[20]

The British government nonetheless maintained that Iceland's threats were of no consequence: 'Alistair Darling, the chancellor, is unconcerned about the legal challenge by Iceland, believing that he acted in a responsible way'.[21]

For Iceland, the misunderstanding with the United Kingdom was serious: Britain's freeze on its assets in the UK caused Iceland significant liquidity problems; in addition, the British government prevented Iceland from obtaining an emergency loan from the International Monetary Fund (IMF). The *Financial Times* reported that 'the loan [was] being withheld until Iceland resolved', in the words of an IMF spokesman, 'the process of determining obligations with regard to foreign deposits'.[22] The Dutch daily *NRC Handelsblad*, however, claimed that the Netherlands and the United Kingdom were 'blocking a loan from the International Monetary Fund (IMF) to Iceland'.[23] London denied any such action against Reykajavík: 'the U.K. government has in no way blocked the IMF's loan to Iceland'.[24]

Whatever the case, the Icelandic government had run out of resources and gave in. It agreed to Britain's conditions and undertook to reim-

---

20 Alex Barker et al., 'Scene set for court battle over deposits', *Financial Times*, October 17, 2008, p. 2.
21 Alex Barker et al., 'Iceland may hold UK store stakes', *Financial Times*, December 29, 2008.
22 An IMF spokesman, quoted by David Ibison, 'Iceland in fresh push to solve diplomatic row', *Financial Times*, November 14, 2008.
23 Cees Banning and Jan Gerritsen, 'Dutch and British block IMF loan to Iceland', *NRC Handelsblad*, November 7, 2008.
24 A British Treasury spokesman, quoted by David Jolly, '$6 billion rescue for Iceland put on hold', *International Herald Tribune*, November 12, 2008.

burse British savers who had been short-changed in the collapse of the Landsbanki. It thus had to find the means to pay for the excesses of its banks, which represented an inordinate extension of the Icelandic state's financial obligations. The agreement then enabled Iceland to obtain the loan requested from the IMF. Although Britain denied it, foreign commentators believed that London had exercised a veto against Iceland to get what it wanted: in this power struggle, which received considerable media attention, the United Kingdom won, but its conduct left Icelanders feeling very resentful and gave rise to long, drawn-out political battles that continue today.

To win foreign public opinion, the Icelandic government used different strategies. It accused the British government of acting in bad faith and being low ('the regulator went behind our back ... to take over our deposits'[25]) and assumed the role of victim unfairly bullied by someone stronger. In an interview with *Le Monde*, Geir Haarde said the British 'had every right to want to protect their citizens, but not to invoke legislation like that against a small country like ours. I highly doubt that they would have used that act with a larger country'.[26] The Icelandic Prime Minister accused the United Kingdom of 'bullying a small neighbour'.[27]

The question remains: did Iceland's assets endanger the United Kingdom to the point where London had no choice but to take such harsh measures? Legal experts deem that the use of anti-terrorism legislation was inappropriate ('The use of anti-terror powers ... is a distor-

---

[25] Sigurður Einarsson, quoted by Alex Barker et al., 'Kaupthing searches for answers', *Financial Times*, October 10, 2008, p. 23.
[26] Geir Haarde, quoted by Élise Vincent, 'Dans un entretien, le premier ministre islandais, Geir Haarde, évoque la grave crise financière que traverse son pays, il y a encore peu de temps l'un des plus prospères de la planète', Économie, *Le Monde*, October 23, 2008, p. 12. The original quote read: 'ont tout à fait le droit de vouloir protéger leurs citoyens, mais pas d'appliquer une loi [antiterroriste] comme celle-là contre un petit pays comme le nôtre. Je doute beaucoup qu'ils se seraient permis d'utiliser cette loi avec un plus grand pays'.
[27] Geir Haarde, quoted by Sarah O'Connor, 'Iceland's leader threatens to sue over "bullying" reaction', *Financial Times*, October 13, 2008, p. 4.

tion of the law's intent'[28]); political analysts saw London's actions as a diversion intended to allay the concerns of its own citizens about the problems in their country. In a piece appearing in *Time* magazine, Catherine Mayer indicated that Iceland was easy prey for Gordon Brown's government: 'There's nothing like an external enemy to make a country pull together, and Britain, fractious and dissatisfied with its Labour government until recently, has found a fresh foe: Iceland.'[29] By playing up Iceland's role in the crisis, Brown and his team gave the impression that they had pinpointed the problem destabilising their country: 'This is a problem that has been caused by Iceland.'[30] The media contributed to strengthening Iceland's image as an enemy of the United Kingdom. *Le Monde* reported the 'ultrapatriotic war cry employed by the *Chronicle*: ... "Millions that belong to you are being held hostage in Iceland"'.[31] Roger Boyes captured the wrath in a vengeful tone, stating: 'The fury of the British has stunned the Icelanders. Suddenly it has become clear ... they are just an island on the outer northern fringe of Europe with sheep, haddock and an orthopedic limb factory.'[32] For columnist A.A. Gill, the British government's strategy against Iceland was petty:

> The act that tipped the last Icelandic bank off the edge of the cliff was delivered by Gordon Brown. ... The Icelanders mind that—they're hurt by that. You see, they always imagined they were one of us, not one of them. But Gordon needed to do something cheap to look

---

28 Jimmy Burns and Michael Peel, 'Warning on use of anti-terror law to freeze bank assets', *Financial Times*, October 10, 2008, p. 3.
29 Catherine Mayer, 'Iceland: Britain's credit crunch scapegoat', *Time*, October 10, 2008.
30 Gordon Brown, quoted in *Herald* (Glasgow), 'Iceland and UK in row over bank assets', October 10, 2008.
31 Marc Roche, 'Les collectivités locales britanniques sont piégées par la défaillance des banques islandaises', Économie, *Le Monde*, October 13, 2008, p. 9. The original quote read: 'cri de guerre ultrapatriote que lance le *Chronicle* : [...] "Des millions qui vous appartiennent ont été pris en otage en Islande"'.
32 Roger Boyes, 'Iceland braces for Brits wanting their money back', *Australian*, October 13, 2008.

competent, so he beat up a smaller kid. Not just a bit of a slap, but a vicious kicking. Showing off to impress the girls. He would never have started it if the banks had been German or French, or even from Liechtenstein.[33]

According to Willem Buiter, Iceland may not have been the source of the United Kingdom's anger. In his opinion, Gordon Brown was leading a country in difficulty that was like Iceland: 'The main question is whether the UK is more like the US and euro area or like Iceland. I would argue that it is more like Iceland.'[34] The image of Iceland's fragility would thus be perceived by the British as a reflection of their own situation. 'It is not much of an exaggeration to describe the UK as a giant hedge fund',[35] wrote Buiter, using the same expression analysts had coined a few months earlier in reference to Iceland.

During and after the crisis, both countries accused each other of doing in the other's financial system. Iceland indicated on several occasions that the British government had forced it to take measures on financial markets that had resulted in destabilising its economy. This position was often reported by the foreign media, particularly the American press. In October, the *Washington Post*, for example, reported the following: 'Haarde, in a news conference later in the day, said the government was forced to take the bank [Kaupþing] over after authorities in London ... froze the bank's assets in Britain, effectively rendering it bankrupt.'[36] Analysts agreed with the assumption that London was one of the parties responsible for the collapse of Iceland's banking system. According to Peter Gumble, 'the government of British Prime Minister Gordon Brown ... used controversial

---

33 A.A. Gill, 'Iceland: frozen assets', *Sunday Times*, December 14, 2008.
34 Willem Buiter, 'There is no excuse for Britain not to join the euro', *Financial Times*, June 3, 2008, p. 9.
35 Ibid.
36 Keith B. Richburg, '"Nordic Tiger" Iceland finds itself in meltdown', *Washington Post*, October 10, 2008, p. A-1.

antiterrorism legislation to deliver the death blow to Iceland's banks'.[37] Willem H. Buiter and Anne Sibert claimed that the use of the legislation was unjustified under the circumstances, stating that it was 'outrageous bullying behaviour by the UK authorities'.[38]

In charge of conducting an inquiry into the flight of Iceland's capital, Norwegian-French judge Eva Joly believed that the British government and, with it, other European governments, had to assume a share of responsibility in Iceland's crisis. For example, she felt that the freeze London placed on Icelandic assets was an 'extreme measure of retaliation'.[39] She asserted that 'Mr. Brown was wrong when he said that he and his government had no responsibility in the matter. Mr. Brown had, first and foremost, a moral obligation'.[40]

The accusation of the United Kingdom in no way alleviated Iceland's difficulties or relieved it of all blame. The conflict between the two countries, however, made it possible to put Iceland's catastrophe in a broader context. In times of crisis, every country tries to keep its economy in balance, while protecting its image in the eyes of its citizens and the rest of the world. Making a small country—supposedly an ally—a scapegoat is certainly reprehensible from a moral standpoint. Unfortunately, it is a solution that some envisage with disconcerting ease.

---

37 Peter Gumbel, 'Iceland: the country that became a hedge fund', *Fortune*, December 4, 2008, http://www.money.cnn.com/.
38 Willem H. Buiter and Anne Sibert, 'The Icelandic banking crisis and what to do about it. The lender of last resort theory of optimal currency areas', *CEPR Policy Insight*, no. 26, October 2008.
39 Eva Joly, 'L'Islande ou les faux semblants de la régulation de l'après-crise', *Le Monde*, August 1, 2009. The original quote read: 'une mesure de rétorsion extrême'.
40 Ibid. The original quote read: 'M. Brown a tort quand il dit que son gouvernement et lui-même n'ont aucune responsabilité dans l'affaire. M. Brown a d'abord une responsabilité morale'.

EUROPE
SEEKING PROTECTIVE SHELTER

'Non-eurozone Europe may not be economically viable during times of crisis.'
Financial Times, November 2, 2008[1]

The debate in Iceland about whether to join the European Union (EU) and use the euro instead of the krona began before the fall of 2008, but gained momentum due to the crisis and became heated. Although the majority of European rules were already being applied by the island, the country's official inclusion in the Union would herald an end to insularity, renunciation of sovereignty maintained with a struggle over the centuries and, above all, endangerment of the fishing industry, the cornerstone of Iceland's economy and identity. Yet, the crisis had severely shaken the country and created a situation that European and even British commentators emphasised repeatedly: the events of 2008 showed that, without the aid of a much larger bloc, a small country is too weak to maintain a high level of growth. Since Iceland was unable to obtain the support it needed to get through the slump from Scandinavia, its European trade partners, the United States or even Russia or China, many analysts claimed that it had no choice but to apply for membership in the European Union. That is what most analysts claimed: as Gérard Lemarquis wrote in an article for *Le Monde*, 'in a country where the press compares the island to a ship that had gone down, Icelanders are seeking a protector. A role that neither the Scandinavians nor the Americans—who closed their

---

1 Wolfgang Munchau, 'Now they see the benefits of the eurozone', *Financial Times*, November 2, 2008.

military base there—seem able to play. That leaves Europe'.[2] The debate about EU membership took place in a global context in which the value of currencies rose and fell at the drop of a hat; the most modest currencies were often hardest hit, increasing the pressure on small countries to join larger blocs—'in Reykjavik, Copenhagen and throughout Europe, the same prayer could be heard: almighty Euro, take us under your wing and protect us from the economic woes of this world!'[3] The pan-European issues were clearly much broader than Iceland's political future, but global market pressures affected the island in particular and it felt compelled to make a rapid decision about whether to join.

Foreign journalists were so unanimous on the issue that almost no one defended Iceland's right to full independence: joining the European Union seemed to be the only option. Its weakened currency appeared to be doomed: as one German analyst predicted, 'we would not be surprised to see the Icelandic krona lose its function as a medium of payment'.[4] The cost associated with maintaining the krona would be unbearable: as Wolfgang Munchau observed, '[in Iceland] people discovered to their horror that monetary independence comes at a crippling cost'.[5] According to university analysts, 'the only way for a small country like Iceland is to have a large internationally active banking sector that is immune to the risk of insolvency [and] to join the EU

---

[2] Gérard Lemarquis, 'Accablés par la crise, les Islandais rêvent de l'euro', Économie, Le Monde, October 29, 2008, p. 13. The original quote read: 'Dans un pays où la presse compare l'île à un navire échoué, les Islandais recherchent un protecteur. Un rôle que ni les Scandinaves, ni les Américains—ils y ont fermé leur base militaire—ne semblent pouvoir tenir. Reste l'Europe'.

[3] Pierre-Antoine Delhommais, 'L'heure de vérité pour l'euro', Le Monde, December 15, 2008, p. 25. The original quote read: 'À Reykjavik, à Copenhague et un peu partout en Europe, on entend la même prière : saint Euro, adopte-nous et protège-nous des malheurs économiques de ce monde!'

[4] Antje Praefcke, quoted by Tom Braithwaite, 'Iceland takes emergency action', Financial Times, October 6, 2008.

[5] Wolfgang Munchau, 'Why the British may decide to love the euro', Financial Times, November 16, 2008.

and become a full member of the euro area'.[6] Such a consensus among economic commentators is rare, but in this case it was conclusive.

The foreign press was full of examples illustrating the need for membership according to two poles of comparison: the countries protected by Europe (and the euro); and the countries left to their own fate. The latter included Denmark, Hungary, Poland and Iceland, whose situation was described by all as being the most perilous:

> Today, countries outside the eurozone, such as Hungary, Denmark and Iceland *have only one dream: being sheltered* from devaluation by entering the fold of the European currency.[7]

> After *turmoil in the currency markets nearly destroyed the Icelandic krona* and undermined the Polish zloty, those two countries are rethinking their opposition to adopting the euro.[8]

> The European countries that do not have [the euro] *suffer even more* than those that do.[9]

Countries protected by the euro, even if they were experiencing severe difficulties, as was Ireland, would not feel market pressures to the same extent as those that are on their own. The most extreme example was Iceland, a small country that chose the wrong camp. And the media used it abundantly in worst-case comparisons:

---

6 Willem H. Buiter and Anne Sibert, 'The Icelandic banking crisis and what to do about it. The lender of last resort theory of optimal currency areas', *CEPR Policy Insight*, no. 26, October 2008.
7 Frédéric Lemaître, 'La revanche de "Super-Trichet"', Analyses, *Le Monde*, November 11, 2008, p. 2. The original quote read: 'Aujourd'hui, les pays périphériques de la zone euro, comme la Hongrie, le Danemark ou l'Islande *n'ont qu'un rêve : se mettre à l'abri* des dévaluations en intégrant le giron de la monnaie européenne'(italics added).
8 Carter Dougherty, 'Buffeted by financial crisis, countries seek euro's shelter', *International Herald Tribune*, December 1, 2008 (italics added).
9 Pierre-Antoine Delhommais, 'L'heure de vérité pour l'euro', *Le Monde*, December 15, 2008, p. 25. The original quote read: 'Les pays européens qui ne possèdent pas [l'euro] *souffrent encore plus* que ceux le détiennent' (italics added).

Without the euro, [Ireland] *would be in the same situation as Iceland today.*[10]

Previously [without the euro] a small country such as Belgium ... would almost certainly have seen a foreign exchange crisis. 'Probably it would have been *a bit like Iceland.*'[11]

But how many Icelands would we have seen had it not been for the euro?[12]

The Central Bank of Iceland conceded that membership in the European Economic Area had enabled the country's banks to achieve strong growth abroad,[13] the basis of even more extensive economic integration. However, some observers believed that the source of the ills lay specifically in the possibilities opened by these markets, in which Iceland was literally swallowed. They criticised the European model for its lethargy during the crisis. Although Iceland was not yet part of the Union, its predicament directly affected Europe, which was forced to take a position with respect to it. According to the *International Herald Tribune*, that was a sore point, because in a global context 'the EU has been widely criticized for showing its limits for united action during the crisis.'[14] In view of Iceland's situation, the EU remained powerless; worse, it let its members back Iceland to the

---

10 Pervenche Berès, 'L'Europe dans un angle mort. La réponse de l'Union à la crise a été une juxtaposition de plans nationaux, sans aucune stratégie', Dialogues, *Le Monde*, November 14, 2008, p. 20. The original quote read: '[L'Irlande] sans l'euro *serait aujourd'hui dans la situation de l'Islande*'(italics added).
11 Ralph Atkins, 'Euro stability helps big and small to forge common goal', *Financial Times*, October 17, 2008, p. 2 (italics added).
12 Carl B. Hamilton, a Member of the Swedish Parliament, quoted by Olivier Truc, 'Le Danemark regrette de plus en plus d'être resté en dehors de la zone euro', Économie, *Le Monde*, October 23, 2008, p. 12. The original quote read: 'Mais combien d'Islande aurait-on vu s'il n'y avait pas eu l'euro ?'
13 See Ingimundur Friðriksson, 'The banking crisis in Iceland in 2008', *Sedlabanki.is*, February 6, 2009.
14 Carter Dougherty, 'EU ministers approve broad measures to combat evolving crisis', *New York Times*, October 7, 2008.

wall. That, at least, is what the person Iceland called in to conduct an inquiry into the crisis, Norwegian-French judge Eva Joly, claimed in a piece published by various European newspapers, including *Le Monde* and the *Telegraph*. Alex Elliott of *Icenews* described Joly's views as follows:

> By forcing Iceland to pay enormous compensation for the Icesave debacle, the countries are helping to reduce Iceland to poverty, increase migration and increase the likelihood that the country will fail, default and never pay back its debts. She also believes they are failing to take responsibility for their own mistakes in the fiasco.[15]

While she was critical first and foremost of Europe, Eva Joly also pointed a finger at Iceland's Nordic partners, stating: 'the Scandinavian countries, usually harbingers of international solidarity, were conspicuous primarily by their failure to react to the blackmailing of Iceland—which puts the generous aid they promised the country in a certain light'.[16] Not involved in covering the debate, the *Australian* expressed mistrust toward the entire European economic system and fear about the interdependence of the countries in it, citing the risky loans to Iceland as an example: 'in Germany alone, financial institutions lent $US21.3 billion to Icelandic banks now collapsing. ... European triumphalism is unfettered by facts'.[17]

What did Icelanders and their leaders think about their country joining the European Union? Without going into the complexities of the country's internal debate, foreign journalists reported, as if to be expected, the growing popularity of EU membership among the people of Iceland, and the mounting pressure such support put on the politicians. The foreign newspapers regularly published the findings of

---

15 Alex Elliott, 'Eva Joly criticises Europe over Iceland debt', *Icenews*, August 4, 2009.
16 Eva Joly, 'L'Island ou les faux semblants de la régulation de l'après-crise', *Le Monde*, August 1, 2009.
17 Janet Albrechtsen, 'Europe worse off than the US', *Australian*, October 29, 2008.

surveys revealing that the idea of joining Europe was gaining ground in Iceland. In February 2008, *Le Monde* stated that '55.1% of people surveyed said they were in favour of Iceland's application for membership in the European Union. ... The percentage had been only 36% in January 2007'.[18] Stable at 55% in September, the rate had risen to 70% by late October, according to the *Globe and Mail*.[19] When the government finally initiated the membership process in May 2009, *Cyberpresse* reported that support stood at 61%.[20]

The reversals in the politicians' positions on the issue were commented on by the foreign press in particular. In October 2008, several cracks appeared in the position of one of the two ruling parties, until then against membership in the Union. At that time, the Minister of Education changed her opinion: '[she] broke with party policy and said the crisis-hit nation should start thinking about membership now'.[21] She was followed shortly thereafter, in December, by Prime Minister Haarde[22] who, according to the *Financial Times*, could not put off the initiative forever, even though in late October he had claimed that 'the EU issue need not be rushed'.[23] In early 2009, the new head of state was hailed abroad as pro EU: 'The new Icelandic government has decided ... to initiate the process of joining the European Union as quickly as possible.'[24] Only a few mavericks proposed an interim

---

18 Agence France-Presse, 'Une majorité d'Islandais souhaite l'adhésion à l'Union européenne', International, *Le Monde*, February 28, 2008, p. 9. The original quote read: '55,1% des personnes interrogées se disent favorables à ce que l'Islande postule pour une adhésion à l'Union européenne [...]. Ils n'étaient que 36% en janvier 2007'.
19 Patrick Lannin and Sakari Suominen, 'Iceland seeks $4-billion more in aid', *Globe and Mail*, October 28, 2008, p. B-18.
20 Agence France-Presse, 'L'Islande enclenche le processus d'adhésion à l'UE', *Cyberpresse*, May 10, 2009.
21 This is in reference to Katrín Gunnarsdóttir (David Ibison, 'Iceland sees rift over EU membership', *Financial Times*, October 30, 2008).
22 David Ibison, 'Bank crisis prompts Iceland EU rethink', *Financial Times*, November 14, 2008.
23 Geir Haarde, quoted by David Ibison, 'Iceland sees rift over EU membership', *Financial Times*, October 30, 2008.
24 Agence France-Presse, 'L'Islande enclenche le processus d'adhésion à l'UE', *Cyberpresse*, May 10, 2009. The original quote read: 'Le nouveau gouvernement islandais a décidé [...] de lancer au plus vite le processus d'adhésion à l'Union européenne'.

solution for Iceland, i.e., unilaterally adopting the euro without joining the European Union,[25] but obviously that option was not voted in by the Icelandic government.

Before the crisis, the gradual 'euroisation' of the Icelandic economy was seen as a blight. In January 2008, the application by Kaupþing bank to record its financial statements in euros instead of the Icelandic kronur[26] was viewed as heresy by the Central Bank, which considered the surreptitious adoption of the euro a risk: 'highly problematic and probably unstable'[27] for the economy. After the crisis, the situation turned around and the euro became, along with a basket of other currencies, a standard enabling the country to maintain a semblance of economic stability.

The euro, however, was not the only issue raised by opponents of EU membership. The fishery, central to Iceland's economy and a strong symbol of its identity, seemed threatened by potential inclusion in the EU. The dozens of coastal villages in Iceland that depend on the industry would have to face new competition—that of the large Spanish and Portuguese trawlers that would be authorized to fish in the island's rich maritime territory. The temptation to join the Union was thus tempered by the desire of Icelandic fishermen to maintain control of the industry, known worldwide for its balanced management, which environmentalists believed could be threatened. As *L'Express* indicated, 'Iceland's application for membership in the EU means wrestling over the fishery.'[28] Iceland also defended its right to practise whaling. That controversial activity—practised by only two other

---

[25] David Ibison, 'Iceland warned against gradual "euroisation"', *Financial Times*, February 14, 2008, p. 6.
[26] David Ibison, 'Iceland delays banks' plan to adopt the euro', *Financial Times*, January 16, 2008, p. 8.
[27] Quoted by David Ibison, 'Iceland warned against gradual "euroisation"', *Financial Times*, February 14, 2008, p. 6.
[28] Agence France-Presse, 'La candidature de l'Islande à l'UE promet un bras de fer sur la pêche', *L'Express*, July 23, 2009. The original quote read: 'la candidature de l'Islande à l'UE promet un bras de fer sur la pêche'.

countries, Norway and Japan—'could', according to *Cyberpresse*, 'also fuel debate'[29] in Europe since Iceland decided after the crisis 'to increase its quotas very significantly'.[30]

While post-crisis Iceland acknowledged the need to consider joining Europe despite the heated debate and high stakes for its future, a question remained: was the country welcome in the Union? On the one hand, there were a few signs indicating that Iceland could benefit from preferential treatment for its application, i.e., from fast-tracking, due to the fact that 'the country already applies three quarters of Europe's policies'[31] and its bid was backed by the other Nordic countries (Sweden, Denmark and Finland). It could also highlight its geostrategic advantage, since it is located 'at the edge of the Arctic Circle at a time when the North Pole is becoming an environmental and economic issue'.[32] However, to minimize the risk of offending other applicant countries—some of which have been waiting for several years for approval of their inclusion—the Nordic countries denied considering Iceland's case a *fait accompli*. Swedish foreign minister Carl Bildt denied any presumption of special treatment, saying: 'There's no fast-track for Iceland, but there's obviously a rather shorter track for Iceland because they're already part of the single market and the Schengen Area.'[33]

On the other hand, some countries, including the Netherlands and the United Kingdom, expressed serious reservations on the matter. Politicians in those countries even wanted to block Iceland's applica-

---

29 Agence France-Presse, 'La CBI vers un ultime effort de négociation', *Cyberpresse*, June 22, 2009. The original quote read: 'pourrait, également fournir matière à débat'.
30 Ibid. The original quote read: 'd'augmenter très fortement ses quotas'.
31 Agence France-Presse, 'La candidature de l'Islande à l'UE promet un bras de fer sur la pêche', *L'Express*, July 23, 2009. The original quote read: 'applique déjà près des trois quarts des directives européennes'.
32 Ibid. The original quote read: 'au bord du cercle arctique, au moment où le Pôle Nord devient un enjeu écologique et économique'.
33 Carl Bildt, quoted by Oana Lungescu, 'EU ministers support Iceland bid', *BBC News*, July 27, 2009.

tion because of the way Reykjavík had treated their depositors during the crisis, a threat still reiterated in July 2009: 'Dutch foreign minister Maxime Verhagen told his Icelandic counterpart that he could block its bid to join the European Union.'[34] Iceland, pressured from all sides to take refuge in a larger bloc, also had to face those who continue to criticise its economic management. Even after the crisis, financial rating agencies assigned the country the worst confidence ratings, which were reported in headlines like 'Moody's cuts Iceland's bond ratings to one notch above junk'[35] and 'Iceland banks flunk at Fitch ratings'.[36]

In the process of being taken aboard the European Union, Iceland is expecting to make a fast entry into the Union, but with a reputation it would have wished to be different.

---

34 *NRC Handelsblad*, 'The Hague threatens Iceland's EU bid over lost savings', July 22, 2009.
35 Mark Brown and Michael Wilson, 'Moody's cuts Iceland's bond ratings to one notch above junk', *Wall Street Journal*, November 12, 2009.
36 The article also states the following: 'The Icelandic banking system was given the lowest rating possible for a developed state at the international agency Fitch Ratings this week. Iceland and Vietnam are in the same category but Tunisia and Ecuador rank higher than Iceland'. (*IcelandReview.com*, 'Iceland banks flunk at Fitch Ratings', November 6, 2009.)

A VERY SMALL COUNTRY
BIG IS NOT ALWAYS BEAUTIFUL

> 'The biggest banking failure in history
> relative to the size of an economy.'
> *Economist*, December 11, 2008[1]

What is Iceland really: a state or simply one big family? Foreign journalists asked the question when they saw that Iceland's public institutions were paralysed by the close-knit ties among people and businesses throughout the country. Michael Lewis of *Vanity Fair* put it very plainly: '[It's] a nation so tiny and homogeneous that everyone in it knows pretty much everyone else. ... Really, it's less a nation than one big extended family.'[2] Such an interwoven social fabric represents an economic risk according to *Le Devoir*, because 'with Iceland being very small, banks and businesses acquired cross-shareholdings, becoming highly interdependent and raising the fear of a house-of-cards effect in the event of collapse'.[3] Going even further, the *Huffington Post* called for energetic action to shake the country out of its characteristic public lethargy and put an end to the seeming system of favours, referring to 'egregious abuses of the financial system for the benefit of

---

1 *Economist*, 'Cracks in the crust', December 11, 2008.
2 Michael Lewis, 'Wall Street on the tundra', *Vanity Fair*, April 2009.
3 Agence France-Presse and Associated Press, 'L'Islande s'enfonce dans la crise', *Le Devoir*, October 9, 2008. The original quote read: 'du fait de la petite taille de l'Islande, banques et entreprises ont pris des participations croisées les unes dans les autres, devenant fortement interdépendantes et faisant craindre un effet "château de cartes" en cas d'effondrement'.

a select few over the past few years'.[4] Analysts Willem H. Buiter and Anne Sibert see Iceland as an example of an economy weakened by four factors; for them, it is:

(1) a small country with

(2) a large, internationally exposed banking sector

(3) its own currency and

(4) limited fiscal spare capacity relative to the possible size of the banking sector solvency gap.[5]

Yet, just a few months earlier, the perception of Iceland's economy was completely the opposite, both on the island and off. While the unfortunate consequences of the imbalance between the size of the country and that of its financial system were denounced in the fall of 2008, the expansion of its economy was a source of national pride earlier that year. 'Think big' read a headline in *Iceland Review*, 'to believe that we *can*, in spite of our smallness'. Before the turmoil, the magazine's editor in chief, Bjarni Brynjólfsson, wrote:

> When one looks at modern Iceland and compares it to Iceland after World War II there is a mammoth difference. How did this happen? In my opinion the answer is not complicated. By thinking big, working hard and using new found wealth to seek the best education. ... We should continue to think big and put faith in our abilities. In the end, we'll get the gold.[6]

'Think big, get the gold.' The mantra, sweet before the crisis, turned sour in the autumn. In October, Brynjólfsson told the *Washington*

---
[4] Íris Erlingsdóttir, 'Iceland is burning', *Huffington Post*, January 20, 2009.
[5] Willem H. Buiter and Anne Sibert, 'The Icelandic banking crisis and what to do about it. The lender of last resort theory of optimal currency areas', *CEPR Policy Insight*, no. 26, October 2008.
[6] Bjarni Brynjólfsson, 'Pipe dreams come true', *Iceland Review*, vol. 46, no. 3, 2008. In reference to the Olympic Games, for example.

Post that 'this is what happens when corporate institutions grow out of proportion to the system designed to regulate them'.[7] A declaration that was particularly surprising in light of his prior statements. At the same time, the *Financial Times* wrote: 'for Iceland ... normal logic is turned on its head. It is a reasonably large banking system with a small country attached. Now that its big banks have failed or are in deep trouble, the crisis for Iceland cannot be underplayed'.[8]

As a result of the expansion of its financial system—associated with ambitions of global conquest—Iceland found itself in a dangerous position of disequilibrium in 2008, caught between the small size of the country and weak power of its institutions relative to the enormous financial empire acquired by its new Viking bankers. The country, too small, was forced into monetary commitments that were too great. For economic commentators, Iceland represents a perfect example of the danger awaiting those who take excessive risk: 'It's a huge motor attached to a tiny buggy'.[9]

After the turmoil, Icelandic politicians and administrators admitted that the country had ventured too far in its conquests. The Prime Minister drew a lesson from it, conceding in October 2008 that, contrary to what he had said early in the year, 'it is not wise for a small country to try to take a leading role in international banking'.[10] He acknowledged that his country became short-sighted and lost its way when he let the financial sector 'become too big'.[11] According to Jon Danielsson, these statements reflect the inability of the Icelandic gov-

---

7 Bjarni Brynjólfsson, quoted by Keith B. Richburg, '"Nordic Tiger" Iceland finds itself in meltdown', *Washington Post*, October 10, 2008, p. A-1.
8 Chris Giles, 'Topsy-turvy logic leaves an unpalatable choice', *Financial Times*, October 8, 2008, p. 4.
9 Friðrik Már Baldursson, quoted by Mark Landler, 'Credit crisis triggers downturn in Iceland', *New York Times*, April 17, 2008.
10 Geir Haarde, quoted in Associated Press, 'Raiding Reykjavik', *Globe and Mail*, October 11, 2008, p. F-2.
11 Geir Haarde, quoted by Deborah Summers and Graeme Weardon, 'Gordon Brown considers legal action against Iceland', *Guardian*, October 9, 2008.

ernment to foresee and manage a crisis; he felt that 'the collapse [had been] brought forward *by the failure of the central bank* to extend its foreign currency reserves'.[12]

Regardless of who is responsible or will be considered as such, Iceland's debacle was a rude awakening for its citizens: 'We felt like we were a big country, and now we've woken up',[13] said one businessman. The dreams of grandeur hit the wall, creating a crisis with serious consequences for islanders: 'Small island, big problem' read a *Financial Times* headline in October, summarising the foreign media's impression of Iceland's instability and imbalance. In the end, the imbalance resulted in a crushing financial obligation for the people of Iceland.

From a political standpoint, the failure of Iceland's economic expansion reduced the country's influence abroad considerably. According to the *Wall Street Journal*, the country should be giving up its official residences in Washington, London, New York and Oslo. Blinded by the growth of its banks, the island had set its sights too high: 'The four homes were perhaps too big for us and unnecessarily expensive for us to run',[14] a consular affairs official told the newspaper. Thus, the crisis brought Iceland's international ambitions to a halt.

Paradoxically—and cruelly—Iceland's failure was reassuring for the large powers, which were dealing with their own bank difficulties. Asserting that Iceland sank because it was too small to withstand the financial storm, French, British and American journalists reassured their readers about their own economic system. They emphasized that what took place in Iceland could not occur in a large country: 'That is *not a question for the United States*, which can print dollars and has a

---

12 Jon Danielsson, 'Why raising interest rates won't work', *BBC News*, October 28, 2008 (italics added).
13 Gunnar Sigursson, quoted by Roger Boyes, 'Iceland braces for Brits wanting their money back', *Australian*, October 13, 2008.
14 Pétur Ásgeirsson, quoted by Christina S.N. Lewis, 'Strapped Iceland lists homes in D.C., New York, London', *Wall Street Journal*, February 27, 2009.

banking system that is the largest in the world but is small in relation to the national economy.'[15] Journalists from large countries constantly repeated warnings, such as: 'Small countries are the biggest victims of the financial crisis, leaving many people looking to bigger nations for economic security';[16] 'Market meltdown teaches Europe that size matters';[17] 'The worst thing at the moment is to be a small country like Denmark or Iceland';[18] etc.

In this particular context, the legitimate aspirations of nations to attain sovereignty tend to be seriously challenged, in particular by countries like the United Kingdom—and even the European Union in general—which have no interest in seeing what they consider to be a part of themselves (like Scotland, in the case of the UK) become fully independent. Consequently, those that so wish can easily find disadvantages with small countries; they can easily find arguments to ridicule them, cast doubt on the competence of their institutions, and question their right to sovereignty and independence.

The debate between the United Kingdom and Scotland offered an ideal forum for maligning Iceland. For Scottish nationalists, Iceland is a model, along with Ireland and Norway; these countries are part of an 'arc of prosperity' to which Scotland aspires to belong should it become independent. The Scottish newspapers expressed concern about the financial crisis in Iceland, a country formerly idealised, but now an embarrassment. However, for opponents of independence, who compared the situation of Iceland's banks taken over by the Icelandic government to that of the Royal Bank of Scotland rescued by London, the crisis shows that Scotland is better protected by remaining within the United Kingdom. *Le Monde* reported that because of

---

15 Floyd Norris, 'Can countries afford to bail out their banks?', *International Herald Tribune*, October 11, 2008. (italics added)
16 Doug Saunders, 'Market meltdown teaches Europe that size matters', *Globe and Mail*, October 22, 2008, p. A-19.
17 Ibid.
18 Colin McLean, quoted in *Bloomberg* and appearing in Ibid.

Iceland's change of fortunes, the leader of the Scottish nationalists, Alex Salmond, lost some arguments: 'the financial crisis, which bankrupted Iceland and saw Norway nationalise its banking system, has weakened his discourse. It's now the "arc of bankruptcy", joked Jim Murphy, Secretary of State for Scotland at Whitehall'.[19] The *Financial Times* also saw a direct link between Iceland's situation and a hypothetically sovereign Scotland, citing the remarks of the British Prime Minister, for whom the Scotland bailout would never have been possible without the 'union':

> An independent Scotland could not have bailed out its struggling banks, Gordon Brown said yesterday in a side-swipe at nationalist plans for independence. ... Labour has also highlighted the problems facing Iceland and Ireland—two countries in what the SNP [Scottish National Party] described as an 'arc of prosperity' of small countries that it aspired to join, which also included Norway and Finland. Mr Salmond, who once worked as an economist for RBS [Royal Bank of Scotland], has refused to comment on Iceland.[20]

This debate, reported by British and Scottish newspapers, reflects the importance of the Icelandic crisis in relations between the United Kingdom and Scotland. London used the Icelandic example to refute the arguments of the nationalists. It may be argued that London had no interest in seeing Iceland come through the crisis easily, which may partially explain its rigid political reaction to the country. Indeed, Iceland's failure was the best guarantee of a united kingdom. Some Scots were not put off balance by these arguments:

---

19 Virginie Malingre, 'Écosse. Le Labour surfe sur la crise', *Le Monde*, November 5, 2008, p. 3. The original quote read: 'la crise financière, qui a mis en faillite l'Islande et vu la Norvège nationaliser son système bancaire, a affaibli son discours. C'est désormais "l'arc de la faillite", a plaisanté Jim Murphy, ministre en charge de l'Écosse à Whitehall'.
20 Andrew Bolger, 'Union made RBS injection possible, says Prime Minister', *Financial Times*, October 15, 2008, p. 2.

> There is something rather distasteful in the way opponents of Scottish independence are currently jumping on the banking failings of Iceland, Ireland and other small nations during the current crisis as proof that Scotland, as an independent nation, would automatically be doomed to bankruptcy. Despite their current problems, I see no sign of Iceland clamouring to rejoin Denmark, Ireland to cede its sovereignty back to the UK or Norway to claim it was all a big mistake and insist it really wanted to be Swedish all along.[21]

Discourse on the problems experienced by small nations in times of crisis was found in a number of articles, particularly those published by *Le Monde*, in which the advantages of the European Union were often emphasised: 'European countries that do not have [the euro] are suffering even more than those that do, starting with *poor, little* Iceland: its economy, whose performance was drawing admiration ... has imploded.'[22]

Icelanders have a sense of humour; they also have pride in being a nation, which they know is legitimate without the support of others. Thus, jokes in the media about small countries and Iceland seeming to be negligible and unimportant can go over. But remarks took on a whole other slant when they question the scope and severity of the crisis that shook the country because of its size: 'Iceland was certainly warned about the risk of bankruptcy, but "it's a tiny country",[23] wrote *Le Monde*. Jokes about Iceland sometimes conveyed a political mes-

---

21 Coupar Angus and Pete Ellis, 'The way ahead', *Herald* (Glasgow), October 16, 2008.
22 Pierre-Antoine Delhommais, 'L'heure de vérité pour l'euro', *Le Monde*, December 15, 2008, p. 25 (italics added). The quote read: 'les pays européens qui ne possèdent pas [l'euro] souffrent encore plus que ceux qui le détiennent. À commencer par la *petite* et *malheureuse* Islande : son économie, dont les performances suscitaient pourtant l'admiration [...], a imposé'.
23 Pascal Gilbert, quoted by Claire Gatinois, 'Les émissions d'emprunts d'État vont se multiplier', Économie, *Le Monde*, October 11, 2008, p. 14. The original quote read: L'Islande a certes alerté d'un risque de faillite, mais "c'est un tout petit pays"'.

sage, for example, when they questioned Iceland's right to independence and its ability to decide for itself. Iceland is a sovereign nation, but for some it was a laboratory to see how far neo-liberal reforms could be pushed. That, at least, is what the *Globe and Mail* indicated in the following dubious assertion: '[Iceland] serves as a useful laboratory for economists.'[24] Other remarks undermined Iceland's sovereignty by comparing the situation prevailing there during the crisis to that of a sham republic. Here, for example, is how the *Times* described it:

> Queues formed at petrol stations as Icelanders rushed to fill up before reported fuel shortages. ... Confusion reigned in the capital among a public unsure whether their savings and investments were safe, even after the Government moved to guarantee deposits. The country's state surgeon even warned politicians and the media to ensure that they did not alarm old people.[25]

Such comments speak volumes about the perceptions abroad and doubts concerning the Icelandic government's ability to manage the crisis and govern the country effectively. Such articles must be considered very seriously because, in harming the image of small countries, they challenge their right to sovereignty.

According to a few media reports, there were not just disadvantages to being small. From a cultural, political and athletics standpoint, having a population of only 330,000 could be an advantage. The Olympic Games in Beijing in August 2008 were an opportunity for journalists to comment on the role of small nations: sometimes to criticise them because they did not win many medals, but often to give them a moment of glory, proof of their importance alongside other nations. The

---

[24] Robert Jackson and Brian Milner, 'Iceland's meltdown', *Globe and Mail*, June 3, 2008, p. B-1.
[25] *Times*, 'Iceland bank shares suspended, state takes control', *Australian*, October 7, 2008.

Globe and Mail reported on a ranking[26] based not on the number of medals per country, but on the number of medals per million inhabitants. China, Russia and the United States thus dropped in the ranking, while Jamaica, the Bahamas and ... Iceland led the way. Jean Dion of *Le Devoir* spoke ironically about Iceland's demographics, stating that as many people live on the island as in a city like Sherbrooke. He added the following, which was his real message: 'it is not known whether Sherbrooke would beat Russia at handball'.[27]

Some newspapers, sympathetic to small, sovereign nations, envied them the cultural independence that large nations lack. For *Le Devoir*, '[Iceland's] creative freedom is due in part to the small size of the local market'.[28] The *Globe and Mail*, citing a sociologist from the University of Iceland, suggested that when a country's population is small, it tends to keep its society and culture alive as a survival reaction to powerful cultures.[29] According to the Glasgow *Herald*, globalisation may, paradoxically, have highlighted the assets of some small nations: 'The advent of globalisation is replacing this with another, something close to: Are you small and smart enough to survive and claim a positive place in common global culture?'[30] All in all, everyone saw something different in the Icelandic example—either disadvantages or advantages of being small.

But the country's serious crisis raises another question: were Iceland's problems due to its size? Most economists think not. The notion of 'small country' is relative, and could easily include countries, such as

---

26 From www.Simon.Forsythe.net and reported in *Globe and Mail*, 'Adding up the Games. Michael, medals, money', August 25, 2008, p. S-4.
27 Jean Dion, 'Hors-jeu. Huit par huit', *Le Devoir*, August 11, 2008. The original quote read: 'on ne sait pas si Sherbrooke battrait la Russie au hand-ball'.
28 Agence France-Presse, 'L'Islande, véritable geyser musical', *Le Devoir*, June 16, 2008. The original quote read: 'liberté de création [islandaise] s'explique en partie par la petitesse du marché local'.
29 Throbjorn Broddason, quoted by Matthew Hart, 'Iceland's next saga. The wounded tiger's tale', *Globe and Mail*, November 15, 2008, p. F-4.
30 *Herald* (Glasgow), 'Our chilling prophecy comes home to roost in Iceland', October 11, 2008.

the United Kingdom, that do not really have the means to support their banks—banks which have become so large they have destabilised the power relationship between themselves and the state. According to Willem Buiter, 'the UK is in many respects comparable to Iceland. It is bigger of course, but still tiny in relation to the global economy, with a sick financial sector that accounts for several times gross domestic product'.[31] The problem would therefore not be so much the size of a country as the equilibrium between its financial system and its capacity to protect it.

It is easy to ridicule the relatively small—a privilege the media rarely pass up. In Iceland's case, that was done by comparing the country to a mere city, by deeming its role in the world to be unimportant[32] or, even worse, by quoting caustic remarks by Icelanders in this regard. In the former case, the element of comparison varied according to local references (for *Le Devoir*, Iceland was Sherbrooke; for the *Australian*, Canberra; for the *Globe and Mail*, 'fewer than half the residents on Vancouver Island—and occupies an area slightly smaller than Newfoundland'[33]) but in all cases, the effect was to revile the country by reducing it to the proportions of a medium-sized city. Reporting the comments of Arney Einarsdóttir, a professor at the University of Reykjavík, the *Dallas Morning News* summarized the jeer as follows: 'Keeping the krona for 300,000 people—isn't that ridiculous? ... Imagine a small city that size in the United States trying to keep its own currency.'[34] It is, however, inappropriate and unfair to compare Iceland in that way, since cities do not have the institutions and pow-

---

31 Willem Buiter, quoted by Wolfgang Munchau, 'Why the British may decide to love the euro', *Financial Times*, November 16, 2008.
32 Despite its impact in the United Kingdom, the *Financial Times* did not consider the crisis in Iceland sufficiently important to highlight it in its year-end review, 'What we will remember from 2008' (Gideon Rachman, *Financial Times*, December 23, 2008, p. 7); the review refers to it only briefly.
33 Robert Jackson and Brian Milner, 'Iceland's meltdown', *Globe and Mail*, June 3, 2008, p. B-1.
34 Arney Einarsdóttir, quoted by Jim Landers, 'Iceland's road to bankruptcy was paved with U.S. ways', *Dallas Morning News*, December 10, 2008.

ers of a sovereign state: 'the oft-cited comparison of Iceland's population—a lowly 300,000—with the combined €118bn balance sheet of its three biggest banks is a distraction. No one draws a similar parallel between, say, Edinburgh and Royal Bank of Scotland'.[35]

Iceland's size led some media to describe the country in childish terms: '*Tiny Iceland*, which is not part of the EU',[36] 'it could be the first country *to be sold and leased back* to another sovereign state',[37] '*the problem child* of the industrialized world',[38] '*the poster child* of the new dark age of global finance',[39] and, in *Moscow News*: 'Moscow needs political heavyweights as friends, *not an island state with a population of 310,000*. But Iceland is *a perfect instrument* to demonstrate Russia's goodwill to the rest of the developed world *at very little cost.*'[40] In all these examples, the newspapers question the fact that such a small country is independent—a flaw, it would seem, in times of crisis. That view sometimes rubbed off on Icelanders themselves. Prime Minister Geir Haarde who, after mentioning that his country was not in a strong enough financial position to deal with the crisis, declared 'we are too small'.[41]

Another means used to run down the Icelandic state was to compare its management to that of a hedge fund. Quoted by the *Financial Times*, one expert asserted that Iceland was 'the world's first country run like a hedge fund'.[42] At the height of the crisis, some of the most

---

35 *Financial Times*, 'Icelandic banks', February 1, 2008, p. 14.
36 Brian Milner and Susan Sachs, 'European (dis)union', *Globe and Mail*, November 8, 2008, p. B-4 (italics added).
37 *Guardian*, 'Kaupthing. The bank that liked to say yes', October 9, 2008.
38 Brian Milner, 'Russia's "imaginative" Icelandic rescue', *Globe and Mail*, October 8, 2008, p. B-10 (italics added).
39 Ibid (italics added).
40 Marina Pustilnik, 'Iceland seeks Russian comfort', *Moscow News*, October 10, 2008 (italics added).
41 Geir Haarde, quoted in Agence France-Presse and Associated Press, 'L'Islande s'enfonce dans la crise', *Le Devoir*, October 9, 2008. The original quote read: 'Nous sommes trop petits'.
42 Quoted in David Ibison and Gillian Tett, 'Indignant Iceland faces a problem of perception', *Financial Times*, March 27, 2008, p. 13.

caustic criticism was found in Canadian and British newspapers, which denounced the inability of Icelandic institutions to deal with the crisis. After judging, in June, that 'the Central Bank of Iceland was slow to react and was caught completely off guard by the credit mess',[43] the *Globe and Mail* let loose in October, stating with respect to the country's monetary policy: 'it is also the latest indication of how ineptly the central bank, Sedlabanki, and the chairman of its board of governors, Davið Oddsson, have handled the banking crisis.'[44] The *Guardian*, for its part, quoted a member of the British parliament as saying: 'It is clear that Icelandic regulators have not done a very good job.'[45]

A small country out of balance, with a disproportionate banking system, accused of almost incestuous relations between its financiers and the regulators who were supposed to monitor their actions, Iceland had to face criticism on all fronts that threatened its sovereignty. The flood of jeers affected its image and credibility. As David Ibison and Gillian Tett wrote: 'Indignant Iceland faces a problem of perception.'[46]

---

43 Robert Jackson and Brian Milner, 'Iceland's meltdown', *Globe and Mail*, June 3, 2008, p. B-1.
44 Brian Milner, 'IMF demand forces Iceland to raise rates', *Globe and Mail*, October 29, 2008, p. B-14.
45 Vince Cable, quoted by Miles Brignall et al., 'Customers face anxious wait over fate of Icesave accounts', *Guardian*, October 7, 2008.
46 David Ibison and Gillian Tett, 'Indignant Iceland faces a problem of perception', *Financial Times*, March 27, 2008, p. 13.

CONCLUSION

THE HUMILIATED COUNTRY

VIOLENCE
ICELANDERS' ANGER

'Iceland "like Chernobyl" as meltdown
shows anger can boil over.'
Bloomberg, December 23, 2008[1]

As foreign journalists reported on the first troubles and subsequent violence that shook the Icelandic capital, they expressed bafflement, amusement, sometimes even glee, but rarely did they convey any sense of concern. They generally saw the anger as a healthy outburst, albeit unexpected in such a tranquil and peace-loving country. In addition, the Icelandic spirit of compromise attracted the international media, which often referred to the good-natured atmosphere of the demonstrations, as reported by *Yahoo News*: 'Demonstrations have been largely peaceful—some protesters were reportedly invited in for coffee when they showed up at President Ólafur Grímsson's home earlier this month.'[2] However, when the police did intervene, their actions were criticized; it became more obvious that there really was a revolt going on and that it was being repressed.

Foreign media coverage of the violence can be summarized quite simply, since it was uniform from one newspaper to the next. The protests were said to be the expression of *natural anger*, on the part of *ordinary people*, aimed at three entities: the government, the Central Bank, and the financiers.

---

1   Ben Holland, 'Iceland "like Chernobyl" as meltdown shows anger can boil over', *Bloomberg*, December 23, 2008.
2   Valur Gunnarsson [Associated Press], 'Icelandic TV program featuring PM forced off air', *Yahoo News*, December 31, 2008.

To explain the underlying issues, *BBC News* gave the example of a typical worker: 'Asta is one of Iceland's many *unlikely protesters*: people who were *never politically active* but who *now find themselves moved to act* in the wake of this country's worst economic crisis in generations.'[3] This observation was echoed in a quote from one of the protesters: 'Jonsson said: "And I want to tell you that the people gathered here are not 'activists' or 'militants', he added, "*they are just ordinary adults of all ages*"'.[4]

The primary target of their animosity was, naturally, the government. The Glasgow *Herald* reported that 'the Icelandic government now faces an angry backlash from the public, who are furious over their economic prospects'.[5] The *Huffington Post* went further, quoting a protester who declared: 'We are calling on the world to help us get rid of this corrupt government'.[6] Now there was talk of 'corruption' and 'incompetence', words very rarely used in political reporting on Scandinavia.

Resentment was also targeted at the Governor of the Central Bank, Davið Oddsson, former prime minister and initiator of the bank reforms that were a part of the country's downfall. And finally the new Vikings, entrepreneurs hungry for foreign conquests, stoked the ire of ordinary citizens who were forced to pay for their errors and who were, as reported by the *Sunday Times,* 'embarrassed by the gluttony and ineptitude of their own businessmen.'[7] In a departure from its usual tone, the *Economist* quoted a schoolteacher who had

---

3 Ray Furlong, 'Unlikely activists fight Iceland woes', *BBC News*, December 19, 2008 (italics added).
4 Sturla Jónsson, quoted by Íris Erlingsdóttir, 'Iceland is burning', *Huffington Post*, January 20, 2009 (italics added).
5 Torcuil Crichton, 'Chancellor pledges £2.2bn to UK depositors in Iceland bank', *Herald* (Glasgow), November 21, 2008.
6 Sturla Jónsson, quoted by Íris Erlingsdóttir, 'Iceland is burning', *Huffington Post*, January 20, 2009.
7 A.A. Gill, 'Iceland: frozen assets', *Sunday Times*, December 14, 2008.

this crude comment: 'If I met a banker ... I'd kick his ass so hard, my shoes would be stuck inside'[8].

Their anger was reflected in an incident, worthy of the sagas, in which protesters threw snowballs at one of the most famous new Vikings, Jón Ásgeir Jóhannesson, as he was fleeing to London. His escape in the middle of the night was reminiscent of the departure of the criminals of old, condemned to exile and the worst punishment meted out to an Islander—banishment from the island. The event attracted ample media coverage:

> One of Iceland's most prominent financiers became the target—literally—of people's anger over the collapse of Iceland's banks Glitnir and Landsbanki when he was hit in the face with a snowball, the DV newspaper reported Thursday. The paper said that prominent businessman and financier Jonsgeir Johannesson [Jón Ásgeir Jóhannesson], 40, was emerging from a joint supervisory board meeting of the two failed banks when three young men hurled snowballs at him. One of the snowballs struck him in the face. The paper cited one of the snowball-throwers as saying that the act felt 'liberating' while Johannesson said he was neither shocked nor hurt by the attack. He immediately flew off to his luxury home in London. With his financial investment group Baugur, Johannesson is regarded both as a chief culprit and as a symbolic figure in the collapse of Iceland's credit-driven investment bubble.[9]

The protests and violence surprised foreign commentators: 'These are highly unusual events in Iceland, normally a very reserved society',

---

8 Sirrý Hjaltested quoted in *Economist*, 'Cracks in the crust', December 11, 2008.
9 Deutsche Presse-Agentur, 'Snowball punishment for Iceland's vilified financial wizard', *Earthtimes*, December 18, 2008.

reported the BBC.[10] Even from the inside they appeared exceptional, prompting the editor in chief of *Iceland Review* to write: 'Fighting in the streets of Reykjavik. It was not the Iceland I know. But then again, what has happened here in the past months is not the Iceland I know, either.'[11] In fact, according to the *Economist*, 'such protests are almost unheard of: the only previous mass demonstrations to shake the country, against NATO membership, took place in 1949.'[12]

The events caused a shift in the media coverage. Suddenly, newspapers began quoting some Icelanders' statements about revolutions in other parts of the world. One financially ruined pensioner spoke to the *Financial Times* of revolution in a wry tone:

> 'The Icelandic people are too lazy', he says. 'Why don't we go to the airport and block it until we get answers? For the first time in my life I have sympathy with the Bolsheviks; with the French revolutionaries who put up the guillotine.'[13]

Journalists from London and Paris, used to rowdy riots, looked upon the small Icelandic demonstrations with amusement and condescension, comparing them to 'squabbles'. *Le Monde* reported a good-natured crowd of protesters making noise with kitchen pots and musical instruments[14] as police intervened, making a bad impression: 'The police, numerous but inexperienced, grasped their transparent shields, soon dripping with broken eggs and dairy products.'[15] The

---

10 Ray Furlong, 'Unlikely activists fight Iceland woes', *BBC News*, December 19, 2008.
11 Bjarni Brynjólfsson, 'The pots and pans revolution', *Iceland Review*, vol. 47, no. 1, 2009.
12 *Economist*, 'Cracks in the crust', December 11, 2008.
13 Örn Svavarsson, quoted by Sarah O'Connor, 'Iceland gives Christmas frosty reception', *Financial Times*, December 23, 2008.
14 Gérard Lemarquis, 'La faillite de l'Islande provoque à Reykjavik les premiers heurts avec la police depuis 60 ans', *Le Monde*, January 24, 2009.
15 Ibid. The original quote read: 'La police, nombreuse mais inexpérimentée, étrennait ses boucliers transparents, bientôt dégoulinants d'œufs qui s'y brisaient, maculés de fromage blanc'.

BBC commented ironically on the 'reinforcements' posted in front of Parliament: 'It is a sign of the times that security has been increased at Reykjavik's small Parliament building, from one policeman to three.'[16] The *Australian*, however, took this increased security seriously and interpreted it as a loss of innocence for Iceland. But it too was unimpressed by the newly deployed security at the Reykjavík exchange: 'Half-joking, half-serious, a newly hired security guard blocked the journalists' path. It was one of his first days on the job. Before trading was shut down last week the exchange was not guarded.'[17]

Nevertheless, once the police retaliation and brutality reached a level never before seen on the island, the media showed more concern in its reporting. The mounting tone in various reports reflected the mounting violence in the conflict between the protesters and their nation's institutions. In early November, the *Australian* reported a demonstration in which a thousand people gathered 'to call for the resignation of government officials and central bank chiefs'.[18] A few weeks later, the Glasgow *Herald* expressed concern over the first signs of violence, when a crowd gathered to demand the release of a demonstrator: 'Protesters angry over Iceland's economic meltdown have clashed with police, with at least five people sent to the hospital with injuries. Police fired pepper spray at the demonstrators as they tried to storm a police building.'[19] After a window was smashed at the offices of the financial supervisory authority in mid-December, the Associated Press put out a news release[20] that was widely circulated abroad: often peaceful, wrote the AP, but more and more violent and reflecting people's growing impatience, the demonstrations targeted banks,

---

16 Ray Furlong, 'Iceland scowls at UK after crisis', *BBC News*, December 16, 2008.
17 Agence France-Presse, 'Reykjavik Exchange resumes trading', *Australian*, October 15, 2008.
18 Agence France-Presse, 'Gordon Brown in Saudi Arabia to calm economic storm', *Australian*, November 2, 2008.
19 *Herald* (Glasgow), 'Five hurt in bid to storm police station', November 24, 2008.
20 Valur Gunnarsson, 'Windows broken at Iceland's financial regulator', *Yahoo News*, December 18, 2008.

government, cabinet ministers, the Central Bank and even businessmen. The tone of this press release, produced and published by one of the largest agencies, was completely unprecedented in connection with Iceland. Foreign readers wrote in to express their dismay at the reversal in the popular perception of Icelanders as peaceful and optimistic. What was happening in Iceland did not fit in any way with what people thought they knew about the country. The crisis had opened up a huge rift between foreign perceptions and reality.

On New Year's Day, the media reported that protests had forced the cancellation of a live television program with the Prime Minister. The incident, reminiscent of an African-style coup d'état, was completely at odds with public opinion: 'Protesters inside and outside the [Borg] hotel clashed with police, who fired pepper spray to disperse the 500-strong crowd', wrote the Associated Press.[21] Finally, on January 23, 2009, Iceland experienced a first that it would gladly have done without and that was carefully noted by the media, who interpreted it as a transition from pacifism to public violence. In grave tones, *Le Monde* reported:

> On Thursday morning, for the first time in half a century, the police of peaceful Iceland—a nation of 300,000 inhabitants having no army and having known only one violent demonstration since its independence, namely the 1949 protests against joining NATO—used tear gas to disperse protesters.[22]

This event, unimaginable just a few weeks earlier, propelled Iceland a thousand miles from its positive image in the world.

---

21 Valur Gunnarsson [Associated Press], 'Icelandic TV program featuring PM forced off air', *Yahoo News*, December 31, 2008.
22 Gérard Lemarquis, 'La faillite de l'Islande provoque à Reykjavik les premiers heurts avec la police depuis 60 ans', *Le Monde*, January 24, 2009. The original quote read: 'Jeudi matin, pour la première fois en un demi-siècle, la police de la pacifique Islande, pays sans armée de 300 000 habitants qui n'avait connu, depuis son indépendance, qu'une seule manifestation violente, en 1949, lors de l'adhésion à l'OTAN, a fait usage de gaz lacrymogènes pour disperser les contestataires'.

RETURNING TO TRADITION
FISHING, MORALITY AND ANTI-CONSUMERISM

'A great weight has been lifted now the money and the desires are gone. We can get back to being who we are.'
The Sunday Times, December 14, 2008[1]

It's a familiar story: a crisis triggers a return to conservatism, which then acts as a counter-discourse. In the case of Iceland, this return was celebrated as an end to the erosion of traditional values, as frugality and fishing were once again respected as symbols of a resilience unshaken by world events. Foreign newspapers were full of testimonials from Icelanders, from humble folk to the Prime Minister, all expressing a desire to revert to the past, or at least to a time *before* the banks embarked on wild expansion abroad, to a *lost era* considered to be more innocent. As the *Australian* reported: 'the Prime Minister has spoken dramatically of returning to Iceland's fishing and farming roots, *rebuilding by simple hard work what may have been lost*'.[2] This attempt at redemption is aimed at wiping out the traces of the crisis and returning to a more harmonious existence. *Iceland Review*, which a few months earlier had been singing the praises of Icelandic entrepreneurship, now joined in this discourse, stating: 'We will have to revert to the old and established values of equality, justice and fairness in trade and commerce. We need to believe that big is not always beautiful.'[3] A sombre time of reflection on what it means to be an

---
[1] An Icelander, quoted by A.A. Gill, 'Iceland: frozen assets', *Sunday Times*, December 14, 2008.
[2] *Australian*, 'Iceland's economic collapse could herald a new round of large-scale acquisitions', October 9, 2008 (italics added).
[3] Bjarni Brynjólfsson, 'The pots and pans revolution', *Iceland Review*, vol. 47, no. 1, 2009.

Icelander, Matthew Hart looked at *what remained* after the crisis: 'a people united by a history of survival and a cherished culture'.[4]

For historians, such pious thinking is reminiscent of the romanticism of the 19th century—another time marked by a new national consciousness. Journalists, ever pragmatic, see it first and foremost as a way of accepting the inevitable: the crisis has forced people to redefine their identity and scale down their ambitions. As Jill Lawless reported in the *Detroit News*, 'Icelanders are cutting back on spending and returning to tradition'.[5] Roger Boyes made a connection between this return to tradition and the nation's insularity: 'Icelanders are returning to their sense of being islanders rather than global players who can throw weight around European capitals. Icelanders, when they return to their roots, know they must accept geographical limitations.'[6]

As Iceland's fallback value, fishing plays a role of near-mythical proportions in the discourse exhorting a return to tradition and ancestral values. An analysis of this discourse shows that fishing is regarded in two ways: as an industry and as an activity integrally related to Icelandic identity. The preservation of fish stocks and the productivity of Icelandic fishermen have often been held up as exemplary by foreigners.[7] However, fishing has also been referred to with a barb of nastiness and derision. In an article for the *International Herald Tribune*, Roger Cohen claimed that 'Iceland, de-banked, has gone back to fishing (if there are any fish left)'.[8] A British investor, quoted by the *Financial Times*, warned that 'the Icelandics had better get their fishing rods

---

4 Matthew Hart, 'Iceland's next saga: The wounded tiger's tale', *Globe and Mail*, November 15, 2008, p. F-4.
5 Jill Lawless, 'Crisis gives Iceland gift of frugality', *Detroit News*, December 25, 2008.
6 Roger Boyes, 'Skating on thin ice', *Australian*, October 10, 2008.
7 See, for example, Gérard Lemarquis, 'L'Islande affronte la baisse des quotas de cabillaud. La bonne gestion des réserves de poisson a transformé les pêcheurs en rentiers... au point d'abandonner le métier', Économie, *Le Monde*, January 15, 2008, p. 5.
8 Roger Cohen, 'Cohen: history and the really weird', *International Herald Tribune*, October 12, 2008.

out. They've got a lot of cod to catch to make up for what we've lost.'[9] Economists cite fishing and other resources as one of the values the nation can rely on, for lack of a productive financial system: 'Icelanders are now talking about falling back on the old industries—fishing, aluminium smelting, and nature tourism.'[10] In October 2008, salvation through fishing was mentioned by Prime Minister Haarde, who admitted that 'it is not wise for a small country to try to take a leading role in international banking',[11] and urged his fellow citizens to turn to activities that were more traditional and even *more Icelandic*.

Paradoxically, for all that fishing appears to be a cornerstone of the nation's identity and economy, it is nonetheless dependent on the uncertainties of foreign policy, especially those related to the question of European Union membership, which was debated with increasing fervour during and after the crisis. The issue is a major one: Iceland's fish catch would be equal to one quarter of the entire combined catch of the European Union countries.[12] Fishing, a fundamental aspect of Icelandic identity, would be compromised within the EU, thus blocking the way to any diplomatic redeployment: 'By joining the European Union,' claimed Sigurdur Sverisson, a fishermen's association spokesman quoted by the Associated Press, "we would not have the controlling rights of the stocks any more."[13] According to Olivier Truc of *Le Monde*, the return to tradition was thus compromised from the outset by the political evolution of Iceland: 'In Iceland, where the krona has

---

9 A British investor, quoted by Tom Braithwaite et al., 'A cruel wind', *Financial Times*, October 10, 2008.
10 Keith B. Richburg, '"Nordic Tiger" Iceland finds itself in meltdown', *Washington Post*, October 10, 2008, p. A-1.
11 Geir Haarde, quoted by Associated Press, 'Raiding Reykjavik', *Globe and Mail*, October 11, 2008, p. F-2.
12 'In 2008, the 5,000 Icelandic fishermen ... caught close to 1.3 million tonnes of fish, which is equal to one quarter of the EU's total catch at present'. The original quote read: 'Les 5 000 pêcheurs islandais [...] ont capturé en 2008 près de 1,3 million de tonnes de poisson, l'équivalent du quart des prises totales actuelles de l'UE'. (Agence France-Presse, 'La candidature de l'Islande à l'UE promet un bras de fer sur la pêche', *L'Express*, July 23, 2009.)
13 Sigurdur Sverisson, quoted by Jill Lawless, 'With fish, Iceland's future is going back', *Globe and Mail*, December 15, 2008.

lost two thirds of its value and where support for joining the EU has strengthened in the past few days, the fishing lobby is making every possible effort to oppose membership in the EU.'[14]

The crisis led to a rebirth of sorts for the fishing industry. Icelanders' perception of fishing was transformed both economically and symbolically after the events of fall 2008. Where for a while it had been barely noticed, it now went from neglected to advantageous and attractive: 'Iceland has had such an economic boom in recent years that towns would rather invest in an aluminium smelter, or in tourism or construction'.[15] As the *Globe and Mail* reported, 'in recent years these proud descendants of Vikings found new fish to catch, scooping up businesses around the world'.[16] Conversely, when the other sectors of the economy went into free fall, fishing re-emerged as the stable value enabling people to recover a certain degree of prosperity and pride. *Iceland Review* saw a rebirth of regionalism in this: 'In many of the small fishing villages along Iceland's coast, life goes on as usual and there is hardly any recession. Moreover, the future looks brighter than it has in many years'.[17] More realistic, Jill Lawless observed that the fishing industry could contribute to Iceland's economic revival. Quoting a fisherman, she reported that 'Mr Sigurgeirsson, 34, has been at sea for 10 years and is bemused by his industry's new image. He says fishermen are being painted as a cross between national saviours and fat cats who haul in big salaries from bumper catches'.[18]

---

14 Olivier Truc, 'Le Danemark regrette de plus en plus d'être resté en dehors de la zone euro', Économie, *Le Monde*, October 23, 2008, p. 12. The original quote read: 'En Islande, où la couronne a perdu les deux tiers de sa valeur et où le soutien en faveur de l'Union s'est renforcé ces derniers jours, le lobby de la pêche joue de toute sa puissance pour s'opposer à une adhésion à l'Union'.
15 Gérard Lemarquis, 'L'Islande affronte la baisse des quotas de cabillaud. La bonne gestion des réserves de poisson a transformé les pêcheurs en rentiers… au point d'abandonner le métier', Économie, *Le Monde*, January 15, 2008, p. 5. The original quote read: 'L'Islande a connu un tel boum économique ces dernières années, que l'on préfère miser ici sur une usine d'aluminium, là sur le tourisme, ou sur le bâtiment'.
16 Jill Lawless, 'With fish, Iceland's future is going back', *Globe and Mail*, December 15, 2008.
17 Bjarni Brynjólfsson, 'Escaping Reykjavik', *Iceland Review*, vol. 47, no. 1, 2009.
18 Jill Lawless, 'With fish, Iceland's future is going back', *Globe and Mail*, December 15, 2008.

Generally speaking, the great return to tradition has also, for many commentators, marked an end to the erosion of the social and moral values that Iceland was built on. Referring to a character in a novel by Nobel laureate Halldór Laxness as an example of what *should be* or what *could be again*, a *Bloomberg* journalist described the feeling of moral degradation undermining Icelandic society: 'Some Icelanders say the easy money of the past decade eroded the island's traditions.'[19] The crisis was a wake-up call that prompted Icelanders into a change of morality based on less materialistic values. That, at least, is how the newspapers described the transition which took place during the most difficult period. *Télérama* provides an example of the 'end of era' moralistic discourse, quoting theatre director Kristín Eysteinsdóttir:

> All our values changed in the space of a few weeks. We spent a decade thinking only about money, buying, always buying, cars, houses, new lines of credit. It's over. We look at Range Rovers differently. Now we call them 'Game overs'. There's no more worshiping of the almighty dollar. We've gone back to something deeper.[20]

The sudden turnaround meant harsh judgement of that time just ended. The reactions were often reported by the foreign media through interviews with Icelanders—from humble fishermen up to the Archbishop of Iceland—all of them unanimous in their condemnation of the conduct prior to the crisis: 'The priorities went askew in the past few years,'[21] said one fisherman. '[Society] was led to believe that it

---

19 Ben Holland, 'Iceland "like Chernobyl" as meltdown shows anger can boil over', *Bloomberg*, December 23, 2008.
20 Kristín Eysteinsdóttir, quoted by Nicolas Delesalle, 'Les révoltés du geyser', *Télérama*, no. 3086, March 8, 2009. The original quote read: 'Toutes nos valeurs ont changé en quelques semaines. On a passé dix ans à ne penser qu'à l'argent, à acheter, toujours acheter, des voitures, des maisons, à prendre de nouveaux crédits. C'est fini. On regarde différemment les Range Rover. Aujourd'hui, on les appelle les "Game over". Il n'y a plus de respect pour le clinquant. On revient vers quelque chose de plus profond'.
21 Kristian, an Icelandic fisherman, quoted by Roger Boyes, 'Skating on thin ice', *Australian*, October 10, 2008.

was unlimited growth forever',[22] stated Bishop Karl Sigurbjörnsson. '[It] is a project that went horribly wrong',[23] declared writer Sjón. The condemnations were accompanied by utopian thoughts of collective moral purification. British columnist A.A. Gill saw the fragility of this remorse, which he reported, tongue-in-cheek, in the form of a tirade he heard from a woman in a Reykjavík bar:

> All the money, all the things and the stuff, *it's very un-Icelandic*. The wanting, the conspicuous consumption, the avarice and ambition, the pathetic jealousy, *that isn't us*. A great weight has been lifted now the money and the desires are gone. We can get back to being *who we are*.[24]

Through the return to tradition, the crisis became an opportunity for moral and ethical renewal and has paved the way for values more conducive to happiness: 'Ever since the advent of the entrepreneurial, dual-income, seize the day ... can't-possibly-meet-you-I'm-so-busy lifestyle, have you, or has anybody else you know, been particularly happy?'[25] That question put to Icelanders contains its own answer (albeit a non-economic and non-financial one) and heralds a return to something essential—a healthy relationship between the individual and materialism. Even though the effects may be ephemeral, a crisis in any country breeds change.

The return to tradition has thus been reflected in self-examination and in the rejection of the heightened consumerism that marked Iceland right up to the last days before the crisis: 'Last year's must-haves, flat screen televisions and games consoles, are on the list of

---

[22] Karl Sigurbjörnsson, quoted by Eric Pfanner, 'Iceland is all but officially bankrupt', *International Herald Tribune*, October 9, 2008.

[23] Sjón, quoted by Matthew Hart, 'Iceland's next saga: The wounded tiger's tale', *Globe and Mail*, November 15, 2008, p. F-4.

[24] An Icelander, quoted by A.A. Gill, 'Iceland: frozen assets', *Sunday Times*, December 14, 2008 (italics added).

[25] Karen Von Hahn, 'Could market meltdown be a chance to slow down?', *Globe and Mail*, October 18, 2008, p. L-3.

things people here call "so 2007". ... This Christmas, people are giving each other books, home-made trinkets and practical presents such as warm socks.'[26] A transitional utopia, this reversion to old times, exchanges, second hand and home-made became a trend during the holidays throughout the 'in' communities of the island. Journalists reported it as they would any new trend: 'Among the things now selling briskly in the capital Reykjavik are horse meat, second-hand clothing and used DVDs of "The Sound of Music"'.[27] Such frugality points to a necessary but difficult back-to-basics and an attempt at ascetic purification which, it is hoped, will erase the nightmarish experience of the past. According to the *Financial Times*, there will be no more whale sashimi, no more extravagant lobster dinners at the finest restaurants in Reykjavík; Icelanders are starting to eat black pudding again, and that almost magically marks a renaissance and a return to self. David Ibison quoted novelist Andri Snær Magnason as saying, 'It reminds us of a generation that came through a crisis with a strong set of values, and helps us realise that these were the real values'.[28] As a discourse of consolation and as a survival strategy, the return to tradition reflects the will never to return to the excessiveness of the recent past.

---

[26] Sarah O'Connor, 'Iceland gives Christmas frosty reception', *Financial Times*, December 23, 2008.
[27] Press Association News, 'Iceland feels chill of recession', *Channel 4 News*, December 11, 2008.
[28] Andri Snær Magnason, quoted by David Ibison, 'Icelanders see Icarus-like plunge of greed', *Financial Times*, October 23, 2008.

IRRESPONSIBILITY
WHO SHOULD PAY THE PRICE?

'The blame game is only just beginning ... Iceland's business and political community bear an important part of the responsibility, even as they now play the victim.'
Fortune, December 4, 2008[1]

Who is responsible for the financial crisis in Iceland and its repercussions abroad? Who should pay the price? Were the nation's institutions and politicians complacent toward the new Vikings? Were the regulations governing the financial system applied with sufficient stringency? Did the entire country lack foresight? Can the blame be placed on others indefinitely? The issue of irresponsibility was discussed in much of the commentary, analysis and news concerning Iceland in 2008. It deeply tarnished the country's reputation for reliability, built up in the past few decades: could Iceland still be considered a reliable partner?

The first reaction of the Icelandic government, faced with accusations of irresponsibility, was to declare that it had not failed in any way. The *International Herald Tribune* had this quote from the Prime Minister: 'Despite the collapse of the banks, Haarde said, 'the country itself is not in default, is not abrogating its responsibilities.'[2] This position was maintained for weeks, even at the peak of the crisis, right up until the government stepped down in January: '[Icelandic] authorities have

---

1 Peter Gumbel, 'Iceland: the country that became a hedge fund', *Fortune*, December 4, 2008, http://www.money.cnn.com/.
2 Eric Pfanner, 'Iceland banks face claims from depositors abroad', *International Herald Tribune*, October 10, 2008.

denied responsibility, but widespread protests eventually forced the government to resign.[3] Two months after leaving office, Geir Haarde accepted some of the blame at a party conference: 'Haarde apologised on Thursday for being partly responsible for events leading to the collapse of Iceland's banks'.[4] The Central Bank, for its part, made a discreet statement that resembled less of an admission: 'The question of when it would have been right to intervene—and how—*is extremely difficult to answer*, however. *No one has perfect foresight*. Many lessons will doubtless be learned from the experience.'[5]

Comments gathered from Icelandic citizens indicate that they were trying to find ways to avoid bearing too much of the blame for their country's financial collapse, despite its impact abroad. Sarah Lyall of the *New York Times* interviewed a secretary who had just lost her job and who failed to understand why the state—and hence its citizens—should have to pay for the imprudence of foreign savers and private bank directors: 'We didn't ask anyone to put their money in the banks', she said. "These are private companies and private banks, and they went abroad and did business there"'.[6] The editor in chief of *Iceland Review* alleged that Icelanders could not have known what was going on: 'we were being assured by our government, bankers and even our Financial Supervisory Authority and Central Bank'.[7] It was common for Icelanders to place the blame elsewhere—in this case, on a handful of people who acted carelessly: 'As economist Vilhjalmur Bjarnason ... says, it was about 20 to 30 people who got themselves

---

[3] Jon Danielsson, 'Waking up to reality in Iceland', *BBC News*, January 26, 2009.
[4] Andrew Roche and Ómar Valdimarsson, 'Iceland's ex-PM apologises for part in bank crash', *Reuters*, March 26, 2009.
[5] Ingimundur Friðriksson, 'The banking crisis in Iceland in 2008', *Sedlabanki.is*, February 6, 2009 (italics added).
[6] Katrín Runólfsdóttir, quoted by Sarah Lyall, 'Stunned Icelanders struggle after economy's fall', *New York Times*, November 9, 2008.
[7] Bjarni Brynjólfsson, 'Bright light to pitch-black night', *Iceland Review*, vol. 46, no. 4, 2008.

into the debt that our nation of 300,000 now has to bear.'[8] However, this sentiment found little sympathy of favour in the media outside Iceland.

The first foreign accusations came from the United Kingdom. Gordon Brown was categorical: 'Icelandic banks have collapsed, and Iceland's authorities must assume responsibility for that.'[9] To force them to do so, the British and their European allies took the hard line, making any international aid conditional upon Iceland's agreeing to fulfil its international obligations: 'In a joint statement, the British, Dutch and German governments welcomed Iceland's commitment to meet its obligations.'[10] Although independent, the International Monetary Fund waited for an agreement between these nations before officially announcing any financial support for Iceland, thus forcing Reykjavík to assume its responsibilities and pay for the errors of its banks.

In February 2009, a news release from the Central Bank of Iceland suggested that it was its proximity to the commercial banks, before the crisis, that undermined the moral authority it needed to impose new rules: 'The Central Bank supported all of these actions wholeheartedly; however, it did not have the statutory authority ... to force the banks to change their conduct.'[11] But this admission came a little too late; at the height of the crisis, financial analysts saw the Bank's attitude as irresponsible complacency on the part of the financial authorities. For Roger Boyes, this state of affairs further weakened the Icelandic government's position abroad, as it came increasingly un-

---

8 Jonas Moody, 'Feature of the week: the author of Revolution', *Iceland Review*, vol. 46, no. 4, 2008.
9 Gordon Brown, quoted in Agence France-Presse, 'Crise. L'Islande nationalise ses banques à marche forcée', *Le Devoir*, October 10, 2008. The original quote read: 'Les banques islandaises se sont écroulées, les autorités islandaises doivent prendre leurs responsabilités pour cela.'
10 Torcuil Crichton, 'Chancellor pledges £2.2bn to UK depositors in Iceland bank', *Herald* (Glasgow), November 21, 2008.
11 Ingimundur Friðriksson, 'The banking crisis in Iceland in 2008', *Sedlabanki.is*, February 6, 2009.

der fire from its own citizens and financial experts: 'Not just because the businessmen and politicians are intertwined like tangled nets, but because the lack of regulatory control during the 1990s privatisations *was so indefensible.*'[12] A lack of independence and laxness in the application of rules were among the shortcomings, according to the BBC:

> The government, the Central Bank and the financial regulator at times seemed to act as cheerleaders for the banks, not as responsible authorities. ... The Icelandic banks were set for failure because of excessive risk taking, inadequate management *and rather lax government supervision.*[13]

The Prime Minister himself admitted that some controls were not sufficiently rigorous: 'The banks always followed the rules. But no doubt we were not paying enough attention.'[14] According to *Le Monde*, the silence of politicians—including President Ólafur Ragnar Grímsson (criticised for his immoderate support of the risky investment abroad[15])—helped create this climate of complacency between financiers and their supposed watchdogs.

The *Financial Times* felt that, from an ethical standpoint, the lack of respect of Icelandic financiers toward their own country was as disturbing as the conduct of the Icelandic authorities. It reported the

---

12 Roger Boyes, 'Iceland braces for Brits wanting their money back', *Australian*, October 13, 2008 (italics added).
13 Jon Danielsson, 'Waking up to reality in Iceland', *BBC News*, January 26, 2009 (italics added).
14 Geir Haarde, quoted by Élise Vincent, 'Dans un entretien, le premier ministre islandais, Geir Haarde, évoque la grave crise financière que traverse son pays, il y a encore peu de temps l'un des plus prospères de la planète', Économie, *Le Monde*, October 23, 2008, p. 12. The original quote read: 'les banques ont toujours suivi les règles. Nous n'avons sans doute toutefois pas fait assez attention'.
15 Gérard Lemarquis, 'La faillite de l'Islande provoque à Reykjavik les premiers heurts avec la police depuis 60 ans', *Le Monde*, January 24, 2009. The original quote read: 'surnommé *"la claque"* pour son soutien immodéré à ces investissements hasardeux à l'étranger'.

insouciance with which the Baugur group planned its departure from Iceland in June 2008, leaving behind vast amounts of debt—as would be revealed by the events of October 2008—to start operations in another country ('either to the UK, Denmark or the Faeroe Islands'[16]), 'to avoid the possibility of Mr Johannesson's [the chairman's] being banned as a company director'[17] by being brought to justice. The international media acknowledged that the lifestyle, management methods and ethics of the '20 or 30 people' mentioned by economist Vilhjálmur Bjarnason might be offensive. For the *Dallas Morning News*, it was the extravagance and arrogance of Icelandic tycoons that was the most difficult to accept:

> The bankers partied by flying in Elton John for a Reykjavik birthday bash. ... Iceland's economists traveled the world with PowerPoint presentations hailing the Icelandic economic miracle. Its 312,000 people were among the world's richest. But their banks owed what amounted to $250,000 for every man, woman and child in the country. ... The party stopped in October.[18]

Foreign journalists also mentioned lack of foresight as one of the causes of the crisis: first of all, that of the Central Bank of Iceland, both in its management and in its role as watchdog: 'a combination of inappropriate monetary policy and an outsized banking system',[19] according to the BBC. For a small country with a small savings protection scheme, the growth of the Icelandic banks was of monstrous proportions and threw the system off balance. According to the calculations provided by Matthew Vincent in the *Financial Times*, 'The

---

16 Tom Braithwaite, 'Baugur in talks over move to Britain', *Financial Times*, June 29, 2008.
17 Ibid.
18 Jim Landers, 'Iceland's road to bankruptcy was paved with U.S. ways', *Dallas Morning News*, December 10, 2008.
19 Jon Danielsson, 'Why raising interest rates won't work', *BBC News*, October 28, 2008.

Icelandic Financial Supervisory Authority has £88m in the scheme. If Landsbanki does declare itself bankrupt, it would need to pay 300,000 customers.'[20] In other words, for just one of the Icelandic banks, the number of foreign customers to reimburse was equal to the entire population of the island.

Time magazine held that the strength of the new Vikings—namely, their neo-liberal will to forge ahead, conquer and acquire—was also their weakness: having no protection against contingencies, they jeopardised their own success and the economy of their country. They were seen as visionaries, but their lack of objectivity ended up being very costly: '[The] country's bankers became too rich too fast, embracing global wealth with little discipline or foresight about what they would do if the economy turned sour'.[21]

Within the Icelandic government, the first reaction upon seeing the magnitude of the crisis was to reproach other countries for their intransigence, their unwillingness to cooperate and their slowness to offer aid. Claiming to be victims of speculators ('Iceland has accused hedge funds of ganging up on its banks and its currency'[22]) and to have followed the rules but were nonetheless punished ('the banks had become too large in relation to the Icelandic economy. ... The European regulatory framework made this possible'[23]), Iceland was finally confronted with the reality that had led to its apparent wealth: the globalisation of its economy. In profiting from the new possibilities offered by the opening of world trade to make loans and acquisitions, the country should have expected that the gears of international finance would exert pressure on its own markets in return. That, at least, was the viewpoint of David Ibison of the *Financial Times*, who

---

20 Matthew Vincent, 'Bank crisis Q&A', *Financial Times*, October 7, 2008.
21 Vivienne Walt, 'A meltdown in Iceland', *Time*, October 8, 2008.
22 James Mackintosh and Peter Smith, 'Australia aims regulatory fire at hedge funds', *Financial Times*, April 10, 2008, p. 22.
23 Ingimundur Friðriksson, 'The banking crisis in Iceland in 2008', *Sedlabanki.is*, February 6, 2009.

maintained that Iceland must assume a greater part of responsibility for the crisis: 'The undeniable fact is *that Iceland is now more internationalised than at any time in its past*. While alleged financial speculation is being rightly investigated, the solution to its challenges does not lie in blaming foreigners.'[24]

Icelanders need not assume *all* the blame for the crisis. Foreign savers who, of their own free will, chose Icelandic banks because they offered higher interest rates must accept the risk incurred. Several pieces in the *Financial Times* corroborate this opinion: 'Depositors must take responsibility for their own choices',[25] 'To amend the old saw: you get what you're paid for'.[26]

In the end, it seems inevitable, according to foreign commentators, that Iceland should have to pay a certain price for its mistakes. The burden is placed on the banks in question, on the government of Iceland and, consequently, on all its citizens: 'its main banks and business tycoons took huge risks and its citizens borrowed to the hilt. Now this island nation is paying the price'.[27] Analysts find few reasons to excuse the excessiveness of recent years. Willem H. Buiter and Anne Sibert simply stated that 'it should not have grown a massive on-shore internationally exposed banking sector'.[28] The government of Iceland therefore has a heavy price to pay, and many fear that it will be unable to meet its obligations. The burden—out of proportion to the size of this nation, as were the branches of its banks abroad—has forced Iceland to endure unprecedented austerity and to solicit for-

---

24 David Ibison, 'Cool under fire Iceland takes the fight back to finance', *Financial Times*, April 9, 2008, p. 7 (italics added).
25 *Financial Times*, 'Saving savers', November 9, 2008.
26 Andrew Hill, 'Why frozen Icesavers deserve sympathy not support', *Financial Times*, October 8, 2008, p. 22.
27 Peter Gumbel, 'Iceland: the country that became a hedge fund', *Fortune*, December 4, 2008, http://www.money.cnn.com/.
28 Willem H. Buiter and Anne Sibert, 'The Icelandic banking crisis and what to do about it. The lender of last resort theory of optimal currency areas', *CEPR Policy Insight*, n° 26, October 2008.

eign loans: 'it's difficult to see how it can refloat without international help'[29] said the BBC. In light of the excuses offered to avoid taking a share of responsibility for the crisis, Iceland's desperate situation elicited little sympathy abroad: 'There is little excuse for Iceland, which essentially turned itself into a highly leveraged hedge fund'[30] said the *Globe and Mail*.

Icelanders must now live with the deeply bitter feeling of having been taken. In the space of a few years, they were passive but sometimes proud witnesses as some of their countrymen rose to dizzying heights. Just before Christmas, they had to register the falseness of the successes of their elite: 'Iceland is paying the price for its role in adding to the world credit crunch by being forced into an austerity Christmas.'[31] Eric Pfanner wrote, in the *International Herald Tribune*, that Icelanders should not be pitied too much, since they too participated in—and profited from—the financial bubble:

> The days when the economy seemed capable of gravity-defying feats are gone. ... Gone too, are the days when ordinary citizens effortlessly joined in the fun, taking out second mortgages to finance their own trips abroad or at least to the Laugavegur, the main shopping strip in Reykjavik.[32]

From the viewpoint of image, all the debate about responsibility for the crisis has been extremely damaging for Iceland, which is now perceived as an unreliable economic partner. The initial reactions of the UK in the Icesave affair took on rapid proportions ('the behaviour of

---

29 Robert Peston, 'Markets call time on Iceland', *BBC News*, October 4, 2008.
30 Dani Rodrik, 'To keep us all afloat. Why must we save emerging markets from Wall Street's follies?', *Globe and Mail*, November 13, 2008, p. B-14.
31 Press Association News, 'Iceland feels chill of recession', *Channel 4 News*, December 11, 2008.
32 Eric Pfanner, 'Iceland is all but officially bankrupt', *International Herald Tribune*, October 9, 2008.

the Icelandic authorities had been unacceptable,[33] proclaimed Gordon Brown), well beyond Britain's borders. The list of bankruptcies and disappearances of Icelandic-controlled corporations grew, leaving bitter souvenirs of the country.

The moral impact of the crisis is therefore not solely financial: it had a bearing on the pride and identity of the Icelandic people, who were at first shocked, then hurt by the whole affair. Writer Einar Már Guðmundsson, who firmly believes that Icelanders must seriously consider the consequences of the crisis, stated: 'What's so serious is how this corrupt administration has deprived us of our reputation and respect as a nation. Self-respect and pride are of real consequence to Icelanders.'[34]

---

[33] Gordon Brown, quoted in *Herald* (Glasgow), 'Treasury officials hold emergency talks on Iceland', October 10, 2008.
[34] Einar Már Guðmundsson, quoted by Jonas Moody, 'Feature of the week: the author of Revolution', *Iceland Review*, vol. 46, no. 4, 2008.

HUMILIATION
THE WOUNDED TIGER

'Iceland—the nordic Zimbabwe.'
The Huffington Post, January 5, 2009[1]

Around the turn of the millennium, Iceland became a sort of success story for small growing nations: egalitarian, rich and ethical, it was seen abroad as the 'Nordic tiger'. Its reversal of fortunes due to the crisis of 2008 thus came as a severe humiliation. Driven upward by delirious economic nationalism until the end of summer 2008, the country was struck down in mid-ascent—a hard blow to its good-natured pride. Iceland's excellent reputation and image changed almost overnight.

Some observers viewed the fall with sympathy, referring to Iceland as a 'casualty of the crisis'. They expressed regret that a country said to be so morally strong, with its citizens seen as so hard-working, should find itself in this situation. Columnist A.A. Gill wrote the following in the *Sunday Times*: 'Iceland and Icelanders have been forged on the anvil of hard knocks. The *unfair thing* about this latest paper calamity is that it happened just when they thought things were going so well.'[2] Others were pitiless: the *International Herald Tribune* expressed severe judgement about Iceland's wealth before the crisis, speaking of 'the extraordinary reversal in the country's fortunes after a decade-long, debt-fueled binge by the country's banks, businesses and some

---

1 Íris Erlingsdóttir, 'Iceland—The nordic Zimbabwe', *Huffington Post*, January 5, 2009.
2 A.A. Gill, 'Iceland: frozen assets', *Sunday Times*, December 14, 2008 (italics added).

private citizens'.[3] But most journalists stuck to the following facts: a rich country, one of the wealthiest in the world, suddenly fell to the bottom of the economic ladder. 'The nordic nation', wrote the *Australian*, 'has in the past week gone from a rich, prosperous country to one that is on the brink of bankruptcy'.[4]

On its humiliating descent, the nation had to suffer injuries to its national currency throughout the year. The drop in the value of the krona in October, accompanied by runaway inflation, led to a temporary soaring of interest rates. Foreign economists expressed concern and saw it as unusual for a prosperous country: '[it is] more typical of a developing economy than one of the wealthiest countries in the world'.[5] Such measures had been seen before 'in places like Argentina and Thailand, [but] not a country that likes to think of itself as close to Europe'.[6] For the *Guardian*, the instability of the krona placed the country among the ranks of the struggling nations: 'it is rated the world's third-worst performing currency—just above Zimbabwe's and Turkmenistan's'.[7]

This apparent collapse was confirmed when the International Monetary Fund (IMF) came into the picture, since it meant that Iceland had exhausted its own resources. Around the world, newspapers emphasized the unusual nature of this aid: 'making it the first Western country to get an IMF bailout since 1976'.[8] Some newspapers made a point of adding that the most recent nation to receive an IMF bailout was the UK, which is precisely the nation many Icelanders hold

---

[3] Eric Pfanner, 'Iceland is all but officially bankrupt', *International Herald Tribune*, October 9, 2008.
[4] Agence France-Presse, 'Reykjavik exchange resumes trading', *Australian*, October 15, 2008.
[5] Eric Pfanner and Julia Werdigier, 'Caught in financial crisis, Iceland tries to tap Russia', *International Herald Tribune*, October 7, 2008.
[6] Eric Pfanner, 'Iceland is all but officially bankrupt', *International Herald Tribune*, October 9, 2008.
[7] Gwladys Fouché, 'Iceland is in the heart of the economic storm', *Guardian*, October 6, 2008.
[8] Marcus Gee, 'The body punches keep on coming', *Globe and Mail*, October 25, 2008, p. B-1.

responsible for their country's economic failure. In any case, the act of requesting and obtaining this aid had symbolic value: Iceland's international status was severely downgraded. The *Globe and Mail* emphasised the rapidity of the change:

> Iceland's economy has deteriorated so dramatically in recent weeks that it is now looking for the sort of emergency bailout more typical of the developing world than of a sophisticated Western economy.[9]

Iceland's recourse to IMF aid was reported by foreign observers as a stop-and-go affair. It can be described as a play in three acts which took place in October and November: act one, denial; act two, acceptance; and act three, recovery and humiliation. Initially, Iceland denied needing aid from the IMF. On October 9, Prime Minister Geir Haarde said, 'we don't think it will come to that'.[10] The next day, the newspapers reported that the IMF was Iceland's last resort; he tried to reassure the markets and asserted that the country had many other options. On October 11, the *Financial Times* had harsh words for the 'other options' considered by Iceland, when the IMF was ready to support the country. Alain Beattie wrote, 'No country likes going to the IMF for help, since it is widely seen as an admission of policy failure.'[11] A bilateral appeal to allied nations, more discreet than the IMF and a means of masking such a policy failure, would have enabled Iceland to avoid finding itself among the needy nations. But pressure was high. On October 16, *Le Devoir* wrote: 'Playing the IMF card would mean national humiliation [for Icelanders] but many economists see it as inevitable.'[12] For the next few days, uncertainty

---

9 Brian Milner, 'Out of options, Iceland leans on IMF', *Globe and Mail*, October 21, 2008, p. B-3.
10 Geir Haarde, quoted by Kerry Capell, 'The stunning collapse of Iceland', *BusinessWeek*, October 9, 2008.
11 Alan Beattie, 'IMF ready to help out emerging market states', *Financial Times*, October 11, 2008, p. 5.
12 Agence France-Presse, 'L'Islande se démène sur tous les fronts pour éviter la faillite',

and confusion reigned: Iceland did not officially request IMF aid, but a team had been on the island for several days to negotiate with the government.[13] Finally, as allied aid was too slow in coming, Iceland gave in and became the first Western nation to request IMF aid in 30 years.

Prime Minister Haarde reacted promptly, attempting to avoid national shame as well as criticism for seeking IMF aid in contradiction to his earlier statements. In an interview with *Le Monde*, Haarde stated on October 23: 'Appealing to the IMF is not a national disgrace. On the contrary, it builds trust.'[14] He was alone in such positive thinking; newspapers around the world quickly changed their opinion of Iceland, ranking it among the developing nations. Comparisons with Eastern Europe, South America, Africa and Asia abounded and tarnished the image of Iceland, which fell from its Scandinavian pedestal to the ranks of the barely surviving.

Although the new comparisons varied from one newspaper and perspective to the next, each one was pejorative: Iceland was included in a 'list of shame' and cited among the 'weaker nations', the 'countries more at risk', and the economies experiencing 'deep-seated solvency problems'.[15] No longer was Iceland generally included among the rich nations—Sweden, Norway, Denmark, Canada and Japan—rather, it appeared alongside Belarus, Ukraine, Pakistan, Hungary, Argentina, Venezuela, Indonesia and Lithuania. In extreme cases, Iceland appeared to be the least favoured among nations. For example:

Le Devoir, October 16, 2008. The original quote read: 'Jouer la carte du FMI risquerait d'être vécu comme une humiliation nationale [pour les Islandais] mais cette option est pourtant jugée inévitable par de nombreux économistes'.
13 According to Johel Sherwood, 'Iceland seen turning to IMF', *Wall Street Journal*, October 17, 2008.
14 Élise Vincent, 'Dans un entretien, le premier ministre islandais, Geir Haarde, évoque la grave crise financière que traverse son pays, il y a encore peu de temps l'un des plus prospères de la planète', Économie, *Le Monde*, October 23, 2008, p. 12. The original quote read: 'Le recours au FMI n'est pas un déshonneur pour l'Islande. Cela crée de la confiance'.
15 Alan Beattie, 'Rescue reforms do not mean cash without strings', *Financial Times*, October 28, 2008.

> Iceland is facing some unfavorable comparisons. Bear Stearns recently suggested the tiny nation was about as safe an investment as Kazakhstan.[16] (*The Guardian*)

> That's a collapse surpassed only by the disastrous demise of the Zimbabwe currency.[17] (*Money Week*)

> Again, it is nothing to boast about. The worst performer is the dollar of Africa's basket-case, Zimbabwe. Among the other big losers are the krona of the near-bankrupt Iceland, the South African rand and the Turkmenistan manat, which after years of rampant inflation is about to be redenominated by dividing it by 5000.[18] (*The Australian*)

Some of these comparisons, of course, are biased; others are unfair and exaggerated. But that means little when it comes to public image. Like the other comments published during the 2008 crisis, these comparisons were added to Iceland's 'record' and contributed to the international perception of the country, now much less positive than it was before.

The Icelandic government quickly understood the benefits it could draw from this reversal of image in its negotiations with the UK and the Netherlands on reimbursement of the savings lost as a result of the Icesave bank's default on payment. It played the sympathy card: a member of Parliament, Pétur Blöndal, told journalists in October 2008 that in order to reimburse the losses of Icesave, Iceland would be subjected to 'the equivalent for every Icelander of three to four times the reparations that were imposed on Germany after the First World

---

16 David Teather, 'Iceland first to feel the blast of global cooling', *Guardian*, April 17, 2008.
17 David Stevenson, 'How Iceland's meltdown affects you', *Money Week*, October 7, 2008.
18 *Australian*, 'Aussie dollar lags the leu, lari and kip', October 31, 2008.

War'.[19] The government tried to use its 'humiliated' status to obtain a reduction in compensatory payments, but did not succeed.

Foreigners were hard on Iceland and had very little sympathy. When the Reykjavík Exchange reopened after a forced three-day shutdown, the *Australian* made a point of mentioning the lamentable state of the Icelandic economy: 'A disfigured Reykjavik stock exchange has reopened, amputated of its once dominant financial stocks that have long made up the cornerstone of Iceland's economy.'[20] The symbols of economic success—subsequently criticized, of course, but which had been sources of national pride, with Glitnir at the top of the list—fell one after the other, dismantled by financial funds that were formerly allies but that were now lured by profit: 'attracted by ... the depressed share price and the weak Icelandic currency'.[21]

More than for any other country, commentators placed Iceland's crisis in a long-term context. They emphasised the nation's great resilience in the face of adversity, sometimes going back to its inception to explain that the catastrophe of 2008 was perhaps neither the worst nor the last that Iceland would have to deal with. Quoting a sociology professor, the *Globe and Mail* stressed the serious breach of honour in the events leading up to and during the crisis: 'The sagas are so much about ... honour, and now we are a dishonoured people. We have behaved like children ... and done damage to people in other countries.'[22] Columnist A.A. Gill wrote that the collapse had been swift and complete, that Iceland had gone from a rich nation to a needy one, 'bobbing in the queue somewhere behind Albania and Moldova'. With typical dry English wit, however, he added that '[it] is not actually the worst thing

---

19 Gary Duncan, 'British savings prove a hurdle to Iceland bailout', *Australian*, October 25, 2008.
20 Agence France-Presse, 'Reykjavik exchange resumes trading', *Australian*, October 15, 2008.
21 David Ibison, 'Glitnir courts international investors', *Financial Times*, May 14, 2008.
22 Þorbjörn Broddason, quoted by Matthew Hart, 'Iceland's next saga. The wounded tiger's tale', *Globe and Mail*, November 15, 2008, p. F-4.

that ever happened to this island. That would have to be the two occasions when the plague wiped out more than half of everybody'.[23]

Discussing an economic crisis in terms of humiliation, pride and foreign image can seem inappropriate unless one remembers the decisive impact of media discourse on a nation's reputation and the degree of trust it enjoys in its dealings with other countries. In Iceland's case, the predominant message conveyed by the media was that of a complete and sudden reversal as the island went from an enviable nation to a humiliated one in the space of a few days. That was not quite the real picture, as Gérard Lemarquis wrote in *Le Monde*: 'There was no lack of warning signs. But Icelanders, hypnotised by mirages of frenzied consumption on credit, never saw a thing coming.'[24] The crisis was nonetheless presented as a sudden reversal of fate—and, according to most foreign commentators, it was experienced as such, too. Examples abound: the *Financial Times*, observing the migration of workers and the large number of Icelanders attracted by offers in Norway, wrote, 'It is a humiliating climbdown for a country that, until a few months ago, imported Polish workers to do its grimy jobs.'[25] This excerpt alludes to the completeness of the reversal, to its suddenness and to a certain lack of moral fibre—three aspects underlying the island's humiliation. In spite of everything, Iceland remains a nation founded on courage and grit. The *Financial Times* summed up the task that lies ahead: 'the nation begins the process of rebuilding its economy and that thing it covets most of all, its reputation.'[26]

The radical change in Iceland's foreign image did not go unnoticed by journalists. *Le Devoir* wrote that 'in the space of a few months …

---

23 A.A. Gill, 'Iceland: frozen assets', *Sunday Times*, December 14, 2008.
24 Gérard Lemarquis, 'Happés par la tourmente, les Islandais lorgnent sur l'Union européenne', Économie, *Le Monde*, October 8, 2008, p. 11. The original quote read: 'Les signes avant-coureurs de la crise n'ont pas manqué. Mais les Islandais, grisés par les mirages d'une hyperconsommation à crédit, n'ont rien vu venir'.
25 Sarah O'Connor, 'Christmas. But not as Reykjavik knows it', *Financial Times*, December 23, 2008.
26 Robert Jackson, 'Letter from Iceland', *Financial Times*, November 15, 2008.

the *small* Nordic country has lost its envied status of success story to become the *sickliest child* in Europe'.[27] *Small* and *sickliest child*—the words leave little doubt as to the drastic nature of the change. It was a hard fall from the image of Viking associated not long before with Iceland's financial wizards: 'The country found itself transformed in a few weeks of headlines from rampaging Viking tiger to global deadbeat—a country whose bankers had annihilated not only the security of their countrymen but the savings of tens of thousands of other depositors.'[28] By the end of the year, Iceland had joined the ranks of the emerging economies. For *La Presse*, Iceland was now 'credit island';[29] for the BBC, the country had earned 'a pariah status in the financial system'.[30] Iceland was now a poor example and its global influence would be harmful. Investors, nervous about its financial straits, fled other fragile economies too, such as Pakistan, Argentina, Ukraine and Latvia, to the great dismay of their governments.[31]

For the people of Iceland, 'insolvency entered the Icelandic vocabulary as did the International Monetary Fund'.[32] But above all, for many citizens, Iceland suddenly lost its status as an obscure nation, quietly minding its own business behind the scenes, to be dragged across the world stage in a humiliating role. This quote appeared in the *New York Times*: 'Years ago, I would say that I was Icelandic and people might say, "Oh, where's that?"' said Katrin Runolfsdottir, 49, who was

---

27 Agence France-Presse, 'L'Islande se démène sur tous les fronts pour éviter la faillite', *Le Devoir*, October 16, 2008 (italics added). The original quote read: 'en l'espace de quelques mois [...] le *petit* pays nordique a perdu son statut envié de success story pour celui *d'enfant* le plus *malade* d'Europe'.
28 Matthew Hart, 'Iceland's next saga. The wounded tiger's tale', *Globe and Mail*, November 15, 2008, p. F-4.
29 Vincent Brousseau-Pouliot, 'Les gagnants et perdants d'une année folle', *La Presse* (Montréal), December 24, 2008. The original quote read: 'l'île du crédit'.
30 Jon Danielsson, 'Why raising interest rates won't work', *BBC News*, October 28, 2008.
31 See, for example, David Oakley, 'Emerging nations hit by growing debt fears', *Financial Times*, October 14, 2008, p. 15.
32 *Financial Times*, 'Iceland, i-banks and jobs', December 30, 2008, p. 10.

fired from her secretarial job on Oct. 31. "That was fine. But now there's this image of us being overspenders, thieves".[33]

Humiliation, a damaged reputation, a demoralised population: what happened to make the global economic crisis choose as its epicentre a small island nation at the edge of Europe, a nation that had been playing according to the rules defined by the big economic powers? David Ibison of the *Financial Times* offered a chilling hypothesis: he speculated that Iceland may have been used as a neo-liberal laboratory by people curious to see just how far their economic theories could be pushed. Iceland's growth would be nothing but an 'experiment' in which honest, hard-working citizens were provided with all the means they needed to test the limits of economic liberalism. In 2008, the results clearly showed that the failure was complete and that certain thresholds could not be crossed in the liberalisation of markets. By November, it could be said that the experiment was finished:

> The huge rescue package and its damaging domestic effect mark the official end of a 17-year experiment in free market economics that transformed Iceland from a fishing-based backwater to a booming tiger economy and now to the humiliation of an IMF-led bail-out.[34]

Icelanders have something to be angry about. Economic humiliation is conceivable and can be gotten over; the country has been through much worse, and each time it has been able to pick itself up. But the humiliation of having been manipulated like puppets, of having served as an experiment set up by invisible hands, is beyond the limits of what is acceptable. The technical, strategic and financial issues underlying the Icelandic crisis no doubt have their importance, but

---

[33] Katrín Runólfsdóttir, quoted by Sarah Lyall, 'Stunned Icelanders struggle after economy's fall', *New York Times*, November 9, 2008.
[34] David Ibison, 'Reykjavik borrows $10bn to stave off economic collapse', *Financial Times*, November 20, 2008. Ibison had already put forth this theory in an earlier article: 'Iceland requests $2bn bail-out from IMF', *Financial Times*, October 24, 2008.

are dwarfed by its effects on a people who have fascinated the world for generations and who have represented a model throughout history for many observers.

The study of a country's image through foreign media contained in these pages also tells us about the limits and inaccuracies that can occur when a crisis is reported abroad wich such unexpected intensity. Much of this discourse may be considered imprecise—or even unsettling—by Icelanders, but one thing remains: this himalaya of foreign discourse constitutes for many foreigners their only image of Iceland, a fact which can no longer be ignored by Icelanders in their relations with others.

CHRONOLOGY

A FEW HISTORICAL POINTS OF REFERENCE

874	Beginning of the settlement of Iceland.
930	Beginning of the 'Saga Age'.
1000	Iceland becomes Christian.
1262	Iceland is brought under the Norwegian crown.
1380	Iceland is brought under the Danish crown.
1944	Following a referendum, Iceland proclaims its independence.
1975-1976	Tense diplomatic relations between Iceland and Great Britain over Iceland's fishery limits, escalating into a 'Cod War' which Iceland wins.
1980	Vigdís Finnbogadóttir is elected President of Iceland—the first woman to be elected a constitutional head of state in Europe.
1982	Davíð Oddsson is elected Mayor of Reykjavík, an office he would hold until 1991.
1989	Jón Ásgeir Jóhannesson and his father, Jóhannes Jónsson, open the first Bonus supermarket, which would become a chain that provided a launching pad for the Baugur conglomerate.
1991	Davíð Oddsson is elected Prime Minister of Iceland, an office he would hold until 2004. Beginning of the bank privatisation policy.
1994	Iceland becomes a member of the European Economic Area.
1996	Ólafur Ragnar Grímsson is elected President of Iceland.
1998	Geir Haarde is appointed Minister of Finance, a position he would hold until 2005.
2001	Davíð Oddsson allows the Icelandic krona to fluctuate on markets.
	Implementation of the *Anti-Terrorism, Crime and Security Act* in the United Kingdom following the September 11 attacks in New York.
2002	Björgólfur Thor Björgólfsson, a 'new Viking' businessman, acquires a 45% share of Landsbanki.
2003	Kaupþing becomes Iceland's largest bank following a merger.
	Baugur becomes the largest Icelandic conglomerate with operations abroad.

2004	Halldór Ásgrímsson is elected Prime Minister of Iceland. He appoints Davíð Oddsson Minister of Foreign Affairs.
2005	Fraud charges are brought against Jón Ásgeir Jóhannesson, most of which would later be dropped. Jón Ásgeir Jóhannesson accuses Davíð Oddsson of orchestrating a vendetta against him.
	Davíð Oddsson is appointed Governor of the Central Bank of Iceland.
2007	Gordon Brown is elected Prime Minister of the United Kingdom. He appoints Alistair Darling Chancellor of the Exchequer.
	Britain-based professor Robert Wade gives a controversial speech in Reykjavík in which he cautions about the risks involved in Iceland's financial expansion abroad.
	Professor Richard Portes and colleagues publish a report entitled *The Internationalisation of Iceland's Financial Sector* for the Iceland Chamber of Commerce.

2008–THE YEAR OF THE CRISIS

January 10	The *Financial Times* reports that the Icelandic firm Gnupur Investment 'was forced to announce an emergency recapitalisation programme yesterday'.
January 29	According to *Le Monde*, Iceland ranks at the top of the United Nations Development Programme (UNDP) index.
	The *Financial Times* reports that, according to Moody's Investors Service, Iceland's rating was at a crossroads 'because of the perceived fragility of the country's banks'.
March 4	A financial adviser tells the *Financial Times* that markets are starting to react badly to Iceland, saying that 'there is a general dislike of Iceland; every movement in the market gets magnified when it comes to Iceland'.
March 6	Moody's lowers Iceland's rating. According to the *Financial Times*, 'the downgrade is the latest in a series of moves by Moody's that indicate it is gradually losing confidence in the ability of the nation to avoid a banking crisis'.
	Following this news, the *Financial Times* reports a drop in the value of the krona, stating that 'Iceland's krona plunged to a record low against the euro after rating agency Moody's changed the country's outlook to "negative"'.
March 8	*Le Monde* reports that Iceland's banking sector now holds assets eight times greater than the country's gross domestic product.
March 23	Iceland is likened to 'one big toxic hedge fund' in an article appearing in the *Telegraph*: 'The story doesn't make sense any more. Nobody wants anything to do with it.'

March 25	Rumours of a crisis erode Iceland's reputation. According to the *Financial Times*, 'the uncomfortable fact for Iceland is that the rumours and talk of a crisis could create the crisis.'
March 28	The *Financial Times* reports that rumours of a conspiracy against Iceland are circulating in the news.
March 29	The *Globe and Mail* reports that the Central Bank of Iceland has raised its key interest rate to 15% in an attempt to support the value of the krona.
April 9	The *Financial Times* writes that 'banking sector assets [in Iceland] have grown from about 96 per cent of GDP in 2000 to about 10 times today—the main source of concern about the country'.
April 11	The *Financial Times* reports that the key interest rate of 15% has not slowed the fall of the krona.
April 17	The head of Landsbanki is quoted by the *New York Times* as asserting that 'it is almost unthinkable to us that we would default'.
April 18	Iceland's rating is downgraded by one credit rating agency after another.
April 21	The *International Herald Tribune* states that four French military planes would be flying over Icelandic airspace to provide protection against hostile Russian aircraft.
May 20	The *Guardian* prints the findings of a study indicating that Iceland is the safest and most peaceful country in the world.
May 28	The *Financial Times* reports that 'Iceland is seeking permission from parliament to borrow up to IKr500bn, its largest ever loan, in a move that would more than double existing foreign exchange reserves and provide further support for its troubled currency and banking system'.
June 3	The *Globe and Mail* wonders whether Iceland's situation could be a sign of a more widespread crisis: 'The question is whether Iceland is the first of several dominoes to fall—or a unique case.'
September 14	The *New York Times* reveals that the American investment bank Lehman Brothers would be filing for bankruptcy protection under the US Bankruptcy Code, signalling a global financial crisis.
September 29	The *International Herald Tribune* reports that the Icelandic government has acquired a 75% stake in Glitnir, the country's third largest bank.
September 30	The *Globe and Mail* expresses concern about the rapid global expansion of the crisis, stating that 'the financial crisis [has] spread like wildfire'.
October 3	The *Financial Times* reports that it now costs Iceland the record amount of 1.3 million euros to service its 10 million euro debt.
October 4	Robert Preston writes on *BBC News* that 'the best way of seeing Iceland is as a country that turned itself into a giant hedge fund', adding that 'it's difficult to see how it can re-float without international help'.

October 5	In an article published by the *Guardian* entitled 'The party's over for Iceland, the island that tried to buy the world', Tracy McVeigh writes that 'Iceland is on the brink of collapse. ... The krona, Iceland's currency, is in freefall and is rated just above those of Zimbabwe and Turkmenistan'.
October 6	The *Financial Times* quotes Antje Praefcke, a Commerzbank analyst, as saying: 'We would also not be surprised to see the Icelandic krona lose its function as a medium of payment'.
	The BBC reveals that six financial institutions in Iceland, including the three main banks—Glitnir, Kaupþing and Landsbanki, have suspended operations.
	The *Financial Times* indicates that the Icelandic government is trying to obtain international assistance to deal with the crisis.
	Geir Haarde states that Iceland could face bankruptcy: 'We were faced with the real possibility that the national economy would be sucked into the global banking swell and end in national bankruptcy.'
October 7	Beginning of tense diplomatic relations between Iceland and the United Kingdom.
	Iceland dominates the headlines of world news: 'All eyes were on the meltdown under way in Iceland', writes the *International Herald Tribune*.
	The *Financial Times* indicates that the krona has lost 45% of its value.
	The *Guardian* announces that the Icelandic government has taken control of Landsbanki, after nationalising Glitnir.
October 8	British Chancellor Alistair Darling tells the BBC that 'the Icelandic government, believe it or not, told me yesterday they have no intention of honouring their obligations here'.
	The United Kingdom invokes anti-terrorism legislation to freeze the assets of the Landsbanki and Kaupþing banks in the U.K.
	The headline of the October 8 edition of the *Financial Times* reads 'Small island, big problem'.
	Willem H. Buiter indicates that the entire world's banking system seems to be at risk, telling the *International Herald Tribune* that 'there is no such thing as a safe bank now'.
	The *Globe and Mail* writes that Iceland 'lined up an emergency infusion of cash from Russia in an increasingly desperate attempt to avoid financial collapse'.
	During an interview broadcast on Icelandic television, Davíð Oddsson declares that 'we will not pay for irresponsible debtors and ... not for banks who have behaved irresponsibly'.
	A financial adviser tells the *Financial Times* that 'Iceland will go down in history as a textbook example of how excess credit can derail an economy'.

October 9	According to *Le Monde*, 'the entire country of Iceland is in bankruptcy today' ('en Islande aujourd'hui, c'est le pays tout entier qui est en faillite').
	Geir Haarde considers the United Kingdom's use of anti-terrorism legislation to be hostile, telling the *International Herald Tribune* that 'we did not consider this to be a particularly friendly act'.
	Bloomberg news agency reports that the Icelandic krona is no longer being traded on markets.
	In an article entitled 'Iceland is all but officially bankrupt', the *International Herald Tribune* announces the government takeover of Kaupþing, Iceland's largest bank, 'completing the nationalization of the country's banking system'.
	BusinessWeek reports that an International Monetary Fund (IMF) delegation has arrived in Reykjavík. Geir Haarde says he does not believe that IMF assistance will be necessary.
October 10	The crisis is considered a global one. The *New York Times* writes that 'we're all in this together, and need a shared solution'.
	Foreign media, including the Russian news agency Novosti, report that Iceland requested a loan from Russia, since it was unable to obtain support from its traditional allies. The news stirs up concern in the West.
October 11	According to the *Financial Times*, Iceland's wealthy entrepreneurs are fleeing the country.
October 13	The United Kingdom is concerned about the conflict with Iceland. The *Financial Times* writes that 'we [the U.K.] always seem to be at odds with this independent-minded nation'.
October 14	The *Financial Times* quotes an Icelandic government official as saying, in reference to the country's economic straits, that 'it's typical, the men make the mess, and the women clean it up'.
	The Glasgow *Herald* reports that trading on the Reykjavík exchange has been suspended, allegedly because of 'unusual market conditions'. From opening, the market index plunged by 76%.
October 15	Iceland's situation worries other countries. *Le Monde* writes that 'Iceland has sunk into a deep coma: it must be revived immediately' ('L'Islande a basculé dans un coma profond : il faut la ranimer au plus vite').
October 16	U.S. *Forbes* magazine publishes a commentary entitled 'Gordon Brown Killed Iceland'.
	Le Monde publishes an analysis on Icelandic women entering positions of power after the crisis, 'Women: The Antidote to the Market Crisis' ('Les femmes, antidote à la crise boursière').
October 17	An Internet user puts Iceland up for sale on eBay, with bidding starting at 99 pence. The news makes its way around the globe.

October 19	Iceland's international image is severely affected by the crisis. The *New York Times* writes: 'Who knew? Who knew that Iceland was just a hedge fund with glaciers? Who knew?'
October 20	Iceland's financial supervisory authority, the FME, announces the creation of three 'new banks': Nýi Glitnir, Nýja Kaupþing and Nýi Landsbanki.
October 22	The crisis provides food for thought about the merits of membership in a large union. One economic advisor tells the *Globe and Mail* that 'the worst thing at the moment is to be a small country like Denmark or Iceland'.
	According to *Le Monde*, Iceland is to announce the implementation of a $6 billion rescue plan 'involving the International Monetary Fund (IMF) and several central banks to help the country through the crisis' ('regroupant le Fonds monétaire international (FMI) et plusieurs banques centrales, pour aider le pays à sortir de la crise').
October 23	Icelandic Prime Minister Geir Haarde tells *Le Monde*, in reference to supervision of the banks, that 'we undoubtedly did not pay enough attention' ('Nous n'avons sans doute toutefois pas fait assez attention').
October 24	The *Financial Times* confirms that Iceland will be the first Western nation to receive IMF assistance since the United Kingdom in 1976.
	The *Australian* believes that Iceland has ruined its reputation: 'But are we to assume that in all the rest of the world [beside Wall Street] only Iceland is comparably immoral?'
October 28	The *Globe and Mail* reports that Icelanders are now in favour of joining the European Union: 'A poll in an Icelandic newspaper yesterday showed public support for entering the EU and adopting the euro at 70 per cent.'
	David Ibison writes in the *Financial Times*: 'Iceland's central bank lifted interest rates on Tuesday from 12 per cent to 18 per cent on the orders of the International Monetary Fund, highlighting the dramatic impact the organization will have on the country's ability to control economic policy.'
October 29	Iceland is now among the countries humiliated by financial difficulties: 'Hungary has joined the "list of shame" along with teetering Iceland, Belarus, Ukraine and Pakistan', writes the *Financial Times*.
November 9	A financial analyst tells the *New York Times* that 'no country has ever crashed as quickly and as badly in peacetime' as Iceland.
November 11	According to the *Financial Times*, there are rumours that the United Kingdom will block the IMF loan to Iceland.
November 13	An article appearing in the *Globe and Mail* calls for Iceland alone to assume responsibility, stating that 'there is little excuse for Iceland, which essentially turned itself into a highly leveraged hedge fund'.

November 15 — Writer Sjón calls for a return to more humanistic values: 'So let's return to what we were—a humanist society.'

November 18 — The Glasgow *Herald* affirms that an Icesave agreement is to be signed by Iceland and the United Kingdom. Iceland will pay back what it owes abroad in order to obtain IMF assistance.

November 20 — Reuters news agency reports that Iceland has been granted IMF assistance of $2.1 billion. Denmark, Finland, Norway, Sweden, Russia, Poland, the Faeroe Islands, Great Britain, the Netherlands and Germany have contributed to a separate emergency fund that is over and above the IMF aid.

November 26 — *BBC News* reports that Iceland's annual inflation rate has climbed to a record level of 17%.

December 1 — Newspapers in different countries, including *Dagsavisen* in Norway, publish a letter by Geir Haarde in which he thanks the countries that have helped Iceland through the crisis.

December 16 — *BBC News* quotes Geir Haarde as saying that Iceland will initiate legal proceedings against the United Kingdom for the collapse of Kaupþing bank.

December 18 — *BBC News* quotes an IMF adviser in Iceland as saying that 'the worst was behind the country'.

December 19 — The decline of the krona spurs a tourism boom. As the *Washington Post* puts it, 'they're calling it [Iceland] Halfpriceland'.

December 20 — *Le Monde* reports that singer Björk has set up an investment fund to 'cure Iceland's economy' ('guérir l'économie islandaise').

December 24 — In its retrospective of the year 2008, *La Presse* (Montréal) indicates that the Reykjavík stock exchange index for 2008 was -94.5%.

December 31 — In its year-end ratings, the *Globe and Mail* grants 'the Alan Greenspan Prize for Bubble Blowing... to Iceland'.

2009—THE YEAR AFTER THE CRISIS

January 1 — According to the *Globe and Mail*, a year-end television broadcast with Geir Haarde was disrupted by a demonstration.

January 9 — The *Economist* forecasts a 10% contraction in economic activity in Iceland in 2009.

January 23 — The *International Herald Tribune* reports that the most violent incidents in Iceland since its independence took place as protesters called for the Prime Minister to step down.

Geir Haarde announces that he will not run in the next election, to be held on May 9.

January 24	An article appearing in *Le Monde* is entitled 'Iceland's bankruptcy prompts the first clashes with police in Reykjavík in 60 years' ('La faillite de l'Islande provoque à Reykjavik les premiers heurts avec la police depuis 60 ans').
January 26	*BBC News* announces the resignation of Geir Haarde and his government.
January 30	*Time* magazine reports that Iceland will have the world's first gay head of state. A new government, formed by a coalition headed by Jóhanna Sigurðardóttir, will take office on February 1.
February 5	The *Independent* reports that the Baugur conglomerate has filed for bankruptcy protection.
February 26	*GroundReport* announces that a new law voted in by the Icelandic government will enable it to dismiss Central Bank governors. The measure is implemented following Davíð Oddsson's refusal to resign. The Central Bank is restructured and new directors are appointed.
February 27	According to the *Wall Street Journal*, the Icelandic government has put some of its properties abroad up for sale.
March 26	*Reuters.com* reports that former Prime Minister Geir Haarde has apologised for being partly responsible for the crisis.
April 10	*Le Monde* reports that Norwegian-French judge, Eva Joly, has been appointed by the Icelandic government to head the commission of inquiry into the crisis.
May 10	According to an article from Agence France-Presse, the new Icelandic government wants to expedite the country's entry into the European Union. According to a survey by RUV national radio, 61.2% of Icelanders are in favour of joining the EU.
July 1	Eva Joly publishes a letter entitled 'Iceland or false pretenses of post-crisis regulation' ('L'Islande ou les faux semblants de la régulation de l'après-crise'), in several newspapers, including *Le Monde* and the *Telegraph*, in which she urges European countries to assume a share of responsibility for Iceland's debacle.
July 23	*L'Express* reports that Össur Skarphéðinsson, the Icelandic Minister of Foreign Affairs, filed his country's application for membership in the European Union in Stockholm.
August 4	*Le Monde* reveals that 'Iceland is dealing with a banking scandal of several billion euros' ('l'Islande [fait] face à un scandale bancaire de plusieurs milliards d'euros'), as unsecured loans were granted by Kaupþing bank to its main shareholders in 2008 just days before the bank was taken over by the government.
September 23	Davíð Oddsson becomes editor in chief of *Morgunbladid*, the main Icelandic daily. A month later, the newspaper *DV* claims that one quarter of *Morgunbladid*'s readership (10,000 individuals) cancelled their subscriptions in protest.

November 6   Fitch Ratings agency gives the Icelandic banking system the worst possible rating, an 'E', the lowest ever assigned in the West.

November 18   The Icelandic newspaper *Morgunbladid* claims that the lawsuits against Landsbanki alone total 35 billion euros.

December 31   The *Guardian* reports that a divided Icelandic parliament voted in favour of settling the Icesave case.

2010

January 5   In an unexpected move, Icelandic President Ólafur Ragnar Grímsson defends the veto and refuses to sign the Icesave bill, forcing the government to hold a referendum and angering the United Kingdom and the Netherlands.

BIBLIOGRAPHY

Agence France-Presse, 'Björk donne son nom à un fonds d'investissement islandais', *Cyberpresse*, December 18, 2008.

Agence France-Presse, 'Crise. L'Islande nationalise ses banques à marche forcée', *Le Devoir*, October 10, 2008.

Agence France-Presse, 'Égalité hommes-femmes: les pays nordiques toujours en tête', *Le Devoir*, November 12, 2008.

Agence France-Presse, 'Gordon Brown in Saudi Arabia to calm economic storm', *Australian*, November 2, 2008.

Agence France-Presse, 'Iceland acting illegally in freezing accounts—UK PM', *Australian*, October 10, 2008.

Agence France-Presse, 'Iceland PM says could sue Britain over savings row', *Australian*, October 13, 2008.

Agence France-Presse, 'L'ambassade de Chine en Islande proteste contre la chanteuse Björk', Culture, *Le Monde*, March 8, 2008, p. 24.

Agence France-Presse, 'L'Islande enclenche le processus d'adhésion à l'UE', *Cyberpresse*, May 10, 2009.

Agence France-Presse, 'L'Islande prend le contrôle d'une quatrième banque', *Le Monde*, March 9, 2009.

Agence France-Presse, 'L'Islande se démène sur tous les fronts pour éviter la faillite', *Le Devoir*, October 16, 2008.

Agence France-Presse, 'L'Islande, véritable geyser musical', *Le Devoir*, June 16, 2008.

Agence France-Presse, 'La candidature de l'Islande à l'UE promet un bras de fer sur la pêche', *L'Express*, July 23, 2009.

Agence France-Presse, 'La CBI vers un ultime effort de négociation', *Cyberpresse*, June 22, 2009.

Agence France-Presse, 'La chanteuse Björk crée un fonds pour "guérir l'économie islandaise"', Économie, *Le Monde*, December 20, 2008, p. 15.

Agence France-Presse, 'Marchés boursiers. Nervosité sans précédent des marchés', *Le Devoir*, October 18, 2008.

Agence France-Presse, 'UN report finds Australia third worst in developed world', *Australian*, December 12, 2008.

Agence France-Presse, 'Une majorité d'Islandais souhaite l'adhésion à l'Union européenne', International, *Le Monde*, February 28, 2008, p. 9.

Agence France-Presse and Associated Press, 'L'Islande s'enfonce dans la crise', *Le Devoir*, October 9, 2008.

Albrechtsen, Janet, 'Europe worse off than the US', *Australian*, October 29, 2008.

Aldred, Jessica, 'Iceland's energy answer comes naturally', *Guardian*, April 22, 2008.

Anderson, Robert and David Oakley, 'Icelandic bank shares and the krona remain in front line of turmoil', *Financial Times*, October 1, 2008, p. 27.

Anderson, Robert and Tom Braithwaite, 'Icelandic bank Kaupthing fights for survival', *Financial Times*, October 9, 2008, p. 16.

Anderson, Robert, 'Big banks break up in effort to restore confidence', *Financial Times*, October 8, 2008, p. 4.

Anderson, Robert, 'Elisa board survives attack', *Financial Times*, January 22, 2008, p. 18.

Anderson, Robert, 'Fears grow of Baltic states' addiction to external capital', *Financial Times*, April 18, 2008, p. 25.

Anderson, Robert, 'Glitnir funds fail to stop fear', *Financial Times*, September 30, 2008, p. 8.

Angus, Coupar and Pete Ellis, 'The way ahead', *Herald* (Glasgow), October 16, 2008.

Associated Press, 'Raiding Reykjavik', *Globe and Mail*, October 11, 2008, p. F-2.

Atkins, Ralph, 'Euro stability helps big and small to forge common goal', *Financial Times*, October 17, 2008, p. 2.

Atkins, Ralph, 'Germans take the credit for crisis jokes', *Financial Times*, December 24, 2008, p. 3.

Australian Associated Press, 'Reykjavik exchange resumes trading', *Australian*, October 15, 2008.

Australian, 'Aussie dollar lags the leu, lari and kip', October 31, 2008.

Australian, 'Iceland's economic collapse could herald a new round of large-scale acquisitions', October 9, 2008.

Bailey, Bill, 'Icelandic bank collapse raises questions for UK', *Financial Times*, October 9, 2008, p. 10.

Balakrishnan, Angela, 'U.K. to sue Iceland over any lost bank savings', *Guardian*, October 8, 2008.

Baldursson, Friðrik Már and Richard Portes, 'Criticism of Icelandic economy does not square with the facts', *Financial Times*, July 4, 2008, p. 14.

Banning, Cees and Jan Gerritsen, 'Dutch and British block IMF loan to Iceland', *NRC Handelsblad*, November 7, 2008.

Barber, Lionel, 'How gamblers broke the banks', *Financial Times*, December 15, 2008.

Barber, Peter, 'On the lookout for a happy ending', *Financial Times*, September 29, 2008, p. 10.

Barber, Tony, 'Note to Europe: we are not all saints', *Financial Times*, December 9, 2008, p. 12.

Barker, Alex, Tom Braithwaite and Jennifer Hugues, 'Kaupthing searches for answers', *Financial Times*, October 10, 2008, p. 23.

Barker, Alex, Tom Braithwaite, Sarah O'Connor, Jim Pickard and Nicholas Timmins, 'Scene set for court battle over deposits', *Financial Times*, October 17, 2008, p. 2.

Barker, Alex, Tom Braithwaite and Michael Peel, 'Iceland frosty as London gets tough', *Financial Times*, October 9, 2008, p. 5.

Barker, Alex, Tom Braithwaite and Anousha Sakoui, 'Iceland may hold UK store stakes', *Financial Times*, December 29, 2008.

Batstone, Jeremy, 'Is Iceland facing a meltdown?' *Money Week*, May 18, 2006.

Bauder, David [Associated Press], 'Dollar goes a long way on winter trip to Iceland', *Daily Times* (Delaware), January 6, 2009.

Beattie, Alan, 'IMF ready to help out emerging market states', *Financial Times*, October 11, 2008, p. 5.

Beattie, Alan, 'Rescue reforms do not mean cash without strings', *Financial Times*, October 28, 2008.

Begg, Alastair, 'Problem of "hidden poverty" in Iceland', *Herald* (Glasgow), October 22, 2008.

Begg, Alastair, 'The real facts', *Herald* (Glasgow), November 5, 2008.

Bekmezian, Hélène, 'L'Islande face à un scandale bancaire de plusieurs milliards d'euros', *Le Monde*, August 4, 2009.

Belton, Catherine and Tom Braithwaite, 'Iceland asks Russia for €4bn after West refuses to help', *Financial Times*, October 8, 2008, p. 4.

Benoit, Bertrand and James Wilson, 'Berlin guarantees savings in effort to avoid panic', *Financial Times*, October 6, 2008, p. 1.

Bertrand, Benoit et al, 'Iceland and UK clash on crisis', *Financial Times*, October 10, 2008, p. 1.

Berès, Pervenche, 'L'Europe dans un angle mort. La réponse de l'Union à la crise a été une juxtaposition de plans nationaux, sans aucune stratégie', Dialogues, *Le Monde*, November 14, 2008, p. 20.

Berglund, Nina, 'Norway sends aid team to crisis-hit Iceland', *Afterposten*, October 22, 2008.

Bérubé, Gérard, 'Panique sur les places boursières', *Le Devoir*, October 7, 2008.

Blitz, James, 'British corporate leaders to visit Russia', *Financial Times*, October 20, 2008.

Bolger, Andrew, 'Union made RBS injection possible, says Prime Minister', *Financial Times*, October 15, 2008, p. 2.

Bounds, Andrew, 'Douglas to spend £150m for Kaupthing savers', *Financial Times*, October 23, 2008.

Boyes, Roger, 'Iceland braces for Brits wanting their money back', *Australian*, October 13, 2008.

Boyes, Roger, 'Skating on thin ice', *Australian*, October 10, 2008.

Braiden, Gerry, 'Icelandair suspends all Scottish flights amid downturn', *Herald* (Glasgow), October 27, 2008.

Braithwaite, Tom, 'Baugur evades Icelandic chill', *Financial Times*, October 4, 2008, p. 19.

Braithwaite, Tom, 'Baugur in talks over move to Britain', *Financial Times*, June 29, 2008.

Braithwaite, Tom, 'Chastened Baugur hopes to navigate debt crisis', *Financial Times*, October 31, 2008.

Braithwaite, Tom, 'Confusion grows over Iceland's rescue plan', *Financial Times*, October 6, 2008.

Braithwaite, Tom, 'Falling krona exposes consumer debt', *Financial Times*, October 7, 2008, p. 5.

Braithwaite, Tom, 'Iceland attacks "friends" for lack of support', *Financial Times*, October 7, 2008.

Braithwaite, Tom, 'Iceland takes emergency action', *Financial Times*, October 6, 2008.

Braithwaite, Tom, 'Iceland's biggest bank gets Swedish loan', *Financial Times*, October 8, 2008.

Braithwaite, Tom, 'Kaupthing goes into administration in UK', *Financial Times*, October 8, 2008.

Braithwaite, Tom, 'Reykjavik steps in with new powers', *Financial Times*, October 8, 2008, p. 4.

Braithwaite, Tom, 'The fraud claims that are taking their toll on Baugur', *Financial Times*, March 19, 2008, p. 27.

Braithwaite, Tom, Kate Burgess and Sarah O'Connor, 'A cruel wind', *Financial Times*, October 10, 2008.

Braithwaite, Tom and Lucy Killgren, 'The men behind the invasion into Britain's retail domain', *Financial Times*, October 4, 2008, p. 19.

Braithwaite, Tom, Andres Magnusson and Sarah O'Connor, 'Johannesson set to cede Baugur control to Green', *Financial Times*, October 13, 2008, p. 22.

Braithwaite, Tom and Elizabeth Rigby, 'BHS chief touches down on mission to Iceland', *Financial Times*, October 11, 2008, p. 15.

Brignall, Miles, Patrick Collinson and David Teather, 'Customers face anxious wait over fate of Icesave accounts', *Guardian*, October 7, 2008.

Brignall, Miles and Hilary Osborne, 'Icesave freezes deposits and withdrawals', *Guardian*, October 7, 2008.

Brousseau-Pouliot, Vincent, 'Les gagnants et perdants d'une année folle', *La Presse* (Montréal), December 24, 2008.

Brown, Mark and Michael Wilson, 'Moody's cuts Iceland's bond ratings to one notch above junk', *Wall Street Journal*, November 12, 2009.

Brown-Humes, Christopher, Joanna Chung and Sarah O'Connor, 'Credit storm rolls across Icelandic landscape', *Financial Times*, March 4, 2008, p. 29.

Brynjólfsson, Bjarni, 'Bright light to pitch-black night', *Iceland Review*, vol. 46, no. 4, 2008.

Brynjólfsson, Bjarni, 'Escaping Reykjavik', *Iceland Review*, vol. 47, no. 1, 2009.

Brynjólfsson, Bjarni, 'Pipe dreams come true', *Iceland Review*, vol. 46, no. 3, 2008.

Brynjólfsson, Bjarni, 'The pots and pans revolution', *Iceland Review*, vol. 47, no. 1, 2009.

Buiter, Willem, 'There is no excuse for Britain not to join the euro', *Financial Times*, June 3, 2008, p. 9.

Buiter, Willem H. and Anne Sibert, 'The Icelandic banking crisis and what to do about it: The lender of last resort theory of optimal currency areas', *CEPR Policy Insight*, no. 26, October 2008.

Burns, Greg, 'Financial fiasco fires up Iceland's ire, civic unrest', *Chicago Tribune*, January 2, 2009.

Burns, Jimmy and Michael Peel, 'Warning on use of anti-terror law to freeze bank assets', *Financial Times*, October 10, 2008, p. 3.

Campbell, Duncan, 'World "more peaceful" in 2008', *Guardian*, May 20, 2008.

Campbell-Johnston, Rachel, 'Wrys and falls of a natural showman', *Australian*, May 1, 2008.

Canadian Press, 'La crise? C'est la faute aux médias!', *Le Devoir*, January 8, 2009.

Capell, Kerry, 'The stunning collapse of Iceland', *BusinessWeek*, October 9, 2008.

Cato, Jeremy and Michael Vaughan, 'Luxury cars', *Globe and Mail*, November 25, 2008, p. F-8.

Charap, Samuel and Andrew Kuchins, 'Russia's peace offensive', *International Herald Tribune*, October 13, 2008.

Ching, Frank, 'It's in China's own interest to extend a helping hand', *Globe and Mail*, October 15, 2008, p. A-25.

Chung, Joanna and Sarah O'Connor, 'Iceland's prime minister calls on its banks to curb expansion plans', *Financial Times*, March 3, 2008, p. 19.

Cienski, Jan and Thomas Escritt, 'New EU members spared worst of crisis', *Financial Times*, October 11, 2008, p. 13.

Clover, Charles, David Ibison and Sarah O'Connor, 'Iceland works on Russian deal', *Financial Times*, October 15, 2008, p. 9.

Cohen, Roger, 'Cohen: history and the really weird', *International Herald Tribune*, October 12, 2008.

Correspondents in London and Reykjavik, 'Another Iceland bank for rescue by Government', *Australian*, October 10, 2008.

Crichton, Torcuil, 'Chancellor pledges £2.2bn to UK depositors in Iceland bank', *Herald* (Glasgow), November 21, 2008.

Daily Telegraph, 'Iceland for sale on eBay for 99p', October 10, 2008.

Danielsson, Jon, 'Icesave and the bankruptcy of a country', *Financial Times*, November 12, 2008.

Danielsson, Jon, 'Waking up to reality in Iceland', *BBC News*, January 26, 2009.

Danielsson, Jon, 'Why raising interest rates won't work', *BBC News*, October 28, 2008.

Davíðsdóttir, Sigrún, 'In a small community, much can be left unsaid', *Financial Times*, March 31, 2008, p. 12.

Davies, Paul J. and Peter Garnham, 'Iceland agrees 1.5bn swap scheme with neighbours', *Financial Times*, May 16, 2008.

DeCloet, Derek, 'Credit crisis. Smells like Norway in 1990', *Globe and Mail*, July 17, 2008, p. B-2.

Delesalle, Nicolas, 'Les révoltés du geyser', *Télérama*, no. 3086, March 8, 2009.

Delhommais, Pierre-Antoine, 'L'heure de vérité pour l'euro', *Le Monde*, December 15, 2008, p. 25.

Delhommais, Pierre-Antoine, 'La solvabilité des États commence à préoccuper les opérateurs', Économie, *Le Monde*, October 13, 2008, p. 12.

Deutsche Presse-Agentur, 'Snowball punishment for Iceland's vilified financial wizard', *Earthtimes*, December 18, 2008.

Devine, Frank, 'Upstart Yanks aren't bowing out', *Australian*, October 24, 2008.

Dion, Jean, 'Hors-jeu. Huit par huit', *Le Devoir*, August 11, 2008.

Dixon, Hugo and Edward Hadas, 'Le syndrome islandais guette le Royaume-Uni', Économie, *Le Monde*, November 18, 2008, p. 17.

Dixon, Laura, 'Iceland's Sterling airline collapses', *Australian*, October 30, 2008.

Dougherty, Carter, 'Buffeted by financial crisis, countries seek euro's shelter', *International Herald Tribune*, December 1, 2008.

Dougherty, Carter, 'EU ministers approve broad measures to combat evolving crisis', *New York Times*, October 7, 2008.

Dougherty, Carter and Landon Thomas Jr., 'Britain earmarks $87 billion to bail out banks', *International Herald Tribune*, October 8, 2008.

Dougherty, Carter and Landon Thomas Jr., 'Britain's bank bailout worth hundreds of billions', *International Herald Tribune*, October 8, 2008.

Duncan, Gary, 'British savings prove a hurdle to Iceland bailout', *Australian*, October 25, 2008.

Dutchnews, 'Iceland may reject one billion euro Dutch loan', *NRC Handelsblad*, November 13, 2008.

Economist, 'Cracks in the crust', December 11, 2008.

Elliott, Alex, 'Eva Joly criticises Europe over Iceland debt', *Icenews*, August 4, 2009.

Ellson, Andrew, 'Icelandic savings bank Icesave crashes', *Times* from the *Australian*, October 9, 2008.

Erlingsdóttir, Íris, 'Iceland—The nordic Zimbabwe', *Huffington Post*, January 5, 2009.

Erlingsdóttir, Íris, 'Iceland is burning', *Huffington Post*, January 20, 2009.

Evra, Jennifer van, 'Seven days: Your guide to the week's entertainment', *Globe and Mail*, April 14, 2008, p. R-5.

Financial Times, 'A woman's work?', October 14, 2008.

Financial Times, 'Iceland', October 7, 2008.

Financial Times, 'Iceland, i-banks and jobs', December 30, 2008, p. 10.

Financial Times, 'Icelandic banks', February 1, 2008, p. 14.

Financial Times, 'Italy's plan', October 10, 2008, p. 16.

Financial Times, 'Saving savers', November 9, 2008.

Financial Times, 'Smoked Salmond; There is less sense than ever to an independent Scotland', October 18, 2008, p. 6.

Fouché, Gwladys, 'Iceland is in the heart of the economic storm', *Guardian*, October 6, 2008.

Friðriksson, Ingimundur, 'The banking crisis in Iceland in 2008', *Sedlabanki.is*, February 6, 2009.

Furlong, Ray, 'Iceland scowls at UK after crisis', *BBC News*, December 16, 2008.

Furlong, Ray, 'Unlikely activists fight Iceland woes', *BBC News*, December 19, 2008.

Gatinois, Claire, 'Les émissions d'emprunts d'État vont se multiplier', Économie, *Le Monde*, October 11, 2008, p. 14.

Gee, Marcus, 'The body punches keep on coming', *Globe and Mail*, October 25, 2008, p. B-1.

Giles, Chris, 'Topsy-turvy logic leaves an unpalatable choice', *Financial Times*, October 8, 2008, p. 4.

Gill, A.A., 'Iceland: frozen assets', *Sunday Times*, December 14, 2008.

Globe and Mail, 'Adding up the Games. Michael, medals, money', August 25, 2008, p. S-4.

Globe and Mail, 'Mortgages, capital and that darn TED spread', October 10, 2008, p. B-3.

Groom, Brian, 'Back to the future. A leader for today', *Financial Times*, October 13, 2008.

Guardian, 'Catch of the day: Sigur Ros take charge', March 7, 2008.

Guardian, 'Darling vows to help Icesave savers', October 8, 2008.

Guardian, 'It could be worse—you could be in Iceland', October 8, 2008.

Guardian, 'Kaupthing. The bank that liked to say yes', October 9, 2008.

Guardian, 'The Icelandic sagas: Europe's most important book?', October 3, 2008.

Gumbel, Peter, 'Iceland: the country that became a hedge fund', *Fortune*, December 4, 2008, http://www.money.cnn.com/.

Gunnarsson, Valur [Associated Press], 'Icelandic TV program featuring PM forced off air', *Yahoo News*, December 31, 2008.

Gunnarsson, Valur [Associated Press], 'Windows broken at Iceland's financial regulator', *Yahoo News*, December 18, 2008.

Harford, Tim, 'Shock news? The media didn't get us into this mess', *Financial Times*, December 13, 2008, p. 12.

Hart, Matthew, 'Iceland's next saga. The wounded tiger's tale', *Globe and Mail*, November 15, 2008, p. F-4.

Hawkes, Steve, 'Failing Iceland calls in the IMF', *Times*, October 15, 2008.

Hay, George, 'L'Islande, victime du "credit crunch"', Économie, *Le Monde*, March 8, 2008, p. 18.

Hay, George, 'Le sang se glace dans les veines de l'Islande', Économie, *Le Monde*, October 7, 2008, p. 17, http://www.breakingviews.com/.

Hay, George, 'Pour l'Islande, mieux vaut le FMI que les Russes', Économie, *Le Monde*, October 10, 2008, p. 15.

Herald (Glasgow), 'Call for Nordic countries to help', October 28, 2008.

Herald (Glasgow), 'Five hurt in bid to storm police station', November 24, 2008.

Herald (Glasgow), 'Iceland and UK in row over bank assets', October 10, 2008.

Herald (Glasgow), 'Our chilling prophecy comes home to roost in Iceland', October 11, 2008.

Herald (Glasgow), 'Treasury officials hold emergency talks on Iceland', October 10, 2008.

Hill, Andrew, 'Why frozen Icesavers deserve sympathy not support', *Financial Times*, October 8, 2008, p. 22.

Holland, Ben, 'Iceland "like Chernobyl" as meltdown shows anger can boil over', *Bloomberg*, December 23, 2008.

Hugues, Chris and Sarah O'Connor, 'Icelandic krona suffers amid turmoil', *Financial Times*, March 20, 2008, p. 27.

Ibison, David, 'Bank crisis prompts Iceland EU rethink', *Financial Times*, November 14, 2008.

Ibison, David, 'Bobby Fischer, chess genius and estranged American, dies in isolation', *Financial Times*, January 19, 2008, p. 1.

Ibison, David, 'Cool under fire Iceland takes the fight back to finance', *Financial Times*, April 9, 2008, p. 7.

Ibison, David, 'Glitnir courts international investors', *Financial Times*, May 14, 2008.

Ibison, David, 'Iceland counters alleged attacks', *Financial Times*, March 31, 2008, p. 6.

Ibison, David, 'Iceland delays banks' plan to adopt the euro', *Financial Times*, January 16, 2008, p. 8.

Ibison, David, 'Iceland fends off hedge fund attack', *Financial Times*, April 18, 2008, p. 6.

Ibison, David, 'Iceland in fresh push to solve diplomatic row', *Financial Times*, November 14, 2008.

Ibison, David, 'Iceland inflation hits six-year high', *Financial Times*, March 29, 2008, p. 2.

Ibison, David, 'Iceland pushes rates to 15% as turmoil bites', *Financial Times*, March 26, 2008, p. 1.

Ibison, David, 'Iceland puts hope in its neighbours', *Financial Times*, October 26, 2008.

Ibison, David, 'Iceland requests $2bn bail-out from IMF', *Financial Times*, October 24, 2008.

Ibison, David, 'Iceland sees rift over EU membership', *Financial Times*, October 30, 2008.

Ibison, David, 'Iceland thaws over clash with UK', *Financial Times*, November 23, 2008.

Ibison, David, 'Iceland threatens direct market intervention', *Financial Times*, April 2, 2008, p. 8.

Ibison, David, 'Iceland warned against gradual "euroisation"', *Financial Times*, February 14, 2008, p. 6.

Ibison, David, 'Iceland wealth fund is proposed', *Financial Times*, April 25, 2008, p. 2.

Ibison, David, 'Icelanders collapse in laughter', *Financial Times*, November 28, 2008.

Ibison, David, 'Icelanders see Icarus-like plunge of greed', *Financial Times*, October 23, 2008.

Ibison, David, 'Icelandic whispers shake faith in boom', *Financial Times*, March 25, 2008.

Ibison, David, 'Moody's blows hot and cold on Iceland', *Financial Times*, January 29, 2008, p. 41.

Ibison, David, 'Moody's poised to downgrade Iceland', *Financial Times*, March 6, 2008, p. 27.

Ibison, David, 'Nordic central banks step in to back Iceland', *Financial Times*, May 17, 2008, p. 2.

Ibison, David, 'Nordic nations work on Iceland bail-out', *Financial Times*, November 5, 2008.

Ibison, David, 'Norway's central bank warns on stability', *Financial Times*, December 2, 2008.

Ibison, David, 'Oddsson defends role in Iceland's collapse', *Financial Times*, October 23, 2008.

Ibison, David, 'Reykjavik borrows $10bn to stave off economic collapse', *Financial Times*, November 20, 2008.

Ibison, David, 'System crisis rated as "low probability"', *Financial Times*, March 25, 2008.

Ibison, David, 'To Iceland from Hong Kong', *Financial Times*, March 28, 2008.

Ibison, David, 'Transcript challenges UK position on Iceland savings', *Financial Times*, October 23, 2008.

Ibison, David, 'UK dispute with Iceland escalates', *Financial Times*, October 24, 2008.

Ibison, David, Sarah O'Connor and David Oakley, 'Rise in CDS spreads fuels Iceland fears', *Financial Times*, June 26, 2008, p. 25.

Ibison, David and Gillian Tett, 'Indignant Iceland faces a problem of perception', *Financial Times*, March 27, 2008, p. 13.

IcelandReview.com, 'Book on Iceland crisis to be published abroad', July 18, 2009.

IcelandReview.com, 'Default claims in Iceland pile up', January 13, 2009.

IcelandReview.com, 'Highest claim to Landsbanki ISK 925 billion', November 18, 2009.

IcelandReview.com, 'Iceland banks flunk at Fitch Ratings', November 6, 2009.

Jackson, Robert, 'Letter from Iceland', *Financial Times*, November 15, 2008.

Jackson, Robert and Brian Milner, 'Iceland's meltdown', *Globe and Mail*, June 3, 2008, p. B-1.

Jacob, Gary, 'Vulture in the air circling West Ham', *Australian* from the *Times*, October 9, 2008.

Jolly, David, '$6 billion rescue for Iceland put on hold', *International Herald Tribune*, November 12, 2008.

Jolly, David, 'Financial tempest spreads to the Gulf states', *International Herald Tribune*, October 26, 2008.

Jolly, David, 'Iceland gets its IMF loan, Turkey awaits its own', *International Herald Tribune*, November 20, 2008.

Jolly, David and Julia Werdigier, '2 European banks warn of tougher market conditions ahead', *International Herald Tribune*, November 4, 2008.

Joly, Eva, 'L'Islande ou les faux semblants de la régulation de l'après-crise', *Le Monde*, August 1, 2009.

Jónsdóttir, Sigríður Vigdís, 'Iceland! Read all about it!', *International Herald Tribune*, May 13, 2008.

Kahn, Annie, 'Les disparités entre hommes et femmes s'atténuent', Environnement et sciences, *Le Monde*, November 13, 2008, p. 4.

Kahn, Annie, 'Les femmes, antidote à la crise boursière', Économie, *Le Monde*, October 16, 2008, p. 20.

Kerr, Christian, 'Signs of success are sunk in mire', *Australian*, October 9, 2008.

Killgren, Lucy, 'Moss Bros says Baugur talks continue', *Financial Times*, April 3, 2008.

Koza, Harry, 'Citigroup's toxic assets should prolong any rescue attempt', *Globe and Mail*, November 28, 2008.

Kristinsson, Stefán, 'Icelandic Central Bank governors fired by parliament', *Groundreport*, February 26, 2009.

Kroll, Luisa, 'Billionaire blowups of 2008', *Forbes*, December 23, 2008.

Landers, Jim, 'Iceland's road to bankruptcy was paved with U.S. ways', *Dallas Morning News*, December 10, 2008.

Landler, Mark, 'Credit crisis triggers downturn in Iceland', *New York Times*, April 17, 2008.

Lannin, Patrick and Sakari Suominen, 'Iceland seeks $4-billion more in aid', *Globe and Mail*, October 28, 2008, p. B-18.

Lawless, Jill, 'Crisis gives Iceland gift of frugality', *Detroit News*, December 25, 2008.

Lawless, Jill, 'With fish, Iceland's future is going back', *Globe and Mail*, December 15, 2008.

Lemaître, Frédéric, 'La revanche de "Super-Trichet"', Analyses, *Le Monde*, November 11, 2008, p. 2.

Lemarquis, Gérard, 'Accablés par la crise, les Islandais rêvent de l'euro', Économie, *Le Monde*, October 29, 2008, p. 13.

Lemarquis, Gérard, 'Happés par la tourmente, les Islandais lorgnent sur l'Union européenne', Économie, *Le Monde*, October 8, 2008, p. 11.

Lemarquis, Gérard, 'L'Islande affronte la baisse des quotas de cabillaud. La bonne gestion des réserves de poisson a transformé les pêcheurs en rentiers… au point d'abandonner le métier', Économie, *Le Monde*, January 15, 2008, p. 5.

Lemarquis, Gérard, 'L'Islande au bord du gouffre', *Le Monde*, October 9, 2008, p. 3.

Lemarquis, Gérard, 'La faillite de l'Islande provoque à Reykjavik les premiers heurts avec la police depuis 60 ans', *Le Monde*, January 24, 2009.

Lewis, Christina S.N., 'Strapped Iceland lists homes in D.C., New York, London', *Wall Street Journal*, February 27, 2009.

Lewis, Michael, 'Wall Street on the tundra', *Vanity Fair*, April 2009.

Lloyd, John, 'How to survive the end of "civilisation"', *Financial Times*, November 29, 2008.

Lucas, Edward, 'Do not let Russia "finlandise" Western Europe', *Financial Times*, October 9, 2008, p. 11.

Lungescu, Oana, 'EU ministers support Iceland bid', *BBC News*, July 27, 2009.

Lunn, Stephen, '"Never say die" trend persists as life expectancies rise', *Australian*, November 26, 2008.

Lyall, Sarah, 'Stunned Icelanders struggle after economy's fall', *New York Times*, November 9, 2008.

Mackintosh, James and Peter Smith, 'Australia aims regulatory fire at hedge funds', *Financial Times*, April 10, 2008, p. 22.

Maddox, Bronwen, 'Snub to Iceland will be costly blunder', *Australian*, October 11, 2008.

Malingre, Virginie, 'Écosse. Le Labour surfe sur la crise', *Le Monde*, November 5, 2008, p. 3.

Mamou, Yves, 'De la difficulté d'anticiper les crises', Économie, *Le Monde*, October 9, 2008, p. 3.

Mason, Rowena, 'Iceland falls out of love with its billionaires', *Telegraph*, October 19, 2008.

Mayer, Catherine, 'Iceland: Britain's credit crunch scapegoat', *Time*, October 10, 2008.

McCrann, Terry, 'Treasury is no longer a bastion of reason', *Australian*, November 1, 2008.

Milner, Brian, 'Iceland at the brink', *Globe and Mail*, October 8, 2008, p. B-1.

Milner, Brian, 'IMF demand forces Iceland to raise rates', *Globe and Mail*, October 29, 2008, p. B-14.

Milner, Brian, 'Out of options, Iceland leans on IMF', *Globe and Mail*, October 21, 2008, p. B-3.

Milner, Brian, 'Russia's "imaginative" Icelandic rescue', *Globe and Mail*, October 8, 2008, p. B-10.

Milner, Brian and Susan Sachs, 'European (dis)union', *Globe and Mail*, November 8, 2008, p. B-4.

Moody, Jonas, 'Feature of the week: the author of Revolution', *Iceland Review*, vol. 46, no. 4, 2008.

Moody, Jonas, 'Iceland picks the world's first openly gay PM', *Time*, January 30, 2009.

Moody, Jonas, 'Iceland to Britain: "We're no terrorists"', *Time*, November 3, 2008.

Moody, Jonas, 'Jóhannarama', *IcelandReview.com*, January 29, 2009.

Moody, Jonas, 'The Republic is dead. Long live the Republic!', *Iceland Review*, vol. 47, no. 1, 2009.

Munchau, Wolfgang, 'Do not be alarmed by Icelandic whispers', *Financial Times*, March 31, 2008, p. 7.

Munchau, Wolfgang, 'Now they see the benefits of the eurozone', *Financial Times*, November 2, 2008.

Munchau, Wolfgang, 'Why the British may decide to love the euro', *Financial Times*, November 16, 2008.

Mychasuk, Emiliya and Emiko Terazono, 'Viking saga', *Financial Times*, October 9, 2008, p. 20.

Naylor, Tony, 'Is this it?', *Guardian*, July 5, 2008.

Norris, Floyd, 'Can countries afford to bail out their banks?', *International Herald Tribune*, October 11, 2008.

Norris, Floyd, 'The world's banks could prove too big to fail', *New York Times*, October 11, 2008.

NRC Handelsblad, 'Provincial government resigns over Icelandic savings scandal', June 11, 2009.

NRC Handelsblad, 'The Hague threatens Iceland's EU bid over lost savings', July 22, 2009.

O'Connor, Sarah, 'Christmas. But not as Reykjavik knows it', *Financial Times*, December 23, 2008.

O'Connor, Sarah, 'Glitnir chief rolls up her sleeves for mammoth task', *Financial Times*, October 19, 2008.

O'Connor, Sarah, 'Iceland accuses UK of financial "siege"', *Financial Times*, October 16, 2008.

O'Connor, Sarah, 'Iceland gives Christmas frosty reception', *Financial Times*, December 23, 2008.

O'Connor, Sarah, 'Iceland's banks feel debt costs heat up', *Financial Times*, March 28, 2008, p. 24.

O'Connor, Sarah, 'Iceland's leader threatens to sue over "bullying" reaction', *Financial Times*, October 13, 2008, p. 4.

O'Connor, Sarah, 'Icelandic banks' 1,000bp CDS', *Financial Times*, July 22, 2008, p. 39.

O'Connor, Sarah, 'Icelandic women will clean up the "young men's mess"', *Financial Times*, October 14, 2008, p. 6.

Oakley, David, 'Emerging nations hit by growing debt fears', *Financial Times*, October 14, 2008, p. 15.

Oddsson, Davið, 'Letter to the Prime Minister of Iceland', *Sedlabanki.is*, February 9, 2009.

Parker, George and Andrew Ward, 'IMF plays down rift loan to Iceland', *Financial Times*, August 1, 2009.

Peel, Quentin, 'Nordic states stay hot on globalisation', *Financial Times*, April 11, 2008, p. 4.

Pfanner, Eric, 'Iceland banks face claims from depositors abroad', *International Herald Tribune*, October 10, 2008.

Pfanner, Eric, 'Iceland is all but officially bankrupt', *International Herald Tribune*, October 9, 2008.

Pfanner, Eric and Julia Werdigier, 'Caught in financial crisis, Iceland tries to tap Russia', *International Herald Tribune*, October 7, 2008.

Politiken, 'Iceland: Denmark has turned its back', November 12, 2008.

Portes, Richard, 'The shocking errors behind Iceland's meltdown', *Financial Times*, October 13, 2008, p. 13.

Press Association News, 'Iceland feels chill of recession', *Channel 4 News*, December 11, 2008.

Prest, Michael, 'Commerzbank accepte les remèdes proposés par l'État', Économie, *Le Monde*, November 5, p. 16.

Preston, Robert, 'Markets call time on Iceland', *BBC News*, October 4, 2008.

Prosser, David, 'Crisis deepens for Iceland as last of "big three" banks is nationalised', *Independent*, October 10, 2008.

Pustilnik, Marina, 'Iceland seeks Russian comfort', *Moscow News*, October 10, 2008.

Rachman, Gideon, 'What we will remember from 2008', *Financial Times*, December 23, 2008, p. 7.

Razon, Boris, 'La journée des blogueurs', *Le Monde*, November 27, 2009.

Reuters, 'How times changed', *Globe and Mail*, October 10, 2008, p. B-11.

Reuters, 'Iceland most peaceful place to live: report', *Australian*, May 21, 2008.

Reuters, 'It could take $24-billion to fix Iceland', *Globe and Mail*, November 18, 2008, p. B-11.

Richburg, Keith B., '"Nordic Tiger" Iceland finds itself in meltdown', *Washington Post*, October 10, 2008, p. A-1.

Roche, Andrew and Ómar Valdimarsson, 'Iceland's ex-PM apologises for part in bank crash', *Reuters*, March 26, 2009.

Roche, Marc, 'Les collectivités locales britanniques sont piégées par la défaillance des banques islandaises', Économie, *Le Monde*, October 13, 2008, p. 9.

Rodrik, Dani, 'To keep us all afloat. Why must we save emerging markets from Wall Street's follies?', *Globe and Mail*, November 13, 2008, p. B-14.

Rothkopf, David, 'The Fund faces up to competition', *Financial Times*, October 21, 2008.

Rozhnov, Konstantin, 'Russia's role in rescuing Iceland', *BBC News*, November 13, 2008.

Saunders, Doug, 'Market meltdown teaches Europe that size matters', *Globe and Mail*, October 22, 2008, p. A-19.

Scoffield, Heather, 'Three stats you just can't be without on a Saturday: The week in economics', *Globe and Mail*, March 29, 2008, p. B-19.

Sherwood, Johel, 'Iceland seen turning to IMF', *Wall Street Journal*, October 17, 2008.

Shrimsley, Robert, 'Saving Iceland', *Financial Times*, March 27, 2008, p. 14.

Soares, Claire, 'Who are you calling terrorists, Mr Brown?', *Independent*, October 24, 2008.

Stacey, Kiran, 'Recession dents image of macho management', *Financial Times*, November 5, 2008.

Stafford, Mikey, 'West Ham deny crisis after Icelandic bank folds', *Guardian*, October 8, 2008.

Stevenson, David, 'How Iceland's meltdown affects you', *Money Week*, October 7, 2008.

Stroobants, Jean-Pierre and Élise Vincent, 'La crise islandaise inquiète de nombreux épargnants du Benelux', Économie, *Le Monde*, October 21, 2008, p. 14.

Stutchbury, Michael, 'Keeping banks afloat our best defence', *Australian*, October 6, 2008.

Summers, Deborah and Graeme Weardon, 'Gordon Brown considers legal action against Iceland', *Guardian*, October 9, 2008.

Surowiecki, James, 'Iceland's deep freeze', *New Yorker*, April 21, 2008.

Talcott, Christina, 'Enjoying Iceland's wonders for less', *Washington Post*, December 14, 2008.

Tan, Cliff, 'Nordic banks must not mistake camouflage for cover', *Financial Times*, May 30, 2008, p. 8.

Taylor, Kate, 'An art collective's SOS', *Globe and Mail*, April 22, 2008, p. R-2.

Teather, David, 'Banking crisis: Iceland takes control of Glitnir', *Guardian*, September 29, 2008.

Teather, David, 'Iceland first to feel the blast of global cooling', *Guardian*, April 17, 2008.

Teather, David, 'Iceland government seizes control of Landsbanki', *Guardian*, October 7, 2008.

Teather, David, 'Icelandic government battles to save the economy', *Guardian*, October 6, 2008.

Thomas, Owen, 'Can Björk save a ruined Iceland?', *Gawker*, December 24, 2008.

Thornton, Henry, 'It's time to restore trust', *Australian*, October 10, 2008.

Thornton, Henry, 'Vexed questions', *Australian*, October 27, 2008.

Tighe, Chris, 'Shoppers sniff at chancellors' VAT cut', *Financial Times*, November 25, 2008.

Times, 'Iceland agrees $US6bn deal with IMF', October 21, 2008.

Times, 'Iceland bank shares suspended, state takes control', *Australian*, October 7, 2008.

Traves, Julie, 'Happy trails?', *Globe and Mail*, February 23, 2008, p. T-1.

Truc, Olivier, 'L'Estonie, la Lettonie et la Lituanie redoutent une "faillite à l'islandaise"', *Le Monde*, November 6, 2008, p. 15.

Truc, Olivier, 'Le Danemark regrette de plus en plus d'être resté en dehors de la zone euro', Économie, *Le Monde*, October 23, 2008, p. 12.

Truffaut, Serge, 'Crise financière. Au secours de l'Est', *Le Devoir*, November 3, 2008.

Urry, Maggie, 'A case of sink or swim', *Financial Times*, September 2, 2008, p. 19.

Valdimarsson, Ómar and Toni Vorobyova, 'Iceland seeks Russian, Nordic help', *Globe and Mail*, October 15, 2008, p. B-14.

Valfells, Arsaell, 'Gordon Brown killed Iceland', *Forbes*, October 16, 2008.

Vincent, Élise, 'Dans un entretien, le premier ministre islandais, Geir Haarde, évoque la grave crise financière que traverse son pays, il y a encore peu de temps l'un des plus prospères de la planète', Économie, *Le Monde*, October 23, 2008, p. 12.

Vincent, Élise, 'Naufragés d'Islande', Horizons, *Le Monde*, October 24, 2008, p. 21.

Vincent, Matthew, 'Bank crisis Q&A', *Financial Times*, October 7, 2008.

Vinocur, John, 'Europe's unlikely attempt to renew a "partnership" with Russia', *International Herald Tribune*, April 21, 2008.

Von Hahn, Karen, 'Could market meltdown be a chance to slow down?', *Globe and Mail*, October 18, 2008, p. L-3.

Wade, Robert, 'Iceland pays price for financial excess', *Financial Times*, July 1, 2008.

Wade, Robert, 'IMF reports uncertain outlook for Iceland', *Financial Times*, July 15, 2008, p. 14.

Waldie, Paul, 'Icelandic banking crisis touches Canada', *Globe and Mail*, October 9, 2008, p. B-11.

Walker, Lamia, 'Crisis gives women a shot at top corporate jobs', *Financial Times*, October 18, 2008, p. 6.

Wall Street Journal, 'Excerpts: Iceland's Oddsson', October 17, 2008.

Walt, Vivienne, 'A meltdown in Iceland', *Time*, October 8, 2008.

Watkins, Simon, 'Iceland's banks top "riskiness league"', *Financial Mail*, March 16, 2008.

Werdigier, Julia, 'Iceland takes extreme steps to save its finance system', *International Herald Tribune*, October 7, 2008.

Westwood, Matthew, 'Made to mingle with electricity', *Australian*, January 10, 2008.

Wikileaks, 'Financial collapse: Confidential exposure analysis of 205 companies each owing above €45M to Icelandic bank Kaupthing, 26 Sep 2008', July 26, 2009.